Primary science and technology

,02

Primary science and technology
Practical alternatives

Di Bentley and Mike Watts

Open University Press
Buckingham · Philadelphia

Open University Press
Celtic Court
22 Ballmoor
Buckingham
MK18 1XW

and

1900 Frost Road, Suite 101
Bristol, PA 19007, USA

First Published 1994

A catalogue record of this book is available from the British Library

ISBN 0 335 19028 6 (pb)   0 335 19029 4 (hb)

Library of Congress Cataloging-in-Publication Data
Bentley, Di.
    Primary science and technology: practical alternatives / Di
Bentley & Mike Watts.
        p.   cm.
    Includes bibliographical references and index.
    ISBN 0–335–19029–4 (hardback)   ISBN 0–335–19028–6 (pbk.)
    1. Science—Study and teaching (Elementary)—Great Britain.
    2. Technology—Study and teaching (Elementary)—Great Britain.
    I. Watts, Mike. II. Title.
    LB1585.5.G7B46   1993
    372.3'5—dc20   93–10657
                                                          CIP

Typeset by Graphicraft Typesetters Ltd., Hong Kong
Printed in Great Britain by Biddles Ltd., Guildford and King's Lynn

We dedicate this book to Samuel and Kenneth

Contents

Acknowledgements

Apple, the Apple logo and Macintosh are trademarks and registered trademarks of Apple Computer, Inc.

We would like to formally record our thanks to Buckingham LEA Science Team for the use of their guidelines in Chapter 3; to Spinfield County Combined School for their science policy in Appendix 1; to Foxes Piece Middle School for their technology statement in Appendix 2; to Rokesly Infants School for their information technology policy in Appendix 3; and to Olney Middle School for their theme plan in Appendix 5.

We thank Janet Patrick for her secretarial support and Grant Alderson for his computing expertise.

We are grateful to the organizations and individuals listed below for permission to reproduce the following figures:

Figures 3.4 and 3.5: Holy Trinity Middle School and Rosemary Denman.
Figures 4.1, 4.2 and 5.1: National Primary Centre.
Figures 6.1–6.3 and 6.8–6.14, 8.2, 9.1: Rokesly Infants School and Sue Marran and her class.
Figures 6.4 and 6.5: Foxes Piece First School and Jenny McGivern.
Figures 8.3 to 8.14: Jane Eaton and the pupils in her class.
Figure 8.15: Spinfield County Combined School.
Figure 11.1: D. Bell/Simon and Schuster and the Association for Science Education.

one

Building on experience

Introduction

Life is never simple and there must be a million ways to make it more difficult than to make it easy. At a time when curriculum change has never been faster and more persistent, what might be needed is a recipe for classroom security and sanity, not another text about alternatives to current practice. Inevitably, this book might serve to complicate what might seem to have been straight-forward. Our aim, though, is quite the opposite. We do not want to make teaching or learning in the classroom more awkward or anxious, but to try to provide a reasonable, positive rationale and description for what is taking place. We believe that in offering a clear, direct perspective and a range of sharply focused case studies, as we do here, we can offer nothing but help at an otherwise complex time.

The rationale we use is framed both by our own experiences of how teaching and learning take place and the developed practice of trusted colleagues in the field. It is a recipe we have used before when writing for secondary teachers (Bentley and Watts, 1989), where we tackled issues in science education through the perspectives of classroom practitioners. Broadly speaking, our work has its basis in a philosophy called 'constructivism' and we discuss this as we go along. The many case study descriptions we have included are taken from our own work and that of good friends and allies in different parts of the educational system. We use these to explore the ways primary classrooms work and examine in particular the styles and systems producing good practice in science and technology in primary schools. Let us begin, though, with distinguishing the audience we have in mind for the book.

Teachers of science and technology

The book is about primary practice and so an instantly obvious audience is the very large number of primary practitioners in schools throughout the UK.

Over the years, we have developed nothing short of admiration for the skills, talents and sheer professionalism of those in the primary sector with whom we have worked. Not only are they specialists in their own right, they are increasingly expected to be specialists in numerous other subject areas and very decidedly expert in a huge range of professional matters. Alongside them work a coterie of other professionals – sometimes experienced in teaching children with particular learning concerns, specific language requirements and/or emotional and behavioural needs. Some are school subject coordinators, advisory teachers, colleagues, or mentors within the school, or educators in higher education and from other parts of the system, and we have tried to address the book to them too. We know that, for many, both science and technology are foreign ground to be trod lightly until some of the terrain becomes familiar. Since, as authors, we both come from a background of science and science teaching, we have tried to be especially careful neither to assume knowledge and understanding that is somewhat distant from our audience, nor to be condescending in our approach to scientific and technological concepts.

We are conscious, too, of our many secondary colleagues who are often drawn into and involved with work across the age phase and we also hope there is something in here for them. While this book is aimed principally at teachers of Key Stages 1 (5 to 7-year-olds) and 2 (7 to 11-year-olds) we hope there is also something of interest for those who teach within Key Stage 3 (11 to 14-year-olds). We feel this is particularly the case when appreciating good primary practice since, we believe, this is some of the very best educational practice to be found anywhere. And last but not least, we are keenly aware that there are numerous similar changes taking place in primary science and technology education throughout the world. We hope that in offering a window onto some of our experiences in the UK we can share in an exchange which will benefit us all. With this final audience in mind we have not detailed hugely the UK's National Curriculum in science and technology. These parts of the system are discussed of course but we have aimed to leave the book more 'timeless' than simply a re-hash of contemporary government documentation. And so, in the jargon of the trade, with talking about science and technology. The broad outline of the book tackles some of the major issues in science and technology education and the main sections we have chosen are illustrated in Figure 1.1.

In the remainder of this chapter we want to consider some of the assumptions from which we work, some of the debates at hand in primary work, and to describe a constructivist approach to concept development. We continue this discussion in Chapters 2 and 3 and raise the issues of differentiation, progression and language. We also examine some of the features of scientific and technological concepts and language in the primary classroom, and ways in which meaning can be constructed. In Chapters 4 and 5 we focus on the planning necessary to bring this about, from whole school policies to professional decision-making in the classroom. Chapter 6 addresses issues of management and organization and we have included some comment on

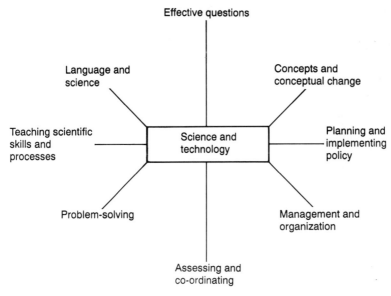

Figure 1.1 Book plan.

resources, storage and safe practice in science and technology. In Chapter 7 we consider posing problems and the nature of effective questions. Chapter 8 takes these processes further through the development of open-ended task-orienated problem-solving. This is a key cross-curricular skill and is best undertaken early in life. In Chapter 9 we consider issues of equal opportunities in science and technology. Chapter 10 rehearses the assessment of the skills and processes and the ways in which record-keeping can be organized and managed. In Chapter 11 the role of science and technology coordinators come to the fore and we illustrate ways in which their work can foster the two subject areas. In the final chapter we take a wide view again, along with a summary of the work covered so far.

In the sections that follow in this chapter we need to make some distinctions in the words we use. So, for example, we need to discuss both science and technology, teaching and learning, planning and performing, themes and topics, concepts and constructs, organization and management, and so on. To set the debate going, then, we start with a discussion of science and technology.

Science and technology: allies or opposites?

Definitions are interesting and useful where they can be clear and concise. In the case of the terms *science* and *technology*, though, this is not the case, both words having large scope and indeterminate meaning. Consequently, we will leave hard definitions aside for a moment. At one level, science is simply what scientists do (whatever that is), though we might also be able to recognize that artists, photographers, journalists and musicians can behave in scientific ways at particular moments in their professional lives. They not only have to *know* some science (about pigments, silver nitrate, computers, acoustics, etc.) but also have to engage in some of the processes of hypothesizing, inferring, testing, experimenting, and so on. It really depends upon how you define the word 'science'. We know, too, that technology is an extensive umbrella term which covers a multitude of activities – in fact the scientist, artist, photographer, journalist and musician might also be acting technologically at different points in their work. We like the following description by Smillie (1991):

> Technology is a combination of knowledge, techniques and concepts; it is tools, machines and factories. It is engineering, but is much more than engineering. It involves organisation and processes. It has to do with agriculture, animal husbandry and health. It is often highly resource-specific. It involves people both as individuals – creators, inventors, entrepreneurs – and as society. The cultural, historical and organisational context in which technology is developed and applied is always a factor in its success or failure. Technology is the science and the art of getting things done through the application of knowledge. It is, according to the American technology historian Edwin Layton, 'a spectrum, with ideas at one end and techniques and things at the other, with design as a middle term'.

There are three broad camps of opinion. In the first, science is seen as dominant and technology is simply 'the appliance of science'. That is, scientists work out the laws and principles that apply in the physical world and then pass these over to the technologist who puts them to good use. Science is hypothesizing, experimentation and theorizing, and technology is the application of this to human good. In the second, it is technology which is the all-embracing discipline and science is just one of the many areas of knowledge upon which it draws. So, while it needs to take account of scientific laws and principles, technology also needs to draw upon its own concepts and ideas, upon principles of art and design, social science, psychology, medical health and safety, economics, marketing, and so on. The third camp of opinion is that the two are interwoven in a complex weave of interrelated ideas and activity. Layton (1988), for instance, concludes that technology is a long way from simply being applied science and that the relationship between the two is 'complex, interactive, symbiotic and egalitarian'. The two are marked by different purposes, different processes and different relationships to bodies of established knowledge but are nevertheless intertwined and inextricably linked. Traditionally, as Layton (1991) says:

> The technologies of instrumentation, yielding clocks, thermometers, barometers, voltmeters, ammeters and the like, allowed greater precision and standardisation of scientific data. Other technological products such

as telescopes, microscopes, vacuum pumps and electric cells extended the range of sensory experience and assisted the reliable reproduction of phenomena. In turn, general scientific theory was redirected towards technological devices and problems, although not always with the success its proponents anticipated.

So, the two should be seen as equal and interactive: technology makes creative use of science; science makes creative use of technology. Both involve evaluation in terms of their end outcomes, both have theories, processes, techniques and competencies which are all their own.

We make a small digression here very briefly for those readers who are not steeped in the very bones of the National Curriculum on a daily basis. Those who are might want to move on to the section on constructivism below.

National Curriculum science – a brief overview

After several changes from its original conception in 1987, the current version of the National Curriculum in science has three main threads in common with all other subjects.

(i) The National Curriculum is divided up into Programmes of Study. These outline broadly the concepts, skills and processes which children are required by law to study through particular stages of their schooling. The Key Stages (KS) correspond to the ages at which they are taught:

KS1 means ages 5–7,
KS2 8–11,
KS3 12–14,
KS4 15–16.

(ii) Each Programme of Study has a series of Attainment Targets (ATs) written through it. (There are now four Attainment Targets in science, one being concerned with skills and processes and the other three with knowledge and understanding.)

(iii) Each Attainment Target has 10 Levels, each Level associated with a particular Statement(s) of Attainment which pupils are expected to know and understand.

In science, each Attainment Target now has a variety of Strands associated with it as shown below.

Attainment Target 1: Scientific investigation
- ask questions, predict, hypothesize
- observe, measure and manipulate variables
- interpret their results and evaluate scientific evidence

Attainment Target 2: Life and living processes
- Life processes and the organization of living things
- Variation and the mechanisms of inheritance and evolution

- Populations and human influences within ecosystems
- Energy flows and cycles of matter within ecosystems

Attainment Target 3: Materials and their properties
  - The properties, classification and structures of materials
  - Explanations of the properties of materials
  - Chemical changes
  - The Earth and its atmosphere

Attainment Target 4: Physical processes
  - Electricity and magnetism
  - Energy resources and energy transfer
  - Forces and their effects
  - Light and sound
  - The Earth's place in the Universe

Within each Strand there are the Statements of Attainment, and those in Attainment Target 1, in most Strands, and in Attainment Target 2 (Strands 1 and 2) have a great deal in common with the National Curriculum technology – as we show in the examples below. The Statements of Attainment tell the child and the teacher what is expected of that Level. So, for example:

AT1, Strand 2, Level 1 states:
  - observe familiar materials and events
AT1, Strand 3, Level 3 states:
  - recognize that their conclusions may not be valid unless a fair test has been carried out

The Levels become progressively more difficult as the child moves from Level 1 to 10. In general terms, the rate of progress in each Attainment Target is not usually one per year; some children progress faster than this, others not so fast. Attaining a level in one Attainment Target in a subject does not necessarily mean that the child is at the same level in all the targets inside that subject. By the time children reach Key Stage 4 (15 years old) the teacher may have to contend with a huge spread of attainment in any one student – and therefore in any one class. For children with Special Educational Needs (SEN), it is widely recognized now that the steps between each Level can be too great and progress for these children may seem to be agonizingly slow.

National Curriculum technology – a brief overview

In technology, there are changes afoot. The original (1990) statutory orders used to have four Attainment Targets. The current proposed version has only two. Each Attainment Target has Strands within it and each Key Stage has associated with it 'design and make tasks' (DMTs), whereby the Programmes of Study are translated into schemes of work and classroom activities. In each Key Stage, DMTs are divided into:

A. Core DMTs where content is prescribed.

B. Supplementary DMTs where the content complements the core to produce a balanced course of study.

Attainment Targets and Strands

Each Attainment Target is divided into 10 Levels and within each Level the Strands are identified so that there is an Attainment Target for each Strand.

1. Designing

   Strand A. Investigating, clarifying and specifying the design task.

   Strand B. Modelling, developing and communicating design ideas.

2. Making

   Strand A. Planning and organizing making.

   Strand B. Using a variety of components, tools, equipment and processes to make products safely.

   Strand C. Testing, modifying and evaluating.

At each Key Stage, there are the Core Programmes of study of designing and making (which have the same name as the Attainment Targets) and Supplementary Programmes. The Supplementary Programmes of study are:

- Business and Industrial Practices (KS4 only)
- Structures
- Control Systems and Energy
- Constructional Materials and Components
- Food

At Key Stage 1 schools must fulfil the Core Programme of two DMTs, one in control systems and one in structures. These tasks represent the skills required to show capability in design and technology. They must also choose one DMT from each of two Supplementary Programmes such as food and structures.

At Key Stage 2, schools must fulfil the Core Programme in five DMTs, in the areas of control (electrics), control (mechanisms) and control (energy) as well as structures and food. They must also choose three Supplementary Programme tasks.

Levels of Attainment: some examples

At Key Stage 1, in design, Strand A, pupils are expected to:

- explain the purpose of what they are making (Level 1)
- discuss their ideas about what is required (Level 2)

Design, Strand B pupils are expected to:

- explore ideas for making by rearranging materials (Level 1)
- follow diagrammatic instructions (Level 2)

Making, Strand B (there is no Strand A at Key Stage 1):

- make products using materials, components and equipment (Level 1)
- make products using hand tools, components and equipment (Level 2)

This has been a very brief overview of the National Curriculum in science and technology and says very little about the reality of what actually happens in classrooms – the way it works, or fails to work. Many of our case studies will illustrate the curriculum in action – not so much 'how to do it' but 'how it has been done well by others'. We hope this helps to ease the transition for many teachers between obligation and inspiration. However, before we move to practicalities, it is necessary to explore a little theory.

Constructivism means to construct

We began earlier by pinning our flag to a constructivist mast, and here we need to say quite what that means. The world of constructivism is fairly broad and unbounded though they who inhabit it probably accept there are several central features, many points of common agreement and some distinct limits to its domain. We have tried to describe elements of constructivism elsewhere (for example in Bentley and Watts, 1989, 1992) and many other writers have made their attempts too (see Adey *et al.*, 1989, for example). In brief, constructivism is a philosophy and a psychology about the way people make sense of the world. We make sense, it says, through our interpretations of what is happening around us. The central point is that people are always intellectually active – they do not learn passively, but go out of their way to try to make some meaning in what is taking place in their environment. Our constructions of life are conditioned and constrained by our experiences and this means that – since we all have different experiences – we are all likely to have different perceptions about ideas, actions, behaviours, incidents, situations, tasks, feelings, and so on.

An example might help here. Teacher separates two children squabbling in the playground:

'It's her fault, Miss, she started it.'
'No I didn't, No I didn't! He started it.'

Getting to the bottom of who did what to whom and who did it first may not be straightforward. It involves interpreting the acts children make, their personalities, their past behaviours, their 'trustworthiness', and so on. Each aspect of the situation – commonplace though it is – needs to weighed and sorted according to the teacher's own frame of reference about 'trust', 'honesty', 'fair play', and so on. And even if the teacher can reach some kind of 'just' interpretation of events, another teacher standing nearby might see things in an entirely different way. One only has to listen to witnesses' vastly different accounts of the same event to realize how varied people are in their interpretative frames.

So, within constructivism we see that learning is always an interpretative process involving individuals' constructions of meaning, which are related to specific occurrences and phenomena. New constructions are built through their relation to previous experience and prior knowledge – and the challenge for the teacher is to focus on students' learning with understanding rather than the more common and straightforward emphasis on 'covering content'. To learn science and technology from a constructivist philosophy implies using concepts and experience we already possess, and which we then change and elaborate on the basis of fresh meanings. These fresh ideas are commonly negotiated through everyday interactions with peers and teachers.

Kelly (1955) used the noun 'a construct' to mean the individual, personal descriptions and perspectives we use in our thinking: the 'perspective of the individual' is central to his work. He suggests that these constructs allow us to build mental models so that we can predict, control and evaluate parts of life – so that we are then able to behave in relation to it. He uses the idea that people can act like scientists, that our models are constantly challenged and revised through our experiences and this process means we are then better able to meet new challenges. Like a scientist's model, this model is subject to change over time since constructions of reality are constantly being tested and modified to allow a better working model to be erected. And better or worse here means how well it serves to predict and sort out what is happening as people go about their daily business. As Johnson-Laird (1983) points out:

> Human beings . . . do not apprehend the world directly; they possess only an internal representation of it, because perception is their construction of a model of the world. They are unable to compare this perceptual representation directly with the world – it *is* their world. (original emphasis)

The revisions that take place derive from previous experiences, interpretations of present circumstances, forecasts of approaching eventualities and assessments of past predictions. As Pope and Keen (1981) say:

> the questioning and exploring, revising and replacing in the light of predictive failure which is symptomatic of scientific theorising, is precisely what a person does in his attempts to anticipate events. The person can be seen as a scientist constantly experimenting with his definition of his existence.

We can apply this idea to children, too, of course and a number of writers have written about 'child-as-scientists', using the idea metaphorically to help describe some of the actions of the child as they are working (see for example Driver, 1985). It produces a very 'child-orientated' view of learning, teaching and classroom activity – the learner is seen to be at the very centre of the learning experience. The emphasis is on the child as a meaning-maker and the stress is on the elevation of the young person and the personal nature of their meaning-making, to the central focus of schooling.

Child-as-technologist

Just as a child or adult can be seen to act like a scientist, so we can carry the metaphor over to technology. Cosgrove (in Cosgrove and Schaverien, 1992), for example, has made an interesting case for viewing children as technologists as they work in school. His work with others (Cosgrove *et al.*, 1985, for instance) leads him to say that children implicitly use the essential elements of a design cycle as they generate ideas, scrutinize proposals, devise prototypes and subject these early models to tests of performance. His case studies of children's activities illustrate how, in turn, children can be seen to be speculators and generators of ideas, discoverers and inventors.

One implication for the curriculum is that children do not need to be taught how to go about designing: they can already do this. As Cosgrove *et al.* (1985) say:

> Rather than teach the child the design cycle, the teacher could help to deconstruct this and other designs so that features of the strategy (such as the sequence) can be examined.

By 'deconstruct' he means to take the process apart and see what the parts do. That is, working closely with children to talk through with them what they are doing, how they do this and what their thought processes are. This is difficult enough with adults and is clearly very demanding when working with young children. However, as we describe later in the case studies, we see that it can be done well. Developing these skills of 'thinking at the same time as doing', Cosgrove calls for a 'know-how' approach to the curriculum, enabling teachers to respond to this way of working. Like Papert (1980) he sees children as building intellectual structures in an extended and enhanced way when they are making something they have designed.

As we have discussed elsewhere (Pope and Watts, 1988), 'being like a scientist', or 'acting like a technologist' is similar to putting on a pair of goggles through which to see the world in a particular way. Our 'ways of seeing' reality can be likened to temporary spectacles which create a window on the world, with which we can alter the clarity and perspective of what we see. In the next section, we look at how knowledge itself can be seen as design. We use this as a useful way to evaluate the chapters that follow.

Classroom constructivism

It is possible to be very purist about constructivism and there are times it is important to develop ideas about the very core of what constructivism means. Whatever else, it is a theory that adapts to everyday practice and we are keen here to explore practice and to leave theory to later. We have five main tenets of 'classroom constructivism' (Watts and Bentley, 1991) which are:

1. Start where the learner is. This is a very common dictum of constructivism and most primary teachers are aware of working this way. They enable individual learning through focused experience and then use children's range of experiences to further understanding.

2. Progression through a process of 'orientation', 'elicitation', 'restructuring' and 'application' (Driver, 1989). This is about structuring the learning environment to encourage the explication of ideas and to provide challenging experiences. So, for example, teachers are used to developing children's language skills in all contexts in order to help children explain and develop their ideas.

3. Design 'bridges' to take the learner to the desired point. The task of the teacher is to know the pupils well enough so that instructional steps are strong and help transport ideas for particular individuals. Primary teachers know their children very well and are commonly able to do this through the careful and targeted questioning of children.

4. Forms of active learning. Learning is not just listening and writing. Group work and collaborative learning are examples of techniques which play upon ideas of active learning.

5. Teacher as facilitator. Classroom management is important: teachers must design and organize situations in which ideas can be discussed without fear and ridicule. We hold now with what we have said previously: many primary teachers are expert. They use sophisticated questioning techniques to lead children along different paths of thinking. They encourage children to explore ideas themselves rather than being directive themselves.

In part, these five points are simply good primary practice. We would like to see them as good workable classroom constructivism.

Knowledge as design

Perkins (1986) has developed the idea of knowledge as design in some quite interesting ways. The principle is not easy at first and takes some accommodation:

> . . . design-coloured glasses are worth wearing . . . if you are the wearer of real glasses you know that a new pair take some getting used to. At first things blur a bit. As you move your head the world seems to move too. Seeing through design-coloured glasses takes some getting used to as well.

The argument goes like this. If we believe (as we do) that thinking, learning, living are constructive processes, then there must be some overall rationale for this construction – there must be some design. If we treat knowledge simply as information then we succumb to a passive view of learning. It is good only for the getting. We believe, though, that knowledge is active – a process governed by a purpose.

Let us take some examples: the road layout in your neighbourhood; your parents' phone number; the rules of badminton; Newton's laws in physics. Let us say you have this information at your beck and call and can summon it whenever you want. From a constructivist point of view, you commonly arrive at this information through a process of active learning. So, even if you memorize a map you still need to walk, cycle or drive the route in order to internalize it. You need to memorize phone numbers so that you can call when you want to; you need the rules of a game so that you can participate in a meaningful way.

But what about academic knowledge, the good, positive understandings of – say – physics or the seemingly 'useless bits of information', good only for general knowledge trivia quizzes? Such data are not devoid of purpose; rather, laden with purpose. As Perkins points out, Newton's laws can be seen as a way of organizing a diverse set of observations in order to explain phenomena of motion. We use this knowledge for the purpose of making sense of parts of the universe we inhabit. If we do not want to do this, or prefer another explanation, we are free to choose – but it is an active choice:

> Knowledge as information purveys a passive view of knowledge, one that highlights knowledge in storage rather than knowledge as an implement of action. Knowledge as design might be our best bet for building a theory of knowledge for teaching and learning.

Perkins offers four main design questions to help unpick understanding of something:

1. What is its purpose (or purposes)?
2. What is its structure?
3. What are model cases of it?
4. What are arguments that explain and evaluate it?

To round off this section, let us take an example – an 'academic' example from science: the concept of energy. Let us talk through the four design questions. First, *purpose*. Nature presents us with a huge variety of phenomena – thunderstorms, clouds, fire, earthquakes, tidal waves, eclipses, sunshine, dogs and cats, lions and tigers, etc. One way of describing the form of these phenomena is to talk about the way that changes take place, their rapidity, intensity, consequences, and so on. Energy is a theory, a 'bank balancing' activity which looks at the 'befores' and 'afters' of such changes and helps to analyse and describe what might be happening. Like any theory it is a tool for producing explanations of a certain rate of phenomena and – as a tool – it is designed for a purpose and with purpose in mind.

Secondly, *structure*. Energy has a central principle: it cannot be created or destroyed. So, the energy before a particular change will always be equal to the energy after the change has taken place. A loudspeaker, for instance, changes electrical signals into sound waves. The 'structure' of an energy analysis means that the energy associated with the electrical circuits before the sound is made must equal the energy associated with the movement of the diaphragm and the air after the sound is produced. There are other parts to the structure, too, so that energy is quantifiable, can be calculated in many different but equivalent ways, will constantly reduce in its 'usability', and so on.

Thirdly, what *model cases* can we use? Here there are countless examples and much of science and technology teaching concerns the teaching of these. Some readers may like Solomon's (1991) excellent book, *Getting to Know About Energy*. We can, though, use the concept of energy to explore how much useful work we might get out of a lump of coal or a litre of petrol, what body processes might result from eating a particular food, what is happening in a chemical explosion or how an ecological system like a garden pond might be described.

Fourthly, what are the *arguments*, evaluations? This can mean 'does the logic of the theory hold up?', 'does the empirical evidence support the theory?' and 'is it a useful concept?' The answer to all three parts of the question is 'yes'. The concept of energy was invented in the mid 19th century and these days is a core concept in science. It is used to discuss the formation of universes, galaxies, atom bombs, fuels, movement, electric circuits, food, chemical changes, biological processes, atoms, molecules, sub-atomic particles and many more phenomena in between. As such, it has stood the test of time for more than a century and is a vital cornerstone concept in the understanding of science.

We can use these four questions, then, to explore the knowledge we are generating. To maximize this and extend the point, we use them to set out a framework for the following chapters of the book. So, as we look at the use of questioning, for instance, we can put forward a particular point of view and then examine this in terms of its design: its purpose, structure, cases models and arguments of value and worth. In particular, we use our five tenets of classroom constructivism to judge the value and worth of our approach in a section at the end of each chapter.

two

Learning and conceptual change

Introduction

If we stretch back in time to all those lectures about concepts and concept development we sat through during our professional training we inevitably come up with names like Piaget, Bruner, Gagne and Vygotsky, to list but a few. It will come as no surprise that there are many mountains of work written about concepts – Piaget alone wrote about a book a year for fifty years, which is no mean feat. What Vygotsky lacked in productivity, he made up in power and Bruner, of course, is still writing and talking today. We cannot hope to survey and review all this work – nor is it all appropriate or pertinent. We have structured this chapter along the four 'design questions' we mentioned in Chapter 1, and begin with a discussion of some of the general purposes behind the book.

Purpose

In broad terms we have allied ourselves to a constructivist camp, as we describe in Chapter 1. This brings with it certain implications and we need to discuss these along the route. We need, though, some general comments before we tackle some of the main underlying principles to this way of thinking. First, not all concepts are the same. This may seem obvious but if we accept that there can be different orders of concept, then it follows that there will be different orders of concept development. So, what sorts of concepts might there be? There have been many different categorizations of concepts and the one we have chosen here is based on a fairly wide survey of work done in the field (Gilbert and Watts, 1983). But where does this take us? Children come to class with personal knowledge and they then proceed to construct and re-construct more personal knowledge from the activities in the class and from the content teachers present during the day. As Driver (1984) says:

Conceptual change involves the learner actively constructing his or her own meaning in any situation whether it is text, dialogue or physical experience.

That

construction of meaning is an active process of hypothesizing and hypothesis-testing and has the consequence that the learner is seen as being ultimately responsible for their own learning.

In our view, teaching involves exploring children's ideas through a range of suitably targeted tasks and then incorporating these ideas into the learning experiences for the class. All this coupled to an empathetic understanding of the learner's motivation and sometimes intuitive view of the world. Teaching involves intervening in and challenging children's meaning-making by suggesting different and powerful spectacles for viewing their everyday world, as well as the world of science and technology. Where their conceptions and models of the world are persistent and durable despite teacher intervention we have to move from teaching science to teaching about science. So, for example, if a child persists with a very animisitic concept of energy, we may have to move from simply trying to teach a 'scientific' concept towards describing why scientists have taken to using the concept they do.

Active and passive learning

We take from what has been said above about classroom constructivism that learning is both purposeful and active – we are firm believers in 'active learning'. Some while ago (Bentley and Watts, 1989) we set out seven markers for what active learning means and we want to use those same ideas here, although they must be modified slightly given the change of context in which we are writing. These seven are that active learners:

(i) *initiate their own activities and take responsibility for their own learning*. This is very much of the 'progressive' view that the task, scheme or activity is directly suited to the learner's own needs and is something that relates to what *they* want to do.

(ii) *make decisions and solve problems*. Active learners, in our view, take responsible decisions and seek to solve problems that crop up along the way. That is, they take some ownership for what they are doing – it becomes their work, their project and their way of working.

(iii) *transfer skills from one context to another*. This is an important element in active learning – it is the learner that sees the links between one context and another. It is a good indicator that learning has been meaningful and that it is seen as intelligible and fruitful.

(iv) *organize themselves and organize others*. That is, active learners can work both as individuals and within a social grouping. They are able to decide if some subset of a task can be done alone or needs the concentrated effort of a group, and are able to cooperate if someone else makes the decision to include them.

(v) *display their understanding and competence in a number of different ways*. They are able to design different outcomes for their learning and can communicate these outcomes to appropriate audiences in appropriate ways.

(vi) *engage in self- and peer-evaluation*. There comes a particular confidence with learning that allows youngsters to be judges of quality of learning outcomes. This self-possession is a criterion of active learning in that it illustrates the capacity to recognize 'fitness for purpose' in activities, and the creativity and innovative work in themselves and others.

(vii) *feel good about themselves as learners*. Confidence in learning is a major motivational factor in any context and is not the pursuit of young children, adolescents or adults. The mode of learning for individuals within any of the three groups will alter considerably where they can become confident in the act of learning itself. At these points, learning becomes fun, thought-provoking, challenging and very active.

We need to make a few caveats in these seven pointers to shape them towards the teaching and learning of very young children. However, we also leave some of this story to be told through the case studies that follow in each of the chapters, where classroom teachers are able to illustrate active learning in situ.

Child-centred learning

It is not fashionable in certain quarters to talk too loudly about 'child-centred learning'. As we write, the general mood is one of 'back to basics', a move away from informal topic and group-based classroom work to formal, subject-based whole-class teaching. Child-centred learning is disparaged as a 'nineteen sixties, wet, libertarian, softies' fad, and that what is wanted today is a tough, pragmatic, systematic 'hard' knowledge approach.

In actuality, most primary schools *are* tough pragmatic places, highly organized and developed in their thinking and commonly use a variety of organizational techniques to suit the learning needs of the children. Sometimes this will be individual tuition, pairs, small-group, team work, class groups and – sometimes – whole-school teaching (and some of the case studies exemplify where and how this is appropriate). Individual attention to one child at a time is frequently impossible in the busy swarm of an active classroom. Where it is important (for example, listening to reading, correcting work, diagnosing particular learning difficulties, giving specific advice, and so on) teachers commonly have a range of strategies to enable this to happen.

However, individually-based learning and child-centred learning are very different. In essence, the difference lies in who has control over what is learned. In child-centred learning the onus tends to lie with the child to drive the direction in which learning will go; in whole-class subject-based learning, it is the teacher or the curriculum which is in charge and then dictates what will, or will not, be taught. It is essentially a difference in philosophy about the nature of learning – do children learn naturally, actively challenging their surroundings? Or do they learn only what they are taught and that which comes directly from teacher or parent?

Given this distinction, we are firmly child-centred in our approach. Children learn from an immense number of sources and some – just some – of this comes from close adults. It is the children themselves who control what they learn and what they choose to forget. This is not to say that significant adults cannot draw them into learning; they clearly can and do every working day. They can provide stimulating surroundings, exciting activities, times of intense hard work, time for fun and creativity. But, in the final analysis, it is the child who must take responsibility for what they learn. And here is the paradox. We actually *want* children to take this responsibility for learning, so that they become self-sufficient and self-sustaining learners. Parents, teachers, educators generally, and employers eventually, do not want people who are highly dependent and cannot take charge of how and what they learn. In society at large, people are expected to know for themselves – if a person is ignorant in some specific area they are expected to tackle that learning as best they can. As they say, 'ignorance of the law is no defence': if you are ignorant of a particular point of legality, it is your responsibility to find out and not the legal system's job to teach you.

To develop these skills for independent learning we need to start early. We must accept that we need to guide children and young people along a route that leads to them growing in confidence in their own capacities. They eventually need to direct all their learning themselves and so to *own* their learning. Nor is this a particularly recent 'bandwagon'; Froebel and Pestalozzi were highly influential in the early 1800s, and they built their work on educators and philosophers who came well before them (Leibschner, 1992). Nor is it particularly 'soft' and 'libertarian'; it is an essential and urgent requirement for civilized life within a democracy. Unless, that is, one holds the view that the average human being inherently dislikes work and will avoid it where s(he) can, preferring to avoid responsibility and having little ambition. As Brandes and Ginnis (1986) point out, if this view is dominant, it commonly means that people must be coerced, controlled, threatened, all in the interests of organizational objectives.

Obviously, this is not our perspective and we prize a high capacity for ingenuity and creativity in solving a wide variety of problems both in school and in outside life. We do not, however, expect the child to arrive at this point alone and teachers are hugely important in teaching children how to be self-sufficient.

Progression and differentiation

To be properly sensitive to children, the National Curriculum needs to be defined in smaller steps. This is a point we made earlier about helping children with Special Educational Needs. In a nutshell, the steps we describe relate to the concepts of progression and differentiation. Progression means advancement by successive steps, where these are related to the child's capacity to change. It is entirely likely that in any one class, each child will require different successive steps to make progress. This, in turn, means the teacher must provide experiences that are shaped to the individual and possibly different in each case. One of the key issues they face is to match the classroom activity to the needs of the child so precisely that progress in thinking, understanding and 'doing' takes place.

Keogh and Naylor (1993) point out the importance of matching, which they refer to as 'attempting to get the degree of challenge and success right for many of the pupils much of the time'. They draw the term from Wynne Harlen's work (Harlen, 1985). She describes matching as a dynamic process in which the teacher attempts to constantly adjust activities according to the pupils' responses. Keogh and Naylor go on to point out that this is an undertaking which matches in a subtle, individual and lesson-by-lesson way. This progress is based upon an assessment of the child's starting point, a judgement of where she or he is trying to reach and how to get there. They outline two main areas where progression is needed: in understanding scientific ideas and accomplishing scientific processes. However, they rely heavily on the 'constructivist approach' as a remedy for ensuring progression. They suggest that, as long as pupils are given the opportunities to clarify, reflect, challenge, apply and review both knowledge and processes, progression will follow.

We take issue here. Constructivism is not necessarily a catch-all panacea which will right all the ills of non-progression in children. The issue is more complex and difficult than this. Children do not necessarily think in a linear progressive way, and to assume that simply because teachers ask questions and provide experiences, that progression will then follow is unfortunately not a case supported by large-scale research evidence.

So what can we do to ensure progression? Probably, it cannot be guaranteed to take place – not least because we believe the learner always has a veto over what he or she chooses to learn. Nevertheless, teachers need to plan, they need to assist children in developing their skills and ideas in science and technology, and they need to do so at rates which facilitate individual children in moving forward.

Harlen's (1993) ideas about how children learn might provide a clue for those searching for how to assist progression. After all, it is sometimes easy to choose a set of activities that make excellent sense to the teacher and which seem to lead on from one to another in logical order. But in our view, there is only progression if the original concept has been clearly understood by the learner, and only if the 'jump' between the first idea and a new one is sufficiently small to allow for progress between the two. Harlen describes this jump as a process of linking. Others describe it as putting in place 'stepping stones', building bridges, or providing scaffolding. Harlen points out that new experiences will 'link' to existing ideas if they have enough in common with these existing ideas, and that testing the links to see if they fit

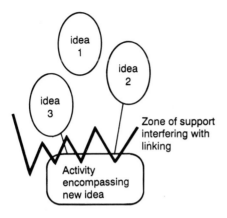

Figure 2.1 Zone of support.

under different conditions is a crucial part of moving to new understandings
– that is, of making progression. She suggests that children's ideas will progress
scientifically if the 'linking and testing' are carried out in a scientific manner.
That is, process skills in science are very similar to the metacognitive processes of linking and testing.

Again – to us – this seems to be overly constraining, relying on constructivism
too much to provide answers which may not be appropriate. However, there
are some possibilities here. What Harlen's model points out is the need for
teachers to know, not just the point children have reached in their ideas and
skill development, but what activities can be provided to introduce new ideas
that overlap sufficiently to form a link between existing ideas and new experiences. That said – and it is a large assumption that teachers can pinpoint
understandings so accurately – they then need to understand what testing
procedures children will need to undertake to be convinced that the new idea
is different, so that they can adapt the old idea and thus make progress.
Testing, however, in our view encompasses a variety of possibilities. The
context and the medium of the test are important here. An activity which
introduces a new context will not necessarily be sufficient to link with an
existing idea. So, for example, children meeting 'measuring and planning' in
technology may not necessarily recognize that as very similar to activities in
maths. In the same way the medium is important. By medium we mean the
presentation of learning experiences to provide a 'zone of support' for the
child so that ideas can be linked. For a child who finds reading and writing
difficult, presenting activities in a written form and expecting the child always
to provide results and feedback in writing could interfere with links, not
support them. In this case, the zone of support will interfere with the link as
Figures 2.1 and 2.2 indicate.

So progression, in our terms, is about assisting the child to make links
(build bridges) between new challenges and old understandings. Those links

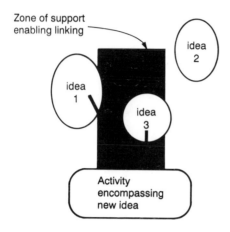

Figure 2.2 Zone of support.

can only be reached and be firm if the teacher ensures that the closeness of fit to the original idea is sufficient and the zone of support which represents the medium in which the idea is presented does not interfere with linking. This inevitably leads to having to present differentiated experiences, since no two children will need either the same support zones or have the same distance between ideas with which to link.

'Zone' design

One way to think about creating an atmosphere for learning is to think of developing a 'zone of learning'. When we set out to make science and technology happen in a classroom, we start from a variety of entry points into a sort of 'space–time zone'. That zone is fixed in some dimensions by the physical nature of the room, the organization of the group, the shape of the curriculum, the timing of the school day, the expectations of the parents and staff, and so on. The zone is flexible, however, in many other respects. Foremost are the nature of sub-groupings the teacher chooses, the quality of the learning environment, the way he or she communicates with the class, the style of teaching and the children's appetite for learning. In the first case study in this chapter, one of us (M.W.) sets out a small exercise in 'zone design': the planning of a series of seven lessons where the intention was to use a problem-solving approach crossing both science and technology. The story is continued in the second part of the study (the plan in action) later in Chapter 8.

The notion of a zone has been around since the work of Vygotsky who used the term the 'zone of proximal development' (ZPD). This is taken from two parts of his writing, first from *Thought and Language* (1986) and, secondly, from a paper published within a compendium called 'Mental development of children and the process of learning' reprinted in *Mind and Society*

(1978). Vygotsky's work seems to go through periods of revival between bouts of neglect and it is currently on the 'up' in such diverse areas as maths and chemistry (Newman *et al.*, 1989). Vygotsky makes his definition of the zone to be the difference between the level of problem difficulty a child could engage in independently and the level that could be reached with adult help. This difference is a fairly specific description of the 'interpersonal learning space' between a pupil and adult: more generally, Vygotsky's concept of ZPD is taken to refer to an interactive system within which people work on a problem which at least one of them could not, alone, work effectively. Cognitive change takes place within the zone, where the zone is considered both in terms of individuals' developmental histories and in terms of the support structures created by the other people and the cultural and pedagogic tools in the setting. The case study that follows describes some early exploratory work where the word 'people' includes adults and pupils within small group and team activities. The work relates to the teaching of the concept of sound in physics. In the UK's current post-National Curriculum era, the 'coverage' of the content of the statutory 'Programmes of Study' is of immediate importance. The central point of this study was to meet the legal requirements while at the same time fostering a constructivist approach through active problem-solving strategies.

CASE STUDY 1

Organizing learning at Spinfield School

Mike Watts, Roehampton Institute

Spinfield School is a co-educational 'combined' school catering for 5–12-year-olds and is housed in modern buildings on the outskirts of a small town in rural England. The class in question comprised 30 charming and well-motivated 11-year-olds and a highly competent and facilitative class teacher. I arrived as the 'man from the university' and guest-teacher for one morning a week for seven weeks.

A real problem associated with the school lies in the design of the school hall – a multi-purpose area which is used for school assemblies, for gymnastics and sports, and as a dining room for school lunchtimes. It is a glass-and-brick construction with a polished wooden floor: not surprisingly, the acoustics in the room are appalling. Such is the problem that communal times in the hall are a misery – even with no talk at all the lunchtime clack of cutlery on crockery alone was deafening. Teachers and pupils together dislike the area, the noise in the hall is inimical to normal conversation and discourse and raised voices simply exacerbate conditions. The general problem, then: how to improve the acoustic properties of the school hall in a feasible and inexpensive way.

The concept of sound is dealt with in the National Curriculum (DES, 1991) and – amongst other things – this requires at this stage of schooling that:

Pupils should learn that sounds are heard because they travel to the ear and that they do so via a variety of materials. They should learn that sounds are made when objects vibrate, and investigate how sounds are changed in pitch, loudness and timbre. [. . .] They should be aware of the obtrusive nature of some sounds in the environment.

The National Curriculum also maintains that at this age pupils should:

Level 3: know that light and sound can be reflected.
Level 4: know that light travels faster than sound.
Level 5: know that sound is produced by a vibrating object and travels as a wave.

I need to say that the research in this area shows that children at this age are rarely able to use a general theory of sound based on the idea of vibrations. Scott and Asoko (1990), for example, maintain that children do not even think of sound travelling (it simply 'happens') and they seldom think that it needs a medium like air or metal to vibrate in order to carry the sound. So their prior knowledge and experience are not in tune with the needs of school science – their starting point (T_1) can be seen to need some considerable development within the 'zone' in order to solve the problem.

Our general principles in setting out the ZPD, our 'zone of learning' for this problem-solving in sound, were to

(i)   provide opportunities for us to explore pupils' ideas and understandings of sound before we began (to establish T_1) and encourage discussions of how sound works;
(ii) promote active, collaborative learning, moving between teacher-directed and pupil-directed activities of various forms;
(iii) teach through the use of open-ended problem-solving, providing sub-problems and team work for different parts of the overall problem;
(iv) encourage a range of communicative techniques within a non-threatening learning environment.

The youngsters worked either as a whole class or in predetermined 'science teams' and the model was one of cooperative learning and social collaboration. Each child had the task of understanding what other members of the group were doing and the answers they had obtained in their work. Our end-point (T_2) for the seven-week period was that we should:

• reach feasible solutions for the sound in the school hall, while also
• meeting the needs of the National Curriculum

In this context we told them they were all 'scientists and technologists for the day', tackling a real problem for the school. The first session was diagnostic – to determine what their ideas were about sound. Then after this the general issues each week concerned:

• the particulate model transmission and velocity of sound
• the working of the human ear
• reflection, echo, reverberation and absorption
• amplitude and frequency
• sound levels, noise, music and the effects on people
• sound in the built environment

Within this 'zone' we put in some structures so that the pupils were able to reach their own solutions with the minimum of help and yet know that there were systems for getting support if it was needed. We had: 'clue cards' ready made with hints of how to make progress; 'skill stations' where they could learn, for example, to use the glue gun or the noise meter; books and materials from the school library; other musical instruments in the music room, and – of course – direct teacher help. On the whole, it was an attempt to enable the pupils to be as independent as possible while still offering that help which was necessary to solve the problem. I describe the outcomes of all this preparation in Case Study 15 in Chapter 8.

Value arguments

We have began to set our stall. We have covered a variety of ideas in this second chapter which forms the initial framework for our views of learning and understanding in science and technology. Several of the ideas we explore here set the scene for the case studies and perspectives we present in later chapters. The chapter set out our thoughts on 'zones for learning' about practical alternatives in science and technology. We hope that our activities in the following chapters are close enough to enable readers to link with their existing ideas and that our zone of support assists, not interferes with that linking.

In all, we have centred learning on the personal, social and environmental zone that we create in order to enable children's structured learning. We recognize that this is not the only learning that takes place and we are keen to build upon their growing experience in the world. We recognize, too, that the individual will always have the power to 'shut down' school learning if the learning environment is threatening or non-supportive. To this extent, we have described early attempts to construct a positive zone of activity to facilitate the learning we want to take place.

three

Conceptual development and language

Introduction

What is the significance of the way that sounds become words and words become meanings? Language is not 'mere sounds or words', of course, but much more – expression, thinking aloud, feelings, ideas, poetry, persuasion, and so on. Our purpose in this chapter is to continue in the vein we have adopted and to explore some of the ways that theories of constructivism can add to our appreciation of language work through science and technology in schools. In Chapter 1 we used Ros Driver's words to make the point that conceptual change involves the learner actively constructing his or her own meaning in any situation, whether it is text, dialogue or physical experience. And that construction of meaning is an active process of hypothesizing and hypothesis testing and has the consequence that the learner is seen as being ultimately responsible for their own learning.

In this chapter we explore more the nature of concepts and conceptual change, some contemporary research, the role of language and how we can put theories into practice in the classroom.

Purpose

In Chapter 1 we described constructivism in the following way: learning is always an interpretative process involving individuals' constructions of meaning. These constructions are commonly related to specific events, happenings, situations and phenomena. New constructions are based upon previous experience and prior knowledge. Learning science and technology the 'constructivist way' means using concepts and experience we already possess, and which we then change and mould on the basis of fresh meanings. Meanings, then, are the core of the theory, and of course words can be at the heart of meanings. As Sutton (1992) says:

Words steer perceptions both positively and negatively and also they influence what people do or do not do as well as what they see or miss seeing.

He means by this that the words in and around science and technology are not plain, simple and straightforward: as with all words they can take on a multitude of meanings. Words like 'energy', 'power', 'force' and 'work', for instance, all have meanings different in science to their everyday meanings.

In his book, Sutton (1992) discusses two general ways of describing language which he calls the 'labelling system' and the 'interpretive system'. The first suggests that words correspond simply to (and describe) features in the external world. Telling works best by efficient, clear transmission from teacher to learner, and the learner must be a good receiver. In this system, words have fixed meanings which can be captured in a clear unambiguous definition. In the interpretive system, however, language is different. Words highlight features and steer thoughts and dialogue. We use them to explore, persuade, suggest, and to influence how we see new points of interest. Learning is the active interpretation and re-expression of ideas by the learner, so that what the hearer constructs may approximate to something like the speaker's intentions, but communication is always partial. Meaning varies from person to person, is fuzzy and debatable, and multiple meanings are important and positive, not an imperfection at all.

What does it mean to say that words shape our ways of seeing the world and are hugely influential on the perspectives we then adopt? One classical example goes as follows. Two people are standing on the seashore watching dusk approach, looking out to sea towards a calm horizon. The question is, are they both watching the sunset, or are they in fact watching the Earthrise? A setting sun implies that the Earth is stationary and that the Sun is moving downwards, so that it eventually 'sinks' below the horizon 'behind' (?) the ocean. Earthrise implies that the sun, for all intents and purposes, is stationary and – as the Earth revolves on its axis – the rim of the Earth passes upwards and away from the line of sight of the sun. So, is it 'sunset' or 'Earthrise'? Or is that just semantics? As a friend joked recently, 'I've nothing against semantics but I wouldn't want my daughter to marry a word'. In scientific terms the expression 'Earthrise' is a better description because it carries with it a model of the way that our part of the Solar System works, rather than a historical version that is no longer seen to have validity. If this seems a little esoteric, then it is only an attempt to show that words carry with them 'packages' of meaning which shape how we think and how we see things.

The difficulty lies in our views of something called 'reality'. Some things we do not doubt are real – hot coffee after a cold winter's playground duty, arguing children outside the classroom door, parent evenings after school – are all pretty real when they happen. Other things (like 'justice', 'democracy', 'accountability') have a more fleeting reality to them and seem to come apart as soon as they are examined carefully. Some things seem concrete and can be pointed at, others are abstract and ephemeral.

Classical concepts

Most of the concepts studied in traditional concept development tasks are completely artificial (patterns of dots on paper, geometrical shapes, colour-coded blocks, etc.). These, and other similar ones, we have called 'classical concepts' because they can be very tightly defined and controlled. They are not too much use to us except the kind of developmental work that may be part of mathematics education in terms of fairly arbitrary sets and groups, etc. Some concepts in science – like the concept of energy in physics – might be thought to be classical in that it is also tightly defined and controlled. We like to think, though, that the meanings that scientists have for the term 'energy' are just sufficiently fuzzy to remove it from this camp and into one we discuss later as 'scientific concepts'.

Natural kinds

A great many concepts correspond to classes of things that occur in the natural world and are part of our reality – however, we want to define that term. As we noted earlier, we have no doubt that reality exists though we are committed to the idea that this will be interpreted by different people in many different ways. Natural kinds correspond to groups of entities that happen in nature and include such things as plants and animals as well as science concepts like elements and compounds. As Keil (1989) points out, there is no simple definition for natural kinds, but nevertheless research indicates the possibility that 'natural kind concepts might have representational structures different from those of other concepts'. This simply means that learners may establish, sort and sift concepts like 'animal', 'cat', 'substance' or 'tree' in ways that would be different from other kinds of concepts. The learning of such concepts is commonly highly contextualized – they happen in particular ways at particular times for any individual so that they become associated with a series of other contextual features which can 'box in' the concept. If we take other examples of natural kinds like 'lemons', 'thunderstorms', 'roses', 'earthquakes' or 'diseases', it is perhaps easier to see that there may be no hard and fast rules about what constitutes, say, a disease. Moreover, any individual's first encounters with – say – a thunderstorm will be very formative in the ways the concept might then be represented. There is a real sense in which young learners develop these kinds of concepts both from the 'concrete' to the 'theoretical' and from 'theory' back to the concrete. So, for instance the concept of 'cat' may grow from encounters with a home or neighbourhood version of a domestic cat and some when associated with the term 'animal'. Over time, differentiation will be made between this and other animals, and distinctions made between cats. The term might then come to cover the 'cat family' and the word 'animal' become more theoretically sophisticated to allow the siting of cats within it more securely. We might expect this kind of yo-yoing to happen all the time. While chairs and tables are not fixed, and classical concepts are quite fuzzy (a tree stump can act as a picnic table as well as a seat for someone) children will oscillate between real chairs they know and the more theoretical term 'furniture'. The important issue here is that the shifts of meaning can happen both ways and we do not necessarily lose the early subjective, immediate and 'concrete' versions just because we can develop more theoretical ones too. Our concepts can often remain very contextualized, despite the sometimes clear overlay of our scientific theorizing.

Concept shifts in science

From the standpoint of our constructivist philosophy we have a particular view about the way concepts 'shift' in science. First, we do not believe that simply because a word is given a particular definition in science that it stays that way for ever. There are countless examples from the history of science to show that terms and expressions are invented, come into fashion only for them later to go back out of fashion and be forgotten.

A common example is that of 'phlogiston'. This was an idea around for a long time, particularly during the mid 17th century, and was meant to be a kind of 'insubstantial essence' which was given up or taken in during chemical reactions. It was a term used to account for heating effects that take place when some chemicals react – why some have a quick rise in temperature and others go cold. However, a French scientist – Antoine Lavoisier – working in the late 1700s during a dramatic era for science, showed that heating, and particularly combustion, depended on measurable substances like oxygen rather than any 'insubstantial' essences like phlogiston. This set Lavoisier towards a theory of chemical combination which did away with phlogiston, and he defined chemicals in the modern way so that the names of compounds reflect the elements they contain. In fact, by the time Lavoisier died on the guillotine during the French Revolution, he had set chemistry along the highly successful lines it follows today.

The point of this story is that it is an example of the way both science and technology change over time. The same can be said of innumerable theories, concepts, terms and expressions in both areas of work – science and technology are constantly evolving and developing. The expressions used when talking this way are that scientific and technological knowledge is socially constructed, is contingent upon the culture of the day and is transient. That is, it is not a body of knowledge fixed as truth for all time, but is changing and developing as new ideas and social imperatives come along.

School science, school technology

There is another kind of concept shift we want to mention here, too. There are many people who argue that what children do in schools is not science or technology at all. If it were, they say, we would not need research scientists in industry or medicine. What an industrial chemist does, they say, bears no relation to the activities of a seven-year-old in a primary classroom. There is, of course, some force to this argument. We would want to say, though,

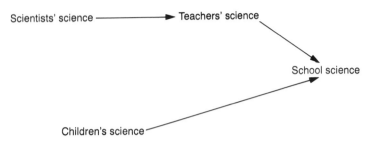

Figure 3.1 School science.

that we are asking children to 'be scientific', to be technologically minded, to be 'scientists and/or technologists for the day'. We know, though, that the content of the activities in classrooms is different, and this is rightly the case.

Figure 3.1 is adapted from the work of Zylbersztajn (1983). He makes the case that 'teachers' science', or textbook science, is really a distillation (often a historical reconstruction) of science itself. So, what appears in biology or physics texts has already gone through a transformation by the authors to make it accessible for teaching in schools. We would not expect to teach straight from contemporary research reports, conference papers or journal articles from *The Lancet*, for example. This transformed knowledge is then transmogrified one more time as the teacher adapts and adopts this for classroom use with the particular group of children present at the time. At this point it becomes 'school science'. So school science is similar to, but not the same as, 'real' science – a sort of distant cousin.

Meanwhile, says Zylbersztajn, children themselves have developed theories for how the world works and they can explain a range of common phenomena (like evaporation, energy, clouds, etc.). These ideas are commonly at odds with 'official' science but nevertheless children bring these to class and use them when doing science. Classroom science, then, is a brew of teachers' and children's ideas and theories – which all need to emerge with some coherence and consistency.

Children's science

We need to know something more about the ways in which children interpret the words in science. For instance, as Asoko *et al.* (1993) point out, to a biologist the term 'animal' refers to any living thing which is not a plant. In everyday talk 'animal' tends to be synonymous with 'mammal', so that birds and insects are not usually referred to as animals. Nor is it just simple labels like this. Metaphors abound both in science and everyday life and we need to know how appropriate they are in use. So for example, Asoko *et al.* note that:

> metaphors and expressions common in everyday talk may suggest ideas which conflict with the science viewpoint. A model which explains how

we see in terms of rays emanating from the eyes is supported by expressions such as 'looking daggers' or 'sending dirty looks'. It is not surprising that a child believes plants get food from the soil if father 'feeds' his tomatoes.

We want to take this last point further and focus on just one part of the forms of language we use in school science – that of animistic and anthropomorphic language.

Animism and anthropomorphism in school science

Animism is when people refer to inanimate objects as if they were alive, as in the expression a 'living flame'. Anthropomorphism is treating inanimate objects not just as alive but having human characteristics, with 'wants' and 'needs' etc. Sometimes these expressions begin as deliberate metaphors and become subsumed within everyday talk – as, for instance, with the terms 'computer memory' or 'computer virus'. The metaphor continues now so that anti-virus programmes are designed to 'disinfect' contaminated files and discs.

What, you might ask, is the harm in all this? On one occasion youngsters were asked to explain why goldfish in a tank tended to occupy the upper reaches of the water rather than the bottom of the tank. The expected answer might have concerned light levels in the water, the presence of food on the surface and so on. Instead, some of the children answered that: 'They probably like the better view they get from there.' Again, if a child is asked, 'Why does an orange float?' and answers, 'It is swimming' or 'Because it wants to stay on top of the water,' then does this really matter?

It is an interesting area because animistic expressions are often seen as a good way of helping children understand what is happening. They go completely against the views of science, are quite scientifically incorrect, and yet we continue to use them all the same to help with certain explanations. It is a kind of 'it's naughty but we like it ' approach. We decided recently (Watts and Bentley, 1993) that there are perhaps three ways forward:

(i) ignore such animistic and anthropomorphic ideas and pupils will grow out of them;
(ii) provide challenges or conflicting ideas to help get them back on the right track;
(iii) use and build on these ideas in order to redirect them towards the correct science.

The first we ruled out because there is now considerable evidence that children do not grow out of these ideas and animism is still 'alive and well' in adult explanations. Moreover, some explanations of this sort are quite powerful and difficult to shift. We ruled out the second on the grounds that it is very difficult to do. How do you prove through counterevidence, for instance that the planet Earth is not living, or that 'Mother Nature' does not exist? It has proved a very interesting experiment with quite mature students to ask them if a candle flame is alive. They normally resort to the standard seven characteristics of living things: movement, respiration, sensitivity, growth, reproduction, excretion and nutrition. We have put them in that order because one of the mnemonics students use to remember these is the acronym 'Mrs. Gren'. However, when you come to put it to the test it is possible to argue that a flame *does* move, *does* exchange gases with the air around like respiration, does respond sensitively to conditions around it (moving air, etc.), can grow into larger flames, can reproduce asexually to produce many more similar flames, and does excrete soot and carbon dioxide and consume wax and oxygen as 'food'. Of course this is stretching issues quite a bit but these sorts of arguments can be enough to convince young scientists that in fact flames *are* alive.

We are left, then, with building on these ideas, using them to help shape thoughts towards more scientific ones. Sherrington (1993), for instance, describes a child who says in response to questions about evaporation: 'evaporation goes up because it wants to be a cloud'.

The child is depicting water vapour as a living object that has wants and needs. Sherrington then suggests that this is a legitimate way forward since it provides the child with another linguistic tool towards more expressive language.

Research on children's science

Animistic thinking is not the only set of ideas which children display. As we have mentioned, they have particular ideas about sound and the way it does or does not travel, about clouds and the ways they move, about evaporation and condensation, about the wind and where rain comes from, how people are able to cling onto the Earth upside down in Australia, how light travels to or from the eye, how shadows are made, why some things sink or float and many more. For example, they have ideas about what happens when things burn and find it very difficult to accept that nothing disappears in burning. 'But the paper turns to ashes', or 'the candle burns down and gets smaller and smaller' they say. They find it very difficult to imagine that if one could collect all the combustible material and the oxygen in the air around before the flames, then there would be exactly the same amount of ashes and smoke after the burning.

Developing language tasks

We are keenly aware that primary teachers are deft and dexterous when it comes to matters of language development and we are not about to add greatly to the store of materials that exists to help develop children's language. So, for example, Bentley and Watts (1992) drew together a range of 'communicative' activities for all four key stages and so feel we can rest a little here. Our only plea is that teachers should be as keenly aware of language and concept development in science and technology as they are in other areas of the curriculum: as we noted above, words like 'force', 'energy', 'pressure', 'work', 'momentum', 'power', and so on, have very particular meanings in science that are different to the way the words are used in everyday life. To come to grips with these particular meanings is not straightforward and often involves revisiting science textbooks again after – possibly – many years away. However, as a 'taster' we suggest that there are many types of tasks that can be used to develop language skills, such as having children tackle a 'fruity' topic, to:

- predict the nature of the inside of a fruit (colour, texture, seeds, etc.) without first opening the fruit. Their hypotheses can be questioned and challenged before the fruit is cut to see what it is like;
- draw cross-sectional cuts of fruit, and describe what they are like;
- classify foods in different ways, ways in which pupils choose for themselves. They can generate reasons for their classifications and then some of the more usual or scientific forms of classification can be introduced;
- observe changes over time. Plant growth, root growth, change of colour of the skin, rate of decomposition, etc. They can measure changes in weight and or appearance over time, for example, grow seeds and describe the changes that take place;
- preserve fruits by cooling, freezing, wrapping in various materials, chemically treat them with sugar, salt or vinegar;
- see what changes take place when fruit is not preserved, so that they can see the way that exposure to oxygen can discolour a cut apple, potato or banana very quickly so that they go brown.

This type of activity works best both with fruit that is familiar and some that is unusual and so not part of the children's normal experience, such as kiwi fruit or pomegranates. However, our case studies offer a very wide range of other suggestions for a variety of language activities as Cindy Palmer, Rosemary Denman, Di Bentley and Amanda Walsh describe below.

CASE STUDY 2

Looking at differences

Cindy Palmer

The work described here arose from a series of interviews which focused on the skills of scientific observation with teachers throughout the infant age range. The questions that I asked were wide ranging and the resulting debates covered all aspects of scientific observation in the classroom. The identification of similarities and differences was discussed in almost all of the interviews. However, I was struck by the firmly held view of both Year 2 teachers that children find it easier to recognize differences than they do similarities. I decided to investigate this theory by working with their children and therefore gathering evidence first hand.

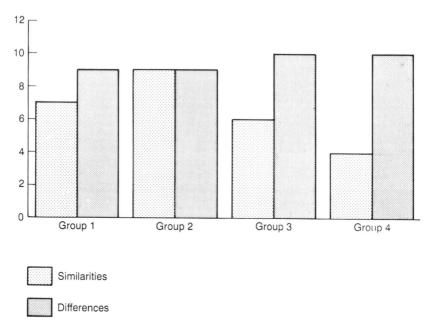

Figure 3.2 Graph.

It soon became clear that children are able to recognize similarities when considering two objects. While, just as the teachers said, they did identify more differences between objects, I realized that children's ability to identify similarities is often underestimated. Perhaps this is because they are rarely asked to demonstrate this skill in the scientific tasks which teachers construct for them.

I worked closely with two Year 2 classes and, for one, I set up a task in which the children were given two red pencils. The pencils had been chosen because the teachers thought that the children would have difficulty identifying any similarities other than the fact they were both pencils.

In the other Year 2 class, I gave the children a pencil and a felt-tip pen. These were chosen to see if the children could find the similarities between them. The teachers thought that the children would only be able to identify the differences.

The children worked in small groups with approximately five children in each group. The groups were given a balance, rulers, magnifying glasses and centicubes. One child was nominated as a reporter to record their findings. The children were free to decide whether they wanted to identify similarities or differences first. Interestingly enough, when given the choice, six out of the eight groups decided to start by identifying similarities.

Two red pencils. The same or different?
In this task, the children found more differences than similarities. However, as the graphs in Figures 3.2 and 3.3 demonstrate, the pattern was not as marked as had been expected by the Year 2 teachers. The following discussions arose when the children were examining the pencils.

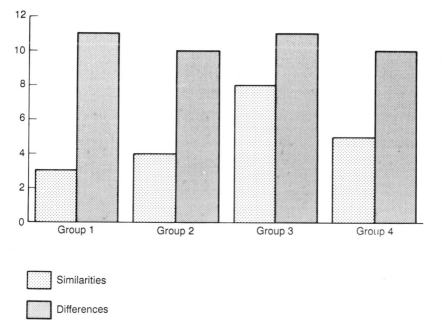

Similarities

Differences

Figure 3.3 Graph.

Looking closely for detail
The children noticed that the two pencils had teeth marks. The teacher encouraged the children to look more closely at them.

SUSAN: They both have bite marks.
TEACHER: Have they? Have a good look. [*There is a long pause*]
SUSAN: They ain't got the same numbers.
TEACHER: So they are the same because they both have bite marks, but different because . . .
SUSAN: They ain't got the same number of them.

The teacher had encouraged the children to have another look, to sharpen their observations. She said that she wanted the children to question what they see all the time, checking their observations and making them more precise. She believed that it was important to provide children with equipment to assist them when making observations.

Using their senses
The teacher checked that the children knew what their different senses were.
She explained that they could use all of their senses when making observations and that she hoped that they would. Not all the children could identify their senses and as a result could not appreciate the differing information each sense could provide them with. At one point the children decided to listen to the pencils.

TEACHER: Do you think that we can hear the pencils? Do you want to try? [*The children try to listen to their pencils*]

TEACHER: Do they make a different sound? How can we test to hear if they make a different sound?

ROYSTON: I don't know.

BERNADETTE: Bang them on the table. [*Children hit them against the table*]

JASMINE: I know, they are different. That one is light, that one is hard. [*Children hit them against the table again*]

JASMINE: That one is louder. That one is lighter.

Another group extended this line of investigation to find out whether weight was a contributing factor to the difference in the sound that the two pencils made when hit against the table.

NICKY: That one is heavier and that one is lighter. [*This conclusion was drawn from the sound the pencils made when they were hit against the table*]

TEACHER: How do you think we can find out if one is heavier?

ANDREW: Weigh it.

SAM: Let's drop it and see what goes down the furthest. [*She means 'fastest'*]

TEACHER: Let's weigh it first.

The children weigh the two pencils. One is heavier than the other by one centicube.

TEACHER: Sam, what are you going to do with the two pencils then?

SAM: I am going to drop them at the same length.

TEACHER: Drop them from the same height and see what?

SAM: See what one drops first. [*Sam drops the pencils*]

RONALD: That one landed, not that one.

PAUL: Do it again. We didn't see.

SAM: All right, I will do it in slow commotion.

TEACHER: Slow 'motion'. [*Sam drops the two pencils several times until an agreement is made*]

The children led their own investigations and came up with a variety of ways to test whether the pencils sounded different. They extended their investigation to discover whether the weight of the pencils had any bearing on the sound they made when hit against the table. This enabled the children to use their skills of measurement. They extended their investigation further. Does weight affect the rate of fall? Throughout, the children were having to verbalize their thoughts so that everyone could hear and understand the ideas being put forward for testing.

Bringing past experiences to bear

The children noticed that the pencils were not sharpened in the same way. This led to a debate as to how they could have been sharpened.

ROYSTON: They are different – one is fatter and one is thin. [*When looking at the leads*]

TEACHER: Why is that?

ROYSTON: Because that has been sharpened a different way. That one has been with a sharpener. When my Grandad hasn't got a sharpener he uses a knife and it comes out like this. When I use a sharpener it comes out like that.

This child has seen the two pencils and can relate to how the pencils are sharpened at home. He can inform the other children why the two look different, relating it to his past experiences. It is important that the teacher encourages the children to reflect on their home and past experiences and to draw parallels between them and what is happening in school.

The children were able to identify many differences between the two red pencils even though they looked very similar. The teachers had thought that the children would have difficulty identifying any similarities between the two, other than the fact they were both pencils. The children found a number of similarities, although not as many as the number of differences. Only one group mentioned that they were the same because they were pencils.

One pencil, one felt tip. The same or different?
Although the two objects were less similar the children found more similarities than with the two red pencils.

The following discussions arose when the children were examining the pencil and the felt tip.

Measuring
All of the children agreed that the pencil and the felt tip were the same length. However, the groups approached their measuring in different ways. Some compared the lengths by laying them on the table to see if they were the same while others measured them using centicubes. Both of these methods enabled the children to come to a conclusion as to whether the objects were the same length. However, only the second method was an attempt at quantification. It is essential that children get into the habit of measuring objects and then quantifying the results.

An interesting debate arose when each group had to decide whether the felt tip should have its lid on or off when it was measured. The group's debate began after the following discovery.

ANNA: It's not the same if you take the lid off the pen.
TEACHER: That's interesting.
ANNA: They aren't the same size. [*Anna puts the lid on the bottom of the felt-tip pen*]
ANNA: The pen is bigger than the pencil now because the lid's down the bottom.
TEACHER: So if you take the lid off?
ANNA: It will be smaller. [*Referring to the felt tip*]
TEACHER: If you put the lid on the bottom?
ANNA: It will make it bigger. [*Referring to the felt tip*]
TEACHER: If the lid is on the felt tip?
ANNA: It will be the same.

All of the groups decided that the lid should be on the felt tip when it was measured. They were all very interested that the position of the felt tip's lid made such a difference to its length.

Listen very carefully
The teacher had encouraged the children to use all their senses when observing the differences between the pencil and the felt tip. The children decided to listen to identify whether the two made the same or different sounds. One child suggested using them to write his name. In order to do this he said that you need to 'listen very carefully'.

AMAL: They don't sound anything. [*Putting the pencil and then the felt tip to his ear*]
MARY: No, you can hear them by writing.
TEACHER: You are going to have to listen really, really hard.
AMAL: Sh, sh.
PHILIP: I can't hear nothing. [*Mary writes her name with the pencil*]
TEACHER: Did you hear the pencil?

PHILIP: I can, I can. It makes a 'cruu' sound.
TEACHER: Let's listen to the felt tip. [*Mary writes her name with the felt tip*]
PHILIP: It's a crackling noise.
TEACHER: Is it the same sort of noise or different? [*All the children shout out 'different'*]
SOPHIE: The pencil sounds like a bee's noise but the felt tip sounds sort of crackly.
TEACHER: So, do they sound the same or different? [*All the children shout out 'different' again*]

The pencil and felt tip were chosen to see if the children could find similarities between them. The teachers had predicted that the children would only be able to identify differences. The children found a number of differences but they were also able to identify similarities. This was despite the objects being quite different.

CASE STUDY 3

Modelling history

Rosemary Denman, Holy Trinity Middle School

The class had been doing some work in history and industry. As a part of the work, we visited a variety of industrial locations in Wales to look at processes and machinery both old and new. The week of the field trip was exhausting, but the children thoroughly enjoyed seeing the history in action and looking at some of the examples of machines that we had talked about in their history lessons. We visited Dinorwig power station at Llanberis and followed that with a visit to the Llechwedd slate mines where we took a visit down the deep mine. The children enjoyed the hard hat wearing! (Figures 3.4 and 3.5.)

We also looked at an overshot water wheel as part of a water mill but unfortunately it was not working at the time. As a finale to the visit we travelled on the Ffestiniog railway and went round Conwy Castle.

On our return to school, the children and I discussed the technology work that was to come out of the visits. They had been told before they went that as part of the follow-up work they would have to produce a working model to show some idea of a machine and its processes or an aspect of history seen on their visits. We spent some time in the first technology lesson on their return just brainstorming ideas. Several very interesting projects were discussed during this time, but not all of them were really feasible. Some either had insufficient work in them, or were too complex to complete in the time scale available. The children had been told that from start to finish they had four weeks (with an afternoon a week) to complete their project from plan to model. Finally, the groups decided on their work. I had already decided to permit the children to work in friendship groups, since part of the differentiated outcomes of the work were to see how they managed themselves and their work, and what level of difficulty they wanted to work at.

The model-making began! As part of the design process, pupils were already used to drawing artistic impressions and plans of the materials and equipment they would need. They also tried to make scale drawings showing front, rear and side elevations using the design planner which all the classes in the middle school used (Figure 3.6).

Figure 3.4 Hard hats.

Of course some groups got to 'working model' stage much faster than others. For some the model-making was prolonged with many false starts and work which needed careful re-examination. I illustrate this later with the example of the process which the water wheel group went through.

By the end of the four weeks, we had a water wheel, the tram car from Llechwedd deep mine, several castles and drawbridges, and a model of the principles of hydro-electricity. In terms of the design and technology process, the work of the water-wheel group shows this admirably. They began with the idea that they wanted to make a model of an overshot water wheel. They built the wheel with no problem, using a wooden base, and cut-out bottle bases for the buckets to catch the water. The rim of the wheel was made from plastic straws originally joined together with wooden cocktail sticks. However, they soon decided that something sturdier was required and built a strong plastic wheel with thick card carriers for the water buckets. They made the new water buckets out of bottle caps, since the others had been too large and unwieldy to tip well. The next problem was to attach the bottle tops to the plastic and card wheel. They accomplished this, and built the tower as a support for the wheel out of card. The water supply for the wheel was a tube of plastic that delivered water from a can that the children kept filled up. Then came the difficult part. They needed to make sure that the water did not flow out of the can and leak, so the seal between the pipe and the can had to be waterproof. This took large amounts of Sellotape and plastic sheeting! Finally, the acid – or water – test. If the water flowed into the first bucket, would the bucket tip and turn the wheel? The first one worked fairly well. The bucket filled, tipped, filled the second

Figure 3.5 Slate mine.

bucket which tipped and poured water all over the floor. The next hour or so was spent in a laborious process of trial and error trying to ensure that the buckets were in the right places to catch the water from the previous bucket. This meant reshaping the card wheel and protecting it better with plastic, as it was becoming very wet. Once the children had decided that they had sufficient buckets and that they were more or less in the right place, they discovered another problem. This consisted of getting the buckets at the right angle to tip properly into one another and not just pour the water in between buckets. They moved the buckets nearer to each other to solve this problem and then discovered that some would not tip properly because they hit others. They were very frustrated at some points during all of this, and really needed to know more science to work out the angle, the volume of the buckets and the force with which the water was being delivered from the bucket above to keep the wheel turning. Without this sophisticated level of knowledge, however, they planned, made, tested, remade, altered angles, evaluated progress, started again, reshaped, altered their ideas and drawings and generally created the design cycle time and again. Throughout the whole activity there was a huge amount of conversation, discussion, argument about ideas and suggestions, which were taken up, refined and owned by the whole group.

Eventually, the class produced a set of finished artefacts. They evaluated each other's products, painted, shiny and glowing – or wet in the case of the water wheel. They had enjoyed the visit, but the follow-up work, in terms of having to rechart part of the scene they had visited, for many fully tested their scientific and technological skills. I found the project an excellent way of combining history and technology whilst keeping the children fully interested and involved at many different levels.

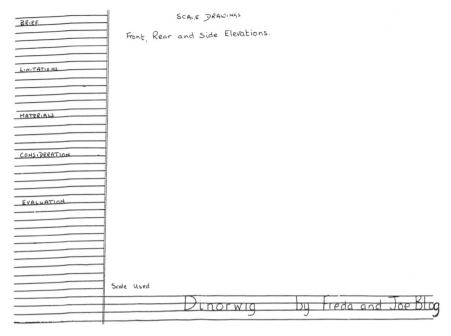

Figure 3.6 Technology design planner.

CASE STUDY 4

Planning and evaluation in technology

Di Bentley, Roehampton Institute

With young children some of the most difficult skills to teach are those of planning and evaluating a product or system. This case study is built from the work of several teachers who developed a series of ideas for teaching planning and evaluation to 6- and 7-year-olds.

Planning
A class of 6-year-olds made a visit to a farm in the Autumn term of the year. Some of them noticed that the goat's stable was fairly rudimentary and, being much taken with two baby kids, they wanted to design a better house for the goat and her kids. The teacher was using the farm visit as a starting point for her technology

project, which was to create a model farm system, and which involved making artefacts and understanding how the system worked. On return to school, during the next day, the teacher asked the children who had been interested in the goats, as a group, to draw a new house. When their drawings were complete she sat with the group and asked each child to describe their goat house from their picture. Some children had simply drawn the outside of the house, others had drawn the inside. From the discussion, she asked them to say what the inside or outside would look like as well. Then they drew the other 'half' of their picture, so that everyone had both an inside and an outside of the house. Sometime later in the week, an adult helper worked with the group. She asked the children to look at their drawings and choose one feature that they liked best from the outside and one from the inside. She produced two large sheets of paper, one with an outline of a 'house' drawn on, as the inside view. After discussion with the children about their chosen feature, a composite goat's house was built up, by the adult helper showing the inside and the outside with everyone's features in. The children were asked to justify their feature as they suggested it, and all the other children were asked for their comments before the feature was added to the composite plan. They were asked, for instance, where it should go on the plan, how big it should be so that, from their own original drawings, the children were now given the opportunity to improve and concentrate on one aspect but directed towards the features necessary for planning a design. The children then proceeded, during the next few weeks, to make various aspects of their composite design.

During the Spring term the same class were making a model of a Victorian kitchen, a technology project initiated by a talk from a local grandmother who had worked in a kitchen in a large house before the Second World War and who told the children stories about Victorian houses and kitchens. Using books and the grandmother's story as source material, the children were asked to draw what they thought a Victorian kitchen looked like. Again the teacher and the adult helper went round working with groups after their drawings had been completed. They wanted each child to take responsibility for making some feature of a Victorian kitchen so that they could transform their classroom into a large replica of the kitchen. This time, however, they directed the children to describe the features of their drawings in terms of size, materials, etc. by asking members of the group to ask particular questions, such as: how big is it?, what is it made of?, how does it work?, what makes it turn?, etc. The children soon adopted the idea and, under the guidance of the adults, each child drew their own feature with information on the drawing that their classmates had stimulated. In this way, the plans began to take on more of the detail needed to realize a design.

Evaluating

In discussion with adults, children can evaluate fairly easily. While they recognize things they like and things they do not, teaching for 'evaluation related to fitness for purpose', for example, or for aesthetic appeal is more difficult. This small cameo traces the development of this skill over two terms in one class of 7-year-olds, where the children ranged in 'evaluating' experience from Levels 1 to 3, and where the teacher had developed a system for getting children to evaluate systematically and progressively. She made the act of evaluation a feature of all their writing and making. So, for example, when talking to children as they were writing – whatever the writing was about – she would ask them which word or letter was the one they had done best, and which needed doing better next time. As they arrived in her class in September, she simply accepted their own evaluation of their work without interjection. By October she was beginning to add some of her own ideas, particularly where they were making artefacts. So, for example, she would ask them what they had done best about the card they were making and then add that she thought that it had been cut out very carefully. She also added things that needed to be improved from time to time. This sounds like the ordinary feedback that all good teachers give to their pupils as a matter of course. Indeed it is. But this particular teacher had another purpose in mind, and the rate of the progress and the features upon which she concentrated were carefully organized and thought out in advance.

By January, she had organized the children into 'helping pairs' for technology. The idea was something along the lines of each child having a critical friend, who would help with evaluation. Helping pairs were given questions on a card to ask during the making or planning of an artefact or other work. Sometimes these questions were general such as, 'How could you make it look better?' Sometimes they were specific such as, 'Does it work well every time – how can you improve it?' At first, the times when helping pairs asked their questions were directed into the work by the teacher to ensure that the questions were indeed asked. This would sometimes be at the start of a session, sometimes at the end. As time progressed over the Spring term, the input of the helping pair became less structured, but by now most children had become used to asking evaluative questions as the process continued. In the teacher's view the value of the questions was to focus the children's attention on the continual need for improvement. She was able to demonstrate some clear changes in work over the Spring term which children had initiated themselves as a result of the questions which their friends asked. She also planned in the Summer term to direct the questions much more towards 'fitness for purpose' in the making of artefacts and to encourage children to ask themselves, rather than having a helping pair. She pointed out that one of the important aspects of an approach such as this was the choice of the pairs. For some children the helping pair could be overcritical, or overhelpful, wanting to make suggestions for improvement rather than ask questions about how the individual might improve. She had had to keep a watchful eye on the progress of some pairs over the term.

CASE STUDY 5

Language and scientific concepts in the primary classroom

Amanda Walsh, Roehampton Gate School

Penny, Hima and Michael play with the class collection of toy cars, boats and aeroplanes. They move the cars along the floor staging several severe crashes, they fly the aeroplanes through the air and sink the boats in the water trough and they enjoy pushing the boats downwards until the water sucks them under. These children are 7 years old and yet each one is able to manipulate complex forces as they push and pull the objects to create the desired effect. Do they understand the scientific concepts involved in their actions, or are they just using information gained directly through the senses?

The children are unable to articulate any information about what forces they are using; they do not have the language to do so. How have they reached this level of understanding without the necessary language? Langer (1969) argues that: 'Before speech there is no conception: there is only perception, and a characteristic repertoire of actions, and a readiness to act according to the perceived world.' Penny, Hima and Michael display this repertoire of actions but these should not be underestimated for they are purposeful and exploratory; is it not through such actions that the child learns?

What is the role of language in understanding science concepts?

Osborne and Tasker (1985) state: 'Before they come near a science classroom children have already developed ideas about how and why things behave as they do . . . often these ideas are arrived at independently of language.' I would agree with Osborne and Tasker in their belief that children construct their own ideas before reaching the classroom but on what basis are these ideas formed if independent from language?

One of the key issues seems to be perception and with that follows expectation, anticipation and also prediction. The children in the classroom were able to manipulate forces because they had formed their own ideas or constructs on previous occasions and as a consequence now had certain expectations of the way the world worked. This, however, does not solve the fundamental question of how the children arrived at their previous constructs without the aid of scientific language.

Linguistic techniques for organizing thoughts

Bruner (1966) argues for a clear pattern in the development of thought and language. Initially the child can use a language which 'embodies powers of organisation he cannot achieve in thought'. Children's abilities in both thought and language then run parallel as they can achieve in thought what is already organized in speech. Finally, Bruner states that 'the powers of organisation in thought come to exceed the powers of organisation in speech'.

Through these stages the child uses language as a tool or instrument for thought. She uses the organizational skills required in speech in order to pattern and classify thoughts and ideas into more generalized concepts. The children playing with toy boats at the water trough maintain a constant flow of talk as they play. This talk is partly fantasy but also is descriptive of the phenomena they are manipulating. Each boat is piled high with Plasticine people until eventually it sinks. After the boats have been sunk many times using Plasticine, Lego bricks and a push from the child's hand, a pattern is identified. As each boat sinks it is acknowledged by using language which classifies it into a group. Classifying and sorting the phenomena in this way allows the children to generalize a connection between cause and effect. Eventually they come to realize that heaviness causing something to sink is a generalization of their experiences. This concept may not be scientifically correct, but it is the *child's* personal construct. Bruner's theory suggests that language comes before thought and consequently the very young child who has not developed language skills will be unable to use these same skills in thought.

To return now to Penny, Hima and Michael with their toy cars, boats and planes. All the evidence suggests that they were manipulating forces due to their perceived world. Each child had a set of expectations about how toy cars, boats and planes behaved under particular circumstances and were able to interact with scientific forces according to these expectations. The children talked about what happened in their play, reflecting on their expectations and recording their experience in order to make meaning and represent it to themselves. The meanings were shared as the children were communicating with each other and were able to anticipate each other's actions and the expected consequences. Similarly, each child has developed the language skills necessary to organize their expectations into patterns. They are able to classify and order but can they organize these patterns into thoughts or concepts?

MICHAEL: Look, it's got six people and it's not sinking yet.
HIMA: I can make it sink. [*She pushes it with her hand*]
MICHAEL: That's not fair, you pushed it down.
PENNY: I've used all my Plasticine now and it's still floating.
MICHAEL: Well the Plasticine floats anyway, 'cos look some of the people from my boat are floating on their own.
HIMA: No they're not, their sinking now look. [*She points to a person just beginning to sink*] It's too heavy.
TEACHER: Could you try and make them float on the water, Hima?
HIMA: No, they only float in the boat.
MICHAEL: That one's floating.
HIMA: No it's not. [*She pushes it gently with her finger but it still floats*]
MICHAEL: See, you can't sink it 'cos it's too big.
PENNY: The bigger ones float but the smaller ones sink.
MICHAEL: Yes, that's right.
TEACHER: There is a very big lump of Plasticine but look it's sunk to the bottom.
MICHAEL: Oh yeh.
PENNY: But it's just a lump. [*She fishes it out and squashes it flat on the table with her hand*] Now it'll float. [*It floats*]
HIMA: That's 'cos it's a boat now, you made it into a boat.
TEACHER: Have you noticed its shape?
MICHAEL: It's squashed and thin.
HIMA: It's boat shaped.
PENNY: It's just flat.

In my opinion Penny, Hima and Michael have developed their own concepts to explain what they observe. They do not use the correct vocabulary or labels, they do not even use language in a scientific context and their frameworks of understanding are certainly alternative to those accepted by the scientific community. But each child has formed concepts based on their own expectations and the language skills needed to organize these expectations.

Driver (1985) argues that: 'Learning is interaction between the learner's experiences and the schemes used to interpret and give meaning to those experiences.' This is an interesting statement as there is no mention of the correct meanings or those accepted by the scientific community. Learning is an individual and personal occurrence, meanings can be conjured in the imagination and need not be representative of scientific fact. I would argue that whilst learning is personal and individuals may have differing interpretations, it is vital that we help children, through language, to evolve shared meanings.

The implications for teaching science 'labels'?
The idea of shared meanings is very significant for teachers and children. Stopping to ensure that we all have a shared definition in the correct context is of tremendous

significance if teacher and children are to communicate effectively especially when many scientific words – such as energy – have a 'common parlance' meaning which is very different and imprecise. However, there are potential hazards which can be encountered when trying to define meaning.

Tolstoy's view is that it is quite impossible to explain the meaning of a word. You may replace it by other incomprehensible words with the connection between them as incomprehensible as the word itself. Falling into the trap of explaining word meanings is to misunderstand the role of teachers. Through negotiation and discussion the child and teacher should agree a shared meaning. There is a further implication when discussing word meanings. When is a word just a label and when is it a concept? For example, if I explained to Penny, Hima and Michael the scientific meaning of the word 'force', would I be labelling phenomena or introducing a new concept? Vygotsky (1978) was very clear on this: 'Direct teaching of concepts is impossible and fruitless.'

Language functions in the classroom

Language operates at different levels in all classrooms. Language used at its lower levels is for everyday communication purposes, such as asking the children to put up their chairs at the end of the day, whilst language used at its higher levels is for complex reasoning or hypothesizing in the abstract.

I observed a child drawing a concept map on sound. She had connected the words 'sound' and 'evaporate'. To explain the link she wrote: 'Sound is like water because they both disappear into the air.' When I spoke to her to try and find out more about her constructs she hypothesized that sound was very strong at first and that when it disappeared it was getting weaker and weaker until it had gone altogether, soaked up by the air and carried away. Here she was using language far beyond its simplest level. Whilst communicating with me she had also organized her thoughts. She made links and identified relationships between her existing knowledge and new experiences. She could classify and generalize the patterns she had identified to form a personal construct. Bruner (1966a) argued: 'It is when one uses language beyond this minimum level that it alters or, indeed transforms the nature of thought processes in a special way.' The special way described by Bruner is thinking abstractly or formally, arguably often required in science.

Cummins (1984) visualizes language proficiency and functions in classrooms along continuums which can be represented graphically.

Contextually embedded ———————— Purely linguistic cues

Undemanding cognitively ——————— Demanding cognitively

Lower cognitive language functions —— Higher cognitive language functions

Labelling ——————————————— Reasoning

Cummins (1984) argues that: 'Verbal activities in the classroom are often context-reduced and cognitively demanding.' This implies that children have to organize language and thought consciously and listen to pure linguistic cues in order to learn new concepts. As a primary school teacher it remains my responsibility to negotiate positions along the continuums with the children in my class. It is important to recognize that these positions are not fixed and may change several times during a single day to accommodate the child, the nature of the subject, the mood of the class and the teacher's beliefs about teaching and learning. As a constructivist I would hope to provide contextually-embedded cognitively-demanding learning. This is based on the way I believe children learn. Through providing this environment, learning is maximized as the child can select experiences and actively construct new concepts. At the opposite end of the continuum a teacher would be reduced to a transmitter of knowledge and would need to adopt this teaching theory in order to provide such a passive learning environment. The teacher and child have to choose the correct positions along each continuum in order that the most effective learning takes place. Obviously the positions may be different for each child every day. I would argue for learning to be contextually-embedded, cognitively-demanding and that language should be used for reasoning, avoiding labelling. Donaldson (1978) disagrees, arguing: 'The child needs to learn to disembed thinking from the context of immediate activity and to operate upon experience, both real and hypothetical, through the medium of words alone.' This would seem to advocate the labelling of phenomena and direct-concept teaching. Perhaps a position along the continuum depends on the age of the child and its previous experience.

Language for negotiation

One of the most significant implications for science teaching is the use of language for reflection and negotiation. Barnes (1976) describes children working in small groups doing science as: 'Talking their way into understanding.' This is an example of children using language for both reflective and communication purposes; a kind of shared inner speech. For the science teacher it is obvious that this talking time for children is very significant if they are to negotiate in their concept formation: 'The shaping of language is a means by which pupils reach deeper understanding of what is already partly grasped' (Barnes, 1976). I promote such quality talk in the classroom by ensuring children are autonomous and active in their own learning. True collaborative talk is rare in some classrooms and needs stimulating; it does not just happen. The children in my class are familiar with the techniques we use to promote such reflective talk. Group concept mapping at the beginning and/or the end of a new area of learning is an excellent way to promote discussion. Similarly brainstorms and fortune lines offer a good basis for communicating and reflection. Simply sitting children together in groups will not promote true collaborative reflection. Talking in small groups becomes increasingly important as the child gets older as language plays a more significant role. I think it is important to mention here that it is not the quantity of speech that is significant but the quality. Increasing the amount of language will not accelerate learning. It is the reflection on experience in negotiation with others which must be at the heart of the interaction.

Scientific concepts and spontaneous concepts

Piaget (1932) believed that there were two fundamental types of concepts: spontaneous concepts are those the child developed alone whilst non-spontaneous concepts are those influenced by adults. Many scientific concepts cannot be easily discovered spontaneously by the child and are therefore classified as non-spontaneous. Vygotsky (1978) classified scientific concepts as formal but believed that everyday concepts and scientific concepts are arrived at in the same way, being affected by both internal and external conditions. From this I conclude that the teacher is one of the external conditions in the classroom and must influence the environment to a greater extent when teaching science because the concepts to be learned are non-spontaneous. How can the teacher influence the environment so that scientific concepts can be constructively learned? As a teacher who promotes active, discovery learning I must minimize the risk of children constructing concepts that are fruitless. This is not to be confused with an early concept which has potential to develop into a fruitful idea at a later date. In order to promote scientific personal constructs the teacher must selectively create the environment, for example, I make sure the children do not discover that all metals sink by providing tin foil at the water trough and metal toy boats. Children commonly discover that metal sinks if all they have to investigate with is metal spoons.

There is a danger of misinterpreting scientific concepts as being ready-made packages, easily transmitted by the teacher and readily absorbed by the child. A concept is a highly complex thought process which cannot be transmitted. In order to learn a new concept in science the child must be active in its own learning, not passively absorbing information. Concept formation is a genuine process of assimilation based on experience with phenomena and the ability to organize thoughts through language.

Language, then, is of primary importance in the formation of true concepts. Whether the skills of language organization be innate in people, as Chomsky (1985) suggested or developed gradually through interaction, it is clear that without language the child has no ability to organize or classify thoughts into patterns and hierarchies. Without the ability to perform these organizational procedures the child cannot formulate concepts, but can only perceive according to a series of expectations.

Value arguments

To what extent can we look at this kind of work for its constructivist value? To examine this thoroughly, we return to our five tenets of classroom constructivism that we posed in Chapter 1. There is no doubt that the learning in each case could be described as 'active'. Active does not just mean being 'activity-based', but means an active challenge to thinking, and different ways for pupils to present their learning. So, for example, some activity-based learning can be very dour, closed and uninviting. These case studies are different – from Di Bentley's challenge to constantly evaluate, to Cindy Palmer's challenge to articulate similarities and differences. The level of facilitation is high, too. Rosemary Denman's water-wheel designers are encouraged to get on and work for themselves, with help from the teacher only in the latter stages. Our five tenets of classroom constructivism, then, still hold up in these model cases. All the exemplars given start from 'where the learner is', from Cindy Palmer's views about what children can hear and thus observe when listening to a pencil and using this to distinguish between different pens and pencils, to Rosemary Denman's provision of an experience through field trips. Amanda Walsh's children's use of language in developing concepts start clearly from children's understanding of meanings. Progression is very evident in Di Bentley's and Rosemary Denman's case studies. In Rosemary Denman's class, the young technologists who try to sort out the problems of the water wheel are progressing their own ideas of force with subtle help from her as she perceives the need for the linking. The zone of support she provides is sufficiently subtle to encourage large amounts of active learning, but still enable a sense of ownership by the children. These themes are evident too, behind the planning that teachers do for the curriculum in the next two chapters.

four

School planning for conceptual change

Introduction

We begin by shaping this chapter with the four design questions posed in Chapter 1, as we look at school planning for conceptual change. We see the overall purpose of curriculum planning to be the link between educational goals and actual classroom practice. So, we want to raise questions about purpose and intent in whole-school planning, the structure of planning and its organization, provide a case example of what we mean by good planning in action and then some discussion of the values and assumptions written into what has been said. The chapter differs a little from others in that the case study is to be found in the section we call Structure. As in other chapters, we adopt and then adapt our general pattern to try to make different points.

Purpose

Our intention in the chapter is to focus on three main aspects of planning:

(i)   planning the curriculum at whole-school level – policy statements and schemes of work;
(ii) planning the best use of resources – staffing, materials, space;
(iii) planning the curriculum at classroom level – weekly and daily planning.

That is, the purpose is to set out the 'whys and wherefores' of planning for science and technology in the primary classroom. Planning is vital because it links curriculum to teaching, and teaching to learning. The thinking, planning and decision-making of teachers makes up a large part of their professional lives and we are all very familiar with the notion of 'taking work home in your head'. The most common form of this mental work-life is planning what next to do, how to do it, what might go wrong, ways in which it has worked before and so on. In many ways, teachers are both are able to make decisions while also having decisions made for them. The balance between the two depends greatly on the nature of the school, the personality and preferences of the headteacher, the disposition of the class teacher and many other factors besides. Our purpose here, then, is to explore planning as a window onto the relationship between schools' and teachers' aims and objectives, and the possible resulting actions in class.

Nowadays, planning is far more complex than it used to be when teachers simply planned which theme or topic to teach in each year. Or, indeed, when they planned whether, in fact, to teach in themes, topics or subjects or a mixture of all three.

Being clear about terms

Words like 'theme', 'topic' and 'subject' in the prose above remind us that we need to explain our use of some terms. As the National Primary Centre (1990) has pointed out, there are a variety of words used to describe such methods of organizing the curriculum, such as:

- topic;
- theme;
- project;
- investigation;
- problem-solving;
- 'our work on . . .'.

We have tried to be more precise than this. So, for instance, we do not agree with Kerry and Eggleston (1988) who say:

> Topic work is characteristically interdisciplinary; it is about hands on experience in the environment. The teacher is less didactic than facilitating and children often tend to work in active investigative groups even if not on group tasks. Topics may be open-ended, flowing in directions determined by children's interests rather than pre-determined schemes of work.

In our terms, what Kerry and Eggleston are describing is an approach to teaching and learning, i.e. more an underlying philosophy than an organizational model of the curriculum. Such definitions, for us, simply serve to muddy the waters created by the advent of the National Curriculum. In our view, definitions need to be more structured and concerned with curriculum organization.

A theme

By 'theme' we mean a broadly-based organization of the curriculum which incorporates a variety of areas of experience and draws upon core and foundation subjects in the National Curriculum. Other aspects such as health education, environmental education and the National Curriculum's (1989b) cross-curricular themes are also included. Essentially, this is a holistic approach which seeks deliberately to draw upon core concepts which feature in several subjects and which learners can use to draw out connections and meanings in their constructed world. Example concepts would be themes like 'Growth', and 'Change'.

A topic

A 'topic', by contrast, is an area of work which draws upon a limited aspect of one or two related subjects. So for example the topic of Electricity would enable children to explore aspects of mathematics, probably some technology, undertake some language work and require a core of knowledge and understanding in science. Its purpose as a topic would be to relate the scientific knowledge to other immediately connected concepts. It would be false, in our view, to introduce art, music and PE into such a topic by making conceptual connections that are tenuous and of little value to children.

A subject

'Subjects' are generally bodies of knowledge and skills which, these days, have increasingly been defined for us by the National Curriculum Council rather than, for example, by the kind of philosophical approach taken by Hirst (1974) and Peters (1967).

Themes vs. subjects

The work of Bonnett (1988) indicates that when teachers plan at classroom level they have, in the past, tended towards particular 'structures' in their planning, and Bonnett refers to five of these:

(i)   teacher-centred;
(ii)   knowledge-centred;
(iii) skills-centred;
(iv)   problem-centred;
(v)   child-centred.

Bonnett's work, though, was conducted before the National Curriculum and the work of Alexander et al. (1992) had gained a real hold on the work of primary schools. Such a description today would probably involve a shorter list, in which (i), (ii) and (iii) are subsumed under a general 'National Curriculum' structure, since all three of these areas are crucial to the planning necessary to deliver the National Curriculum. And the last of the list (child-centred planning) – as we discussed in Chapter 1 – has become more and more difficult to introduce into planning structures. The Alexander Report (1992) has made that goal even more difficult to achieve, calling as it does for a major change in the 'delivery' basis of the curriculum, away from topic/theme work and into a more subject-based approach. Nevertheless, as we continue to say, we believe it is still possible to achieve a child-centred structure to curriculum planning and this remains one of the main thrusts of this chapter and the next.

Since the introduction of the National Curriculum, the general debate has focused on the organization of the curriculum in primary schools. This debate was heightened by the publication of the DES discussion paper (1992) which followed Alexander's (1991) original research into primary education in Leeds. The DES discussion document did much to dispel myths that 'progressive teaching' abounded in primary schools and that classes were taught only as small groups, where 'topic work' and not subject-based teaching dominated. HMI findings showed that very few schools in the country organized their curriculum entirely through topic work: practically every school taught separate subjects at some point during the week. The DES report, however, in dispelling some myths also attempted to create others. In paragraph 63, for instance, the report states that current practice in primary education is hostile to subject teaching for young children:

> Subject divisions, it is argued, are inconsistent with the child's view of the world. Children must be allowed to construct their own meanings and subject teaching involves the imposition of a received version of knowledge. And moreover it is the wholeness of the curriculum which is important rather than the distinct identity of the individual subjects.

In the report, the authors contest such assertions:

> First, to resist subjects on the grounds that they are inconsistent with children's views of the world is to confine them within their existing modes of thought and deny them access to some of the most powerful tools for making sense of the world which human beings have ever devised.

This in itself is an assertion which needs contesting. First, it does not necessarily follow that children are confined within existing modes of thought in areas where they are not taught in subjects. Teaching itself and the very model of learning of which the paragraph makes so light, is about extending experiences from the child's own conceptual frameworks. How can this be constraining? Secondly to refer to 'subjects' as 'the most powerful tools for making sense of the world' borders on the crass and simplistic. What is the level of 'subjectness' being referred to here? Developments in the secondary science curriculum have succeeded in questioning the subject divisions of science. Is it just physics, chemistry and biology – or physics, chemistry, botany, zoology, astronomy, geology, meteorology, etc.? Where does 'subjectness' begin and end? The issue is that the National Curriculum – which could have started from the excellent HMI premise of 'areas of experience' – was in fact designed from a model of knowledge in which subjects were the foundation. In our opinion it is a notion of a curriculum which better serves the 1950s than the 1990s. Given that this is the case, and that the administrative burden of dealing with the National Curriculum is so huge, it is – in our view – easier to simply take the subject-based model for granted and work at producing planning strategies that will make its teaching easier. It is, after all, no weakness to know that the curriculum model is neither the right one, nor a helpful one, but simply one we are stuck with by law. It is therefore in the interests of pupil achievement and teacher time that we should plan to organize schooling in a way that is least painful. And if that means teaching by subjects, then so be it. If Alexander *et al.* are trying to be critical of teaching approaches used in schools (rather than the organizational models of the curriculum) then they should be more specific. That is why, in our definitions above, we are careful to restrict ourselves to organizational models rather than make any further comment about philosophical approaches or assumptions about teaching and learning.

Pragmatism in planning for practice

At the very least, planning in practice needs to take account of *all* the children in a year group, however they are then re-grouped and sub-grouped. Planning must also take account of all the aspects of the National Curriculum, before such things as 'routes' and 'progress maps' can be designed. Moreover, planning must now take place for development through 'Key Stages' rather than simply for a calendar year – especially where children are vertically grouped as they are in so many schools.

A complex business indeed! Not one about which to despair, however. There are several words of encouragement to be had from a variety of sources. The Alexander Report (1992) itself, for example, says:

> Curriculum planning is one aspect of primary teaching which . . . is now improving significantly . . . HMI report that one of the first visible improvements in primary schools has been curriculum planning in relation to the National Curriculum core subjects.

and similarly, HMI (1991) have said:

> Planning was more closely focused, yielding better continuity and progression. More schools tried to link planning to the findings of assessment . . .

So progress is on the way. Broad curriculum changes, however, have not made the task easier. The Alexander Report (1992) also focuses on the way in which planning at whole-school level takes place as being an area for considerable future development:

> Further developments in the quality of curriculum planning depend upon the management of whole school planning across all National Curriculum subjects and both key stages.

Whole-school planning

Undoubtedly, the complexity of the National Curriculum and the very specific nature of some of the knowledge and understanding required (for

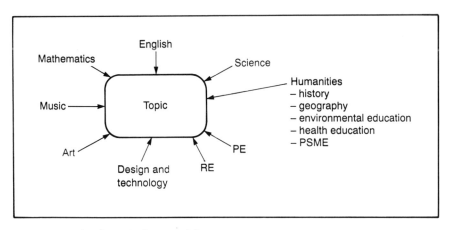

Figure 4.1 School curriculum model.

example, in history core study units) has made whole-school planning increasingly difficult. The opportunity for schools to retain a largely theme-based approach for all their teaching is lessening as time goes by.

This leads us to a very pragmatic position. The National Curriculum is in place, the Programmes of Study for each Key Stage are required to be taught by law. What is needed is an organizational model that will best suit what has to be done whilst allowing teachers the freedom to teach in as holistic way as possible and still deliver the National Curriculum. The National Primary Centre (1990) has suggested that curriculum organization is different in different stages of the primary school. For example, they have shown the first school curriculum as being depicted as in Figure 4.1 whereas the older pupils have a different model, rather more subject based in the core areas as shown in Figure 4.2.

In our view, what is required now that we know the details of the National Curriculum is a much more mixed model. If that sounds like a 'cop out', or a compromise, then perhaps so. There is no denying, though, that some aspects of the National Curriculum involve fundamental concepts across several subjects which can and should be looked at from a variety of viewpoints. These areas can be taught as themes. Other parts of the Programmes of Study have close conceptual links to some subjects but not to others. To stretch these links too far would be superficial at best and false at worst. These aspects are best taught as topics. Finally, there are some parts of the National Curriculum best taught separately and related only to themselves as separate subjects. So our mixed model would look like that depicted in Figure 4.3.

The key to getting such a pragmatic approach right is to ensure that the objectives behind the programmes of study are expanded into schemes of work for all subjects, so that the conceptual and skill 'overlaps' are clear. Planning for subjects, topics and themes can be done against the necessary

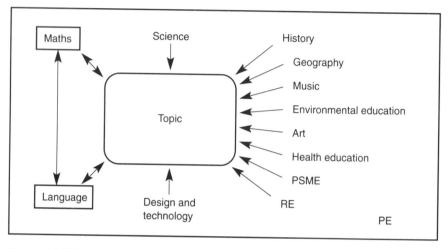

Figure 4.2 School curriculum model.

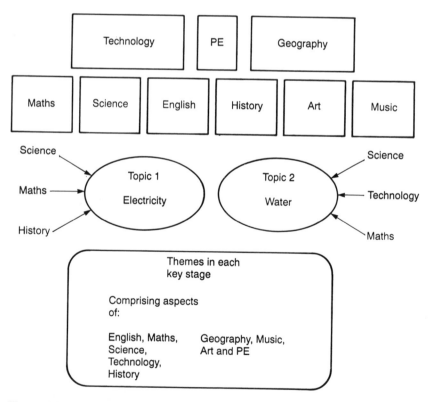

Figure 4.3 Mixed model.

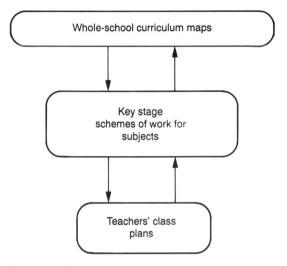

Figure 4.4 Planning layers.

background of continuity and progression. There are two implications of this pragmatic approach. The first is that every subject should be taught within this mixed model. No one subject can be taught solely as a subject. That means that teaching English and maths on their own as separate subjects would no longer take place. Often these areas are taught through commercially-prepared schemes at a specific time of the day or week. If the mixed model is adopted with regard to these areas too, this will make the knowledge more relevant for pupils and the practice of the language and mathematics easier and more productive. Secondly, there are three layers to the planning as Figure 4.4 demonstrates.

The whole-school planning area, in terms of how to deliver a curriculum, which for example, fits around our mixed model, is covered in our case study in this chapter by Jenny Saady.

CASE STUDY 6

Making the curriculum work across the whole school – the role of planning

Jenny Saady, Spinfield Combined School

When I took up post as Headteacher of Spinfield school, the National Curriculum was just beginning its way through the myriad of steps it has since pursued. In those days, planning was much more straightforward. In essence, the Headteacher determined, by consultation with staff, the curriculum, themes and topics agreed but the classroom teacher as an individual decided how those themes and topics were translated into classroom work for children in groups and as individuals. In my school, in those days, there was a clear and obvious place for field trips – every child, every year, if possible had the opportunity to go away either for days, or residentially to study some aspect of the curriculum in depth and work with others in social and work situations. It was a part of the school's developed philosophy and one that parents willingly supported with help on the trips, as well as funding for their offspring. It made our school different from others around and made the education at Spinfield a unique experience for children.

With the advent of the National Curriculum in the core subjects, we made some adjustments to our planning methods. We organized ourselves into year teams and had joint planning sessions for science in particular because everyone felt unfamiliar with what was required of them. Led by our curriculum coordinator, however, we soon became used to understanding the Programmes of Study and the 14 – or for teachers in Year 7 (our LEA changes schools at 12) 17 Attainment Targets. There is no doubt, that in that first year of the National Curriculum's introduction, we planned against the Attainment Targets – despite the advice of HMI and our local advisers! It seemed so much easier. The Statements of Attainment were clear and manageable, and in those days we thought we understood what had to be done! We had school policies in a variety of curriculum areas, but during that first year we learnt what it meant to convert them to the National Curriculum and begin to use them more fully to gear our planning.

All in all, as far as planning was concerned, the first year passed peacefully enough. Then technology arrived on the curriculum map. Unfortunately, at the same time so did assessment at Key Stage 1. We found our technology planning to be much easier than the science planning since the design process, as a process, was much more adaptable to a theme-based approach. The technology context could be adapted to almost any theme successfully. However, it did increase the number of Attainment Targets we had to assess, but not by a huge amount, so we still regarded it as manageable. We concentrated too, on the challenges brought about by managing the use of computers in the classroom. As a headteacher, I had to face the resource challenge, but again parents were very supportive. As a staff, we had to face the progression challenge in our planning, especially as many of our children had computers at home and were already fairly proficient – or could get expert adult help at home – much more expert than much that we could provide. This pushed us into working across our year teams much more than we had done previously, simply because the need to plan for individuals and groups made us want to know what children were facing in the next class.

Although we had already begun our assessment processes, we nevertheless found the first set of SAT tests very overwhelming – if nothing else, by the sheer weight of work. However, we learnt a great deal, not the least of which was that although we thought we had understood the Statements of Attainment, perhaps we had been mistaken in some cases.

Whilst our learning curve was steepening, the school was growing. We were having to institute classes of mixed age groups. This in itself posed no particular problems for us, until we saw the National Curriculum standing orders for history. Immediately it became obvious that with such a prescribed curriculum, our planning would need to be more meticulous and much tighter about when we did things, how we communicated with each other about our planning and what we did. I was, as usual, collecting the staff's weekly plans and reading them. I realized that everyone needed a similar experience, so we got together as a whole staff, in

June of the year before we faced history and geography and tried to bring a whole school perspective to bear. We had a library floor covered in pieces of paper, yellow Post-it notes, and much frustration. We tried to look for overlap so that we would not have to repeat ourselves, and for work that could be done in assessment across subject boundaries. On top of that we tried to devise a system that would tell us which group of pupils had done which study units in history and, when to pass on to the next teacher. When we had decided all that we felt, we could decide on themes. I realized after that experience, that our whole curriculum map needed re-examination. Not only did curriculum time audits show that the time we were devoting to different subjects was fluctuating without any real rationale, but themes and topics were becoming less viable as ways of organizing the whole curriculum. We were constantly having to top up our work in the themes with subject-specific work. Similarly, as we faced the prospect of more and more Attainment Targets to manage and plan for, our work load was becoming too great. We needed to move to a different planning unit and streamline the process in a way that helped us. Lastly, staff were beginning to seriously question whether field trips, with all the prior planning and post-trip work were viable at all any longer. This would represent a major change in our philosophy and we were anxious to avoid this if possible.

I saw the way forward to be a three-phase issue. First, move away from a planning unit of year teams into Key Stage planning. This would have the advantage of putting first school teachers together with middle school teachers – not a huge advantage since we all worked together closely anyway, and the disadvantage of making Year 7 teachers still a year team – unless they worked more closely with secondary colleagues. The planning base for the Key Stage would be the Programme of Study in each subject. Secondly, the development of schemes of work for each subject. Developed on a subject basis these would allow us the flexibility of planning our themes from a variety of subjects in detail and avoid overlap, by not planning the theme first and then introducing subjects. Thirdly, there was the movement of the curriculum from thematic approaches to subjects and themes.

I organized a staff meeting, and explained to staff what I saw to be the way forward. However, as is always the case, the Headteacher's ideas need to be tempered by the practical experience of staff, their vision and their time constraints. We agreed to compromise. We have moved to a mixed-delivery model, and we are auditing the curriculum carefully to see that it works. We are tracking pupils through the curriculum, by developing reporting systems for what children have been taught, as well as what they have learnt. But Key Stage planning and schemes of work are a little way off yet. However, we do feel more on top of what we do. We have managed to cut down overlap and make the National Curriculum manageable for us and the children. And our field trips? Unresolved. We do them if we can, but we recognize that they will need very careful planning if we are to make the most of them and the follow-up work. We are not there yet. The work continues!

Jenny's case study puts into perspective the difficulties of organizing and conceptualizing a curriculum map which allows space for the school's own agendas as well as the needs of the National Curriculum. Such a curriculum map at least enables a school to see where change is possible, overlap occurs and deletion can be managed.

We cannot look at planning issues and not consider either the school development plan or the role of the governors. Since all school development plans have the curriculum as a significant part of their process, the links between the school development plan and Key Stage planning for different subjects need to be made explicit. If one were to look at science and technology as examples for whole-school planning, what would the process look like? Below, we suggest a general plan and then provide a 'worked example' to show what the plans might look like.

Timetable for a development plan

December: Start of new school development plan for next academic year. Involvement of all staff in the discussions of areas requiring further work or development. Technology identified as an area that is underresourced and needing more staff development and equipment purchase. Science to be maintained on its present resource budget but to undergo a curriculum review during the next year.

February: Finalization of new school development plan for coming school year against school budget share.

April: Allocation of maintenance budget to science for resources and development budget to technology for purchase of new equipment and INSET provision.

May: Key Stage teachers meet to develop the whole school curriculum plan for delivering the Programmes of Study against the schemes of work. Decisions are made regarding which themes will be used across the Key Stage, what topics will be taught and which areas of science and technology skills will need to be taught as separate areas.
   Whole staff meet to look at the curriculum map and decide where overlap between subjects allows for efficiency of assessment tasks, fulfilling of objectives from more than one subject to streamline the curriculum map for the next two years.

June: Year teams meet to plan the themes and topics in detail, organize assessment tasks for the year, dates for moderation of assessed work in different classes in the year, plan team teaching with the subject specialist.

July: Coordinators of science and technology use the information from each year team to ensure that resources are available for the required teaching. Where demand outstrips resource, negotiation takes place. Technology coordinator organizes purchase of new resources and sets up INSET sessions for colleagues.

Two of the most important tools that the Key Stage teachers will need are the schemes of work for science and technology, and the policy documents for each subject. The science coordinator in our example given above will need the policy document, since it is against this she will evaluate or review the curriculum with staff in the coming year. Policy documents have been in

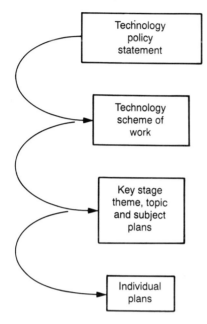

Figure 4.5 Document fits.

place for science and technology for a while now, and indeed in many schools have had more than one revision. However, it is easy to become confused about what is necessary in each of the levels of documentation. As we see it, the documents fit together in the way indicated in Figure 4.5.

Values and arguments

Planning for a whole-school perspective is no easy matter. We have tried to provide in this chapter a series of models and suggestions by which the massive change between a thematic integrated curriculum in the primary school can become curriculum maps which meet the requirements of the National Curriculum. As Jenny Saady found, in Case Study 6, the road is not an easy one. Even if there is light at the end of the tunnel, not everyone can see it yet, and staff may quail at the thought of developing schemes of work that lead to even more work before they can contemplate a rest. In a changing world where two of the core subjects and one of the foundation subjects have already changed radically just when people had got used to them, staff need to persevere under very difficult conditions. However, whole-school planning is only half of the story. The real work goes on not at policy whole-school level, but in the classroom. Our next chapter deals with classroom planning.

five

Planning for the curriculum and the classroom

Introduction

In this chapter we look at the development of policies for science and technology and their role in shaping the curriculum. We consider how schemes of work follow from policy and look at the implementation of these in planning for the activities of children in classrooms.

Purpose

What should a policy statement contain? Basically, it needs to represent guidance that would enable a new teacher to see how the subject fits into the overall curriculum, and what standards of teaching and resource she can expect to have to work to. It provides the necessary standards against which a school can judge its progress in the teaching and learning of that particular subject area. In this chapter we include advice on developing a science policy document, although much of this advice can equally well apply to technology. In Appendices 1, 2 and 3 there are three examples of policy statements from schools, some of which are at different stages of development – not least because the world of National Curriculum technology is changing even as we write.

We can think of no better way forward to suit our purposes here than to present a useful example of how to develop a school policy. This set of hints and suggestions comes from Buckinghamshire Science Team, and we have presented it in full, as follows.

DEVELOPING A SCHOOL SCIENCE POLICY DOCUMENT

Some hints and suggestions

Why have a policy document?
Any policy is an essential working document. It describes the nature, purposes, organization and management of science within the curriculum. It should be valued and accessible and be a guide to new teachers to the school and other interested parties. Through the document they should understand the role of science in the children's learning and how it is structured within the school. It does not give details of content. This is covered in schemes of work and detailed teaching plans. This implies three separate, but related, stages in planning for science:

- the policy document
- schemes of work
- detailed plans for teaching and learning

What informs the science policy?

- the National Curriculum for science and associated circular 17/91
- the school's aims and objectives
- children's needs
- any existing policy
- LEA Science Policy
- governors' recommendations
- HMI discussion papers
- Non-statutory Guidance for Science 89 and 91

What should it include?

- a statement defining the meaning of science
- the place of science in the curriculum
- aims of science education in the school
- details explaining how these aims are met, which will include:
  - DES requirements as defined by the National Curriculum
  - local agreements to ensure continuity and progression
  - children's needs
  - organization at school and class level
  - teaching and learning strategies
  - planning for continuity and progression and access
  - differentiation
  - relationship of AT1 to the other ATs and strands
  - assessment procedures
  - recording and reporting attainment
  - equal opportunities (gender and culture)
  - relationship to other curricular areas
  - resources
  - safety
  - monitoring and evaluation
  - role of the Co-ordinator
  - liaison with partner schools

How should it be developed?

(a) Science Co-ordinator (SC) reviews current situation.
 Is there a current policy? When was it written? Does it need updating? Why? Are there parts which should be retained/reconsidered?
(b) SC negotiates with Headteacher.
 What should be the first step? Are staff meetings needed? How many? What should be the focus at each?
(c) SC produces a draft policy.
(d) SC plans staff meetings/discussions in detail.

How long should it be?
The length will be determined by your answers to the following questions. However, about 4 to 6 sides of A4 would seem to be reasonable.

Details of the policy

1. What is science?
A brainstorming session which could be useful in identifying where the staff's thinking is at present. A statement should be agreed and written down. Schools will find the LEA Science Policy and the Non-statutory Guidance useful here.

2. The place of science in the curriculum
How much curriculum time is to be devoted to it? How is it to be incorporated into the curriculum throughout a school year? How can you ensure that this occurs?
 Remember that science is a core subject, like English and maths, so it should be continuous.

3. Aims
Two or three statements which state what you intend children will gain from their science activities. They are likely to be related to the needs of the children and reflect the aspirations of teachers and parents as well as the wider aspects of the local community.

4. DES requirements as defined by the NC
Taking into account the age range within your school, which Key Stages and Programmes of Study are appropriate for your children to enable them to meet the Attainment Targets at the range of levels specified for each Key Stage.

5. Local arrangements to ensure continuity and progression
What arrangements will you make regarding coverage of the Programme of Study for each Key Stage to ensure continuity and progression when children transfer to another school?

6. Children's needs
Have you established key principles by which children learn? How can you ensure that your science teaching encompasses these principles? Which attitudes would you hope to develop through science work?

7. Organization
Where do science investigations take place?
How are the children organized?
Is this the same for all age groups?

Are there any science specialists on the staff? What is his/her role?
How are adult helpers deployed?

8. *Planning for continuity and progression*
What is the school's policy on schemes of work and detailed plans for teaching and learning?

(a) School level
How do you plan as a whole school for balance throughout a Key Stage in terms of:

- coverage of PoS [Programme of Study]
- coverage of ATs
- process/content

How is this ensured?
Is there planned coverage of the PoS for each Key Stage?
Does this involve matching the PoS with the Statements of Attainment in order to determine which parts of the PoS are best dealt with earlier and which later in the Key Stage?

(b) Year/Team level
How do teams/years plan their science? How is the Co-ordinator involved?
Is there a common format for termly/half-termly schemes of work?

(c) Class level
How does each teacher plan in detail from the agreed schemes of work? Is there a common format? If so, what?
How is science defined within a topic, if this approach is used?

9. *Teaching and learning strategies*
What teaching methods are to be used? Why? Is there a balance?
The key here is 'fitness for purpose'. See Section A of Non-statutory Guidance (NCC, 1989c).

10. *Differentiation*
What arrangements are made in planning and classroom practice for children at different stages of development? (Differentiation by outcome and by task are both important.)
How is formative assessment used to aid this process?
What special arrangements have been made for children who would benefit from working above or below their normal Key Stage?

11. *Relationship of AT1 to other ATs*
How are you ensuring that sufficient emphasis is given to AT1 in relation to ATs 2, 3 and 4? Circular 17/91 states that schools may wish to be guided by the weightings recommended by NCC when considering the relative importance of the Attainment Targets.

Key Stages 1 and 2
AT1   50 per cent
ATs 2, 3 and 4   50 per cent

How are investigations built into schemes of work so that the teaching of the skills and ideas in AT1 is given as much consideration as the teaching of the knowledge and understanding in ATs 2–4?
How are investigations linked to children's knowledge and understanding?
In the teaching programme is there a balance between illustrative and investigative activities?

12. *Assessment: planning for, and procedures used*
Why and how are children assessed? (What different methods are used?)
How is assessment built into planning?
How do you ensure that judgements made are consistent?
When are children assessed? (Is it continuous?)
How is assessment used formatively in planning future activities?
How do you ensure that the assessment of AT1 is within the context of whole investigations?
Who assesses? (Are children involved in setting targets and making assessments about attainment against clearly defined criteria?)
Are any particular materials used?

13. *Recording and reporting attainment*
What should be recorded?
When? How often? By whom – are children involved?
Is there a common format? What is it?
What information is retained in school?
What is passed on to teachers/parents/other schools?
Is there clarity about the use of summative and formative records?

14. *Equal opportunities*
How do the school and teachers plan so that a variety of contexts are offered which will appeal to both girls and boys?
What strategies are employed so that girls and boys take an active part in science investigations?
What strategies are employed to present a positive image of women in science?
What strategies are employed to draw on a range of cultures in presenting science?
What strategies are employed to avoid stereotyping other cultures?
What strategies are employed to present a positive image of the contributions of other cultures to science?

15. *Relationships to other curricular areas and the cross-curricular themes identified by NCC*
How does the school build in meaningful links between science and other curricular areas?
How is the integrity of science maintained within topic and thematic work?
How do activities in science contribute to the cross-curricular themes?

16. *Resources*
Equipment: Where stored? Retrieval system?
Teachers' reference materials – where available?
Children's references – where?
Address lists
People as a resource, e.g. Health Education Officer, Road Safety Officer
   (Draw up a list of resources and give to each teacher after discussion.

Discuss and agree arrangements for the retrieval and return of resources.
How do you educate staff and children in their use?)
Has the full potential of the school grounds been exploited?

17. *Safety*
Refer to:
  ASE publication *Be Safe*
  CLEAPSS booklets
What activities/materials are appropriate at what stages?
Which items may be used by children? Which are teacher only?
Which are not suitable for primary schools?
What precautions need to be taken? (Identify special activities, e.g. with flames, hair tied back.)
How should certain items be stored for safety (e.g. glassware, certain chemicals)?
What are the procedures in case of accident? To whom do you turn for extra advice?

18. *Monitoring and evaluation*
How will you monitor the science planning, teaching, learning, and assessment within the school?
How often?
Who should be involved?

19. *The role of the Co-ordinator*
Is the role of the Co-ordinator defined and clear to all staff?

20. *Liaison with partner schools*
How does the school liaise with its partner schools, in the same and different phases, to ensure that progression and continuity of curriculum coverage, teaching and learning and assessment are realized?

We are not suggesting that this set of hints is totally perfect or exhaustive – we do think, though that it represents a good template which schools might want to adjust and amend for their own purposes. We next look at how we might move forward from this and begin with writing a scheme of work.

Writing a scheme of work

What should a scheme of work contain? Ideally it should be based on the Programme of Study and show how the development of the knowledge, skills, understanding and processes will be developed across the years of the particular Key Stage. Important, too, are identified areas of assessment and tasks, cross-curricular opportunities and resources. The general teaching approaches to be employed need to be identified and the pupil outcomes specified. Clearly it is important to get all this information into as manageable a format as possible so that it is a useful document rather than a weighty tome no one ever opens. The purpose of the scheme is to help teachers fit both continuity and progression into their work. The scheme does not name themes or topics to be used and thus it can be developed differently every year. What the scheme does do is identify the attainments in skills and knowledge pupils should have reached at any one time of year – and the resources needed to provide for this development.

Planning staffing resources

Any move which places greater emphasis on subject specialisms will have a profound effect on the use of staffing resources. For example, it will be necessary to decide which parts of the curriculum are to be taught by a class teacher in the first instance. This will vary between Key Stages: current political agendas appear to favour an approach which is predominantly 'subject specialist' at Key Stage 2, with a reduced curriculum model at Key Stage 1, to allow time for pupils to learn the core subjects. If this is the case, then headteachers and staff will need to organize class bases carefully in order to maximize both stability and expertise. One possibility would be to adopt a secondary model of the curriculum entirely in which pupils were taught maths and English by the class teacher as well as PSE, while all other subjects were taught by the specific subject co-ordinator. This would represent a major departure for most teachers and schools and would have several implications. For example:

1. Co-ordinators would need to assess pupils in every lesson which they taught with a class since the contact with the class would be infrequent.
2. The subject co-ordinator would be responsible for assessing every child in the school in their own subject.
3. The moderation of subject assessments would have to take place on a between-schools basis, thereby adding to the expense, since there would be no other teacher against whom judgements could be compared in any one school.
4. The problems of small primary schools would mean that consortia would need to be established to allow subject specialisms to be shared between different staff, relieving individuals of the burden of having more than one specialism.
5. Headteachers and governors would need to ensure that full use was made of staff expertise and time, if specialists were moving around from class to class and that proper amounts of time for each subject were included in any one class timetable.
6. It implies that all teachers, as they will all be subject co-ordinators in one area at least, must possess the expertise to teach across the age range of a Key Stage.

Alternatively, subjects could be considered on our 'theme', 'topic' and 'subject' criteria outlined above (p. 49). In this case, the themes would be taught by the class teacher, with specialist input only for subject specialist areas (which may be the most difficult concept areas) or for both topic and subject areas. This would create a greater opportunity for stability in a class group, since the class teachers would spend most of the time with their class during theme time – which could be as much as half the week. Subject specialists would then have the opportunity to work with classes during the rest of the week. This has several advantages as far as assessment is concerned:

- it allows moderation to be internal, since both specialist and class teacher are assessing the same subject area and the judgements of each can be tried against the other;
- it relieves the burden of assessment on subject co-ordinators;
- it creates the opportunity for the subject co-ordinator still to have a role in advising staff whilst having the opportunity to monitor the progress of children across the school.

Another area of staffing to be considered is that of the professional development of staff. In areas such as science and technology, staff often feel a lack of confidence in their own conceptual understanding of the subject area. This is understandable, especially where staff teaching Year 7 need to teach up to Level 6 in many Attainment Targets. Conducting a staff audit with regard to staff perceptions of their confidence and understanding of the issues is a good idea. Such an audit will help the school to target its expertise in teaching better and to provide useful INSET and training for staff in content areas of knowledge. A questionnaire outlining the types of questions that might be used in such an audit is included below.

Staff audit

1. What subject area did you originally follow in your training?
2. What other areas of expertise do you feel you have acquired over the last few years?
3. What curriculum training courses have you attended recently (within the last four years)?
4. Were any of these extended, e.g. '20 Day' courses?
5. Did any of the courses address your own knowledge of the subject?
6. How would you describe your subject knowledge now in the subject in which you trained?
7. Are there any areas in which you feel you lack confidence about teaching the National Curriculum?
8. Is your lack of confidence concerned with your own subject knowledge or is it, for example, in managing it in the classroom?
9. If you could design a 'tailor-made INSET course' for yourself in the subject in which you feel least confident, what would it contain?

Planning at classroom level

Our main concern here is to be certain that plans made for each class contain all the relevant and important detail that teachers need to take into account, without producing a huge amount of work for little gain. So, we can ask the question: what is necessary for good comprehensive classroom planning to take place? Here we consider six main areas that every curriculum plan needs. These are:

1. *Reference to a scheme of work.* This ensures that the necessary aspects of the Programme of Study are covered and may be as simple as a paragraph reference.
2. *Pupil and teacher activities.* This includes grouping arrangements, aims of learning and the actual activities pupils will be expected to do. It includes the skills being learnt, and the processes being developed.
3. *Differentiation.* This shows where there are separate activities or questions or tasks for different groups of pupils.
4. *Assessment.* This refers back to the scheme of work to show what assessment activity is taking place in that lesson, at which group it is directed and what Attainment Target and level is being dealt with. It may not always be filled in as a column on the plan, but given the amount of teacher assessment necessary across a year, there ought always to be something available for assessment once teachers know their class.
5. *Cross-curricular issues.* This is a reminder that cross-curricular issues are an important feature of the work of schools and, as increasingly the work of a primary school becomes even more directed towards subject specialisms, it is precisely those aspects which will slip most easily off the agenda. Often a simple reference is all that is needed. For example, if the work draws on particular multicultural materials, the word 'multiculture' would be sufficient. Or if, for example, pupils are being asked to cost the production of an artefact and check this against market prices, then 'economic awareness' would be sufficient. It serves as a useful checklist later to show what areas have been covered frequently as well as those that have been left uncovered.
6. *Resources.* The books, materials, time and other essential components of the work also need planning.

The difficulty with having six major areas of work like this is that there is potential for a huge amount of writing for teachers on a regular basis. However, just as having a scheme of work saves time once it is established and operating, so there are short cuts to any planning document. For example, many of the teacher and pupil activities can be written by means of a short statement and a code for the grouping and type of activity of learning approach. This implies that all staff have agreed on a regular range of learning approaches and class management strategies which are to be used, such as small group, individual, whole class, and writing, listening, problem-solving, investigating, planning, drawing, role play, discussion, etc. as learning approaches and activities. A sheet attached to the plan makes the use of this type of code easy, it saves time and also provides a good opportunity for year teams or co-ordinators to access information when evaluating work. One useful example is that drawn from the work of the National Primary Centre, shown in Figure 5.1. Although this checklist applies to assessment/recording activities, it is easy to see how, with a little adaptation, it could fill more than one purpose.

However, discussing plans and the arrangement of information in them

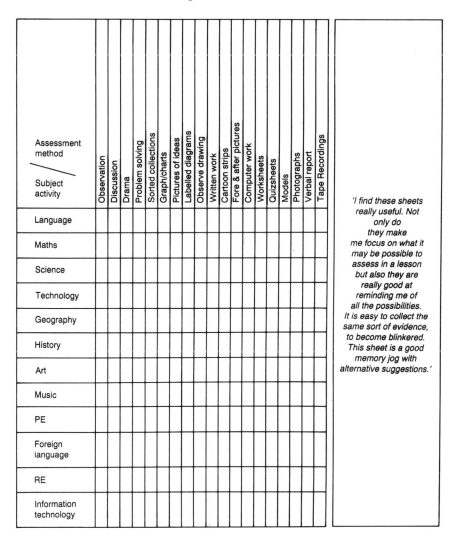

Figure 5.1 Assessment card.

is all well and good in the abstract, but real examples are important. We include in Appendix 6 an example of the work of Olney Middle School in Buckinghamshire. There the teachers have produced a 'theme plan' which goes further in detail than even our recommendations. It seems to be able to provide a large amount of detail with the minimum amount of writing. It ensures that recording devices (such as topic/theme webs – a useful device for seeing the curriculum at a glance) and the all important evaluations are included in the work of the school. More importantly, the booklet also acts as a record of what particular groups and or classes have achieved. This record can be stored by the school so that a full track of the pupils' work can be kept across a Key Stage. The National Primary Centre's work also includes such overview records but we feel that the work at Olney supersedes this. It keeps all the work together without the necessity for completing other forms such as the one provided by the NPC.

Further aspects of curriculum planning for the classroom

The National Primary Centre focuses on three further aspects of planning. These are:

(i)   continuity and progression;
(ii) a broad and balanced curriculum; and
(iii) the involvement of children in the process of planning.

They point out the importance of knowing what pupils' past learning activities have been before effective planning for continuity and progression can take place. As we stated in Chapter 1, it is not just previous activities that need to be known. Clearly, no-one wants to provide learning activities that pupils have already undertaken. This is hardly motivating. What is just as important however is determining what children know and understand, not just from their previous activities but also from all the other sources of scientific and technological experiences in their lives. As Jane Eaton mentions in Case Study 14, it is not uncommon to be in classrooms where several pupils have a wide range of experiences of a computer. As she points out, teachers can draw on that experience to help those who do not have access to such equipment outside school and also, sometimes, for helping themselves to manage and organize the environment.

As we begin to plan more and more at an individual progress level, some documents become essential tools to have before we begin the plans. Earlier in the chapter we mentioned the policy document and schemes of work, but teachers also need other things before they work out their day-to-day activities for children.

Essential documentation

It might be helpful here to consider what are the essential documents needed. They are:

- Policy statement for science or technology
- Schemes of work for the Key Stage being taught
- Last year's teacher assessment sheets for science and technology
- Information on which group the child was in last year within a class

This is crucial information if classes are vertically grouped and children move as a group within the school to another class at some point either at the end of or during the year. Also:

- Theme or topic plans from last year
- Any prior concept information available

This may simply be 'brainstorms' by the children, or posters that they have drawn that illustrate what they know or understand about a particular area of work in science or technology. This is crucial information for real differentiated planning since, as we explained in Chapter 1: it is this which gives a teacher access to the conceptual understanding of the child. Finally,

- Resources list
- Library list

These documents provide a framework, but they only represent prior information. The 'here and now' of the pupils in the class, their views and their involvement is the most important influence on the planning that teachers do. So how can pupils have a hand in the planning?

Involving pupils in planning

One way is to be clear about the areas of the scheme of work to which the planning relates, but also to begin the first steps into the work with a problem-solving session in which the children help make decisions. They can decide, for example, how the groups will be organized, what types of activities are necessary, which resources they will require and so on. In our six areas covered above, the children then share responsibility, with guidance from the teacher, for planning the activities and the resources. Several of the case studies have already illustrated the kinds of involvements that are possible when pupils are encouraged to have a responsible level of autonomy for planning their own activities and pace.

Values and arguments

This chapter has been about tools. Tools to help teachers and children achieve the tenets of classroom constructivism and thus more effective learning. Tools to plan learning effectively. If constructivism in the classroom is to be effective as a model of learning, then detailed planning is crucial. Planning is necessary too if our five tenets for constructivism in the classroom (p. 10), which shape the values and arguments of our chapters, are to be achieved. The move, in this chapter, from policies to teachers' weekly plans, shows the importance once again of our tenets. The purpose of the scheme of work is to ensure that those small stepping stones or bridges, so essential to the learner, are in place – an essential tool if the progress and differentiation is to take place. Similarly, the teachers' weekly plans focuses particularly on how to help pupils be active learners, to take a part in the planning for themselves and to start from where the learners are. And the policy statement? What role does this have in our five tenets? This is the 'zone of the support' which helps all teachers to be facilitators – to provide similar learning experiences within an agreed school framework.

six

Classroom organization and management

Introduction

In several areas of this book we refer to the importance of teachers being managers of the classroom environment. In this chapter we focus particularly on those aspects of classroom organization and management specifically related to technology and science. If we return to our four design questions, we ask what purposes lie behind knowing about classroom organization and management? For us, there are several.

Purpose

First and foremost is our preoccupation with environments where pupils learn progressively and which encourages them to become autonomous learners. This presupposes a type of organization to the classroom, its working practices and its resources, which permit and encourage learner autonomy. In science and technology this is particularly important with regard to two aspects: safety and 'direct skill' teaching. Further, however, each teacher needs to build on the experiences that pupils have already as they develop autonomy. So, as well as 'progressive autonomy', there needs to be consistency and continuity between classrooms and teachers. The National Primary Centre (1992) has stated the purposes of good classroom management. Good management can create an environment where:

- pupils are led to ask questions and seek answers individually and/or in cooperation with others;
- their thinking is guided and informed sympathetically by teachers and other adults;
- pupils are encouraged to become self-confident, self-disciplined and courteous; to set their own high standards and learn to recognize when they have achieved them.

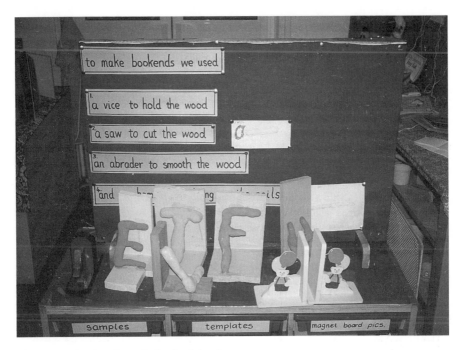

Figure 6.1 Bookends at Rokesly School.

In all our case studies so far, teachers have used different organizational strategies for managing pupils' activities safely and in ways which allow support for learning. In general, these have moved between whole group, small group and individual divisions of the class. Whilst carrying out activities, teachers have – for the most part – found that small groups work best. This appears to be in contrast to the current trends we have already discussed, in which much more whole-group teaching is advocated. There has been, over a number of years, criticism of small-group teaching. Classroom observations have revealed that frequently too many and varied activities were taking place at any one time in a class to permit the effective use of teacher input. However, some of this debate concerns the very nature of group work itself. If group work is, as it is in so many classrooms, a small collection of pupils seated around tables all carrying out the same individual tasks, then in our view, this is not 'group' work. If the activities are designed so that they can only take place by virtue of collaboration between pupils then that is a different matter. Most of our case studies describe collaborative group work. It is interesting, too, that in teaching science and technology in the National Curriculum and in dealing with assessment, teachers have found such organizational strategies to be the most effective in ensuring that pupils learn (Figure 6.1).

Structure

In looking at classroom organization and management, we deal with three main areas, using throughout this chapter case studies to bring alive some of the main features:

(i) classrooms, the physical environment and pupil organization;
(ii) resource organization;
(iii) safety organization.

First, to set the overall scene, we have pulled one case study away from the others. It looks at a First School which undertook a major piece of work in classroom organization and management. Doreen Wootton, the headteacher, talks about the INSET and development opportunities she provided with staff to focus on children's achievement. From this focus, issues of organizing the learning environment and pupil working practices came very much to the fore.

CASE STUDY 7

Organizing for pupil achievement

Doreen Wootton, Foxes Piece First School

When I took over the school as headteacher it was not long before I realized that many of the pupils were underachieving. I did not feel that it would be the correct approach to take to tackle this underachievement as it stood. What was needed was a much more overall approach. I noticed from my visits to classrooms in the school that the level of responsibility that pupils had in the classroom was not high in many classes, although practice differed across the school. I determined that I would deal with pupil underachievement through the overall umbrella of classroom management and organization.

In trying to get the issue started in the school, I noted in my daily 'pop-in' visits to classrooms, the practices of staff in the management of pupils, the organization of their classrooms physically and the access that pupils had to resources without using the teacher as a go-between. I soon became aware that the geography of the building with two classrooms and a shared area together in one building and these buildings joined by linked corridors did not facilitate the sharing of good practice. There were many differences between the staff in their teaching styles. Whilst this is not necessarily a bad thing, many staff as individuals did not use a wide range of styles in their everyday repertoire and were not learning new ones from one another. As children moved from class to class, their experiences were very patchy. I realized that if continuity and progression were to be helped and achievement improved for all pupils, there was a need for some common elements of classroom practice to develop. I began the process of change, as so many processes have begun, with a staff meeting. We looked generally at the issue of classroom organization across the school and I used the examples drawn from my regular classroom visits. I focused on what I saw in these visits, children asking the teacher where things were, their inability to find equipment for the simplest tasks without help and the consequent extra load for teachers at a time when they needed all the spare time they could get.

At the staff meeting we agreed to make classroom organization and management the INSET issue for the whole school across a year. We undertook several planks to this INSET. We used outsider evaluators, such as our attached adviser and visiting experts, partly to remove the element of critique from my visits to classrooms. We also joined with another school for twilight evening sessions on organization and management of classrooms. We held the INSET sessions alternately in each other's schools, giving everyone an opportunity to see each one's classrooms and pick up ideas. This approach greatly facilitated the sharing of ideas and made staff feel less vulnerable. We also took visits to other schools on our INSET school day. We did this as a whole team so that everyone could share the same experiences when we got back to school. As an exercise in team building it was very successful and we learnt a great deal from watching how others managed their classroom environments and their pupils. I had hoped that the changes would be fast and that by the end of the year I could expect to see all the classrooms with consistent practice such as cupboards appropriately labelled for pupils to obtain equipment, areas of the room clearly designated, space for larger material work maximized and the management of pupils being flexible between groups, whole class individual and other arrangements. But I had forgotten how much change people were having to cope with in the National Curriculum and the security of their own ways of working and their familiar environments was very powerful. So change at this stage appeared slow. At the end of one term I had a staff meeting to review progress and look at the next stage. We chose to focus on the pupils' access to resources and using classroom space. Everyone agreed that the teacher's desk was unnecessary now – to my surprise. So during the holiday break the desks were moved out and the new term started without them. I provided cover for every member of staff to spend time observing each other with the brief: what can you observe that will be useful to you in your classroom? The expectation was that when they returned to their own class, they would make a change to their ways of dealing with pupils or to the classroom environment.

At the end of that first year, the final staff meeting shared the progress so far. I was surprised I suppose that we had in fact accomplished a great deal. For instance, all the classrooms looked pleasant and worklike when you entered them. The equipment was better arranged and stored. All equipment was labelled, most of it in pupil-accessible language. One teacher used a mixture of adult language and pupil language. Adult language for some resources, pupil for others, but used this feature as a definite teaching point for the children, so that they began to recognize different words and a different register of language. The management of groups had improved. Pupils were clearer about what was required of them on a task. They managed themselves and their time better. When they had finished a task, after showing the teacher and obtaining feedback on their work, they would put it away and get on with the next task or a continuation activity from a previous day, without being told. They used the different areas of the room more appropriately too, so that in my visits around, or my teaching of colleagues' classes I would see many areas of the room in use at any one time, as pupils selected particular activities and carried them out close to the resources or in the space that worked best for them.

But, considering that my aim was the improvement of pupil achievement, more was needed! For the second year of our work, we began to look at the quality of learning and the learning environment as aspects of classroom organization and management. We discussed amongst ourselves what quality meant, and had an outside presentation on issues of quality in the learning environment. Again we visited other schools although we did not this time work in tandem with any one particular school, although that had been very helpful last year. We realized as the year progressed that the issue of whole-school planning had become crucial to raising the quality of pupils' work. We needed to know what was happening in advance and in each other's classes if we were to see how quality of learning could get better. We decided to undertake a quality work survey and look at the work of several children from each class to see if we could diagnose what each child needed next in terms of progression if the child was to be really stretched and challenged. This was a very successful piece of work. Discussing what activities or tasks a particular child needed and how we could manage that in a classroom with a whole range of needs made staff use each other's experience well and draw on each other's ideas. We discussed classroom-management issues like, group work, individual work, whole-class teaching, how to present work to children so that they managed their own learning better and could move on to designated tasks at a smooth rate and differentiation could be more effective. As a result of this activity, we began to review our criteria for good practice in classrooms. We started off with the County criteria, asking what others would expect of us in our classroom management and then relating this to what we expected of ourselves.

During this year, as a result of this work, there has been a marked improvement in the children's standards of work and consistency of practice in the school is much better now. Just as importantly, the children access equipment much more themselves. In science and technology activities you can watch the children developing an idea of something they want to do – measure or weigh an object, for example, to find out more about it, or use a different type of fastener – glue, a staple or a paperclip, and go to find the necessary equipment without having to ask the teacher's permission because they know where it is kept and can access it easily. This had made a tremendous difference to the speed at which children work and the ways in which they feel they own what they are doing. It is their work because they can develop it in different directions. This is very noticeable in technology where the outcomes of ideas can now be very different within a class from the same original starting point.

There is also far more group work in evidence and a wider range of activities being undertaken by children in the classes. By group work I mean activities in which children have to cooperate to complete the task, not just working on the same task at the same table. I worry about the present moves in terms of class teaching. We have always, of course, done whole-class teaching when it is appropriate, but there is a very useful place in terms of improving achievement, for group working practices if they are well done. I suppose now that we feel we are doing them quite well we can see the benefits. If they are badly done the children do not benefit and learning does not take place. Well-managed and organized classrooms and working practices for children improve achievement. I do not think we should lose sight of that.

Doreen Wootton's case study gives us a wide range of examples of changes to the organization and management of classrooms and children's work that Foxes Piece First School undertook under her leadership. We pick these up in more detail in the next three sections and explore some of the value arguments in the final part of the chapter.

Classrooms, the physical environment and pupil organization

The effective organization of the classroom not only creates a work-centred environment which is pleasant for pupils, teacher and visitors, it also facilitates ease of access to resources, safe and careful storage, easy movement and autonomy for children. As Doreen Wootton points out, they begin to 'own' their classroom. Here we ask four questions of the environment.

General aspects

First, what in general are the aspects to consider in the room? Clearly, good access is required. This is not only about access 'ins and outs' of the classroom, but also access to resources, which need to be carefully labelled and at pupil height. What the label says, too, is important. Many classrooms have drawers and cupboards with labels on but frequently these are designed for the benefit of adults: they say 'maths resources' or 'science equipment' for example. Whilst this is understandable for teachers, the use of pupil level cupboards, labelled in this fashion is not helpful in encouraging autonomy, unless, as in Doreen Wootton's case study it is deliberately used as a teaching point.

Movement

Secondly, what is movement around the room like? Can pupils and teachers move freely to collect equipment and more importantly make good use of it? In Case Study 8 below, the issues of safe working in technology became real issues in the classroom due to restricted access for pupils and teacher.

Furniture

Thirdly, furniture, too, is important. It needs to reflect the purposes for which it will be used. If there are tables for the pupils they need to be of the right material, wipeable and colourful and of the right height. The shape of the tables can be important too. Whilst round ones are useful in many ways, they are essentially space-wasting. Tables which fit into a hexagon shape are often the best in small rooms, so that space can be maximized both for working and for giving pupils a comfortable space in which to sit, and which they can feel is theirs. Two other points about furniture concern the position of the teacher's desk and the overall amount of furniture. Several classrooms, such as those in Foxes Piece First School, have dispensed with a teacher's desk altogether, since the teacher moves around taking advantage of different areas from which to teach: the reading area, the board area, the flipchart and display area. However, dispensing with the teacher's desk still means that there needs to be a place where schemes, current work, daily plans and other needs have to be kept.

The quantity of furniture in a classroom is an aspect that often needs re-examination. In many classrooms some furniture (such as cupboards) are

Figure 6.2 'Hungry caterpillar' display at Rokesly School.

there for historical reasons, rather than the real need for the class to use them. In classes where the only storage is provided by movable trays and cupboards (all of which take up floor space) the number needs careful consideration. So too do the types of chairs for different activities. When children are reading in a quiet area, are the chairs the same or different from those they normally sit on? Are 'bean bags' useful or do they take up too much room?

Most classrooms these days have been carpeted, since this cuts down noise level and provides easily for quiet areas where children can spread out and work with larger equipment and games or read informally. Nevertheless, floor covering is an issue to think about, especially in areas where science and technology are taking place. Given the nature of the activities, floor covering that can easily be swept, washed and that is non-slip is important.

Display

Fourthly, display is an obvious feature of the physical environment in a school. Displays not only make the environment interesting, they also convey messages about the ethos of the school. More importantly from a science and technology viewpoint, they can provide real opportunities for observation, particularly those parts of the display that are three-dimensional and designed to be tactile or kinetically stimulating. The opportunity to develop thought-provoking displays which challenge children's thinking by posing questions about scientific phenomena or technological instrumentation should

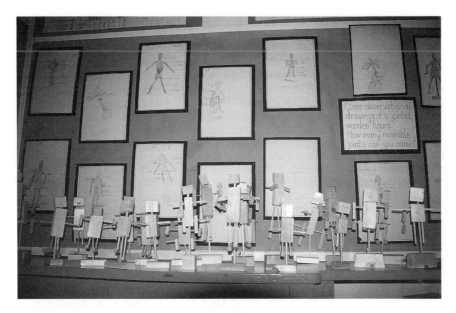

Figure 6.3 Jointed wooden figures at Rokesly School.

be exploited in classrooms. Such displays can be accompanied by hand-lenses, balances and other equipment. Several of our illustrations give examples of the kind of displays which teachers in several schools have used to extend children in their observational skills and scientific and technological knowledge.

Here we include our second case study in this chapter, drawn from one of the classes at Foxes Piece First School to show how the work the staff did has manifested itself within technology teaching for 5 and 6-year-olds. Figure 6.3 shows the work done by some of the youngsters at Rokesly School discussed later in Case Study 10.

CASE STUDY 8

Technology, classroom management and organization

Jenny McGivern, Foxes Piece First School

I have found the major problem with teaching technology to 5 and 6-year-olds is to provide similar learning experiences for pupils but also enable originality to develop. Because the children watch each other's work, it is sometimes difficult to make sure that they can develop their own ideas sufficiently at this age. They pick up on the ideas that children in other groups develop so easily. I suppose that this means they are observing well, but often they need a push to make sure that they are actually thinking for themselves as well.

I am a firm believer in direct skill teaching. I think it is difficult for small children to enter into an open-ended project if they do not have the necessary initial understanding of some basic ideas. Like for example ideas about fasteners and tools. At an early point in the year, I get the children to work in small groups with a support assistant. We get out a range of fasteners, such as Sellotape, hole punches, paperclips, treasury tags, and get the children to investigate what fastens things best. Similarly with tools. We have a board behind our technology table where the tools are displayed and drawn around so that everyone knows where they live and their return can be easily checked. But the children's vocabulary with regard to tools often centres just around ideas that tools are things kept on the technology board. They do not classify scissors as tools, or staplers, so we work with them in small groups to help increase their vocabulary in terms of tools, what they are, what a wider view of them is, what they are best at doing. We want to encourage them to have a familiarity with ideas of tools and some simple skills and processes like fastenings before they begin to really get to grips with more extensive project work in technology.

I do encourage the children, despite the worries I have about originality to collaborate within a group and build on each other's ideas. I usually start group sessions by introducing the work and getting them to pool ideas about how it might be done. I think another part of the technology process that young children need to understand from very early on is that the process of technology is a process which involves trying, evaluating and re-trying. I make sure that we constantly reinforce the message that it does not matter if something is not perfect the first time.

Our most recent project has arisen from the story of the three bears. We have been making the three bears' chairs. That is quite difficult for small children, to get all four legs the same length and in proportion to the seat size, and then to fasten the legs and seat together with each other and the appropriate fasteners. They need to use all the skills of tool use and fastening that we have encouraged. When we made the chairs, the children worked in groups of six with a support assistant, and a helping mother, each group having a different opportunity during the day to do some work on technology. They had cutting boards each and a hacksaw each with some balsa wood. They had to measure the size that they wanted – was it Daddy, Mummy or Baby bear's chair? We also showed them pictures of chairs. Some wanted to make high chairs for Baby bear, and that involved some extra work and fasteners. The safety issues of small children and hacksaws are potentially difficult, but we supervise very carefully, and our early skills work on tools means that they feel much more confident when they come to a real project.

Once they have been able to complete something like a chair, using hacksaw tools, I move them on to a potentially simpler project, by asking them to make a picture frame out of card and decorate the frame. This requires them to use scissors, paste, or staples, measure sizes and work out an appropriate decoration, as well as the right thickness of card. Finally, as the next problem, I ask them to work out a way of making the picture frame stand up. This again taxes their understanding of materials and fasteners. How can they attach more card so that a picture can still be put into the frame, but the frame will stand up?

Our most exciting project this year has come from work done in conjunction with older pupils. We have a local policemen who as part of his community work wants children to see him in another light. He offered to come and help with technology teaching. The project was to make a wheeled vehicle of some sort out of appropriate

Figure 6.4 Wheeled vehicle.   **Figure 6.5** Wheeled vehicle.

materials and involved pairs of younger and older pupils working together. The policeman worked alongside the pupils suggesting, assisting in the skills of gluing, cutting, designing. The younger children got a great deal out of this. They felt very proud of their finished products (see Figures 6.4 and 6.5), learnt new skills on a one to one basis with an older child and established a good set of relationships within the school which persisted for a long time.

The implications for classroom organization in this work are quite tremendous. Because we are encouraging the children to develop as much independence as is appropriate given the relevant safety issues, we need to be very well organized. We keep basic tools such as fasteners, scissors, etc. in the classroom, and they reside in boxes in a drawer at the kind of height that is accessible for the children. The drawers are labelled. Card, paper, Sellotape are all in labelled cupboards, paper for spreading out on worktables is kept in a large box and the children get used to establishing a routine for when they are doing technology. Each member of the group has a responsibility. One is responsible for covering the table, another for sweeping up after everything has been put away, and so on. It takes time to establish these routines, but once established they all contribute to the autonomy of work that we are trying to encourage throughout the school.

Work as concentrated as this would be impossible to undertake without the use of small groups and support helpers or mothers and fathers. The safety issues in making sure that hacksaws cut balsa wood not fingers mean that whole-class teaching in this area would be almost impossible, leave alone the resource issues. It is necessary for each child to develop their own skills and experiences. That can only be done at first hand. Whole-class teaching does take place at other times, but not for this area of the curriculum in project and skill work.

The two case studies used so far in this chapter have described work in science and technology which takes place in classrooms. But in some middle and upper parts of the primary school, there is increasingly a trend – particularly in technology – to have specialist areas. This poses particular kinds of challenges.

Specialist and non-specialist locations

Where science and technology are taught in a school obviously determines the kind and level of activity that can take place, the resourcing issues and the safety needs. If there is a specialist area, this has immediate advantages in terms of storage of unfinished work and safety aspects that have been designed into the room. There is also the issue of supervision. Where a specialist room exists, it is much more economic of time to teach in a whole-class group, although this may be subdivided into smaller groups, than have a class in which one group is doing English, another history and a third science. Clearly pupils cannot be left to work in a specialist room alone, and using support staff in these circumstances often has insurance complications. In ordinary classrooms, however, the teaching of science and technology can cause difficulties of wet areas, and in some classes water supply. In temporary classroom accommodation, there is rarely any water, and many teachers have found large five-gallon water containers (such as are used in caravanning) with washing-up bowls helpful under these circumstances. In some classrooms where the usual organization is in small groups, areas of the room are dedicated to science or technology, simply for ease of access to resources such as a vice or worktable and tools. In other rooms this is not possible and the safety aspects need to be very carefully watched. The placing of science and technology dedicated equipment for classroom use is a whole-school decision under such circumstances. Often the shared area can be put to such uses, especially if staffing between classes which butt onto the shared area is managed well. This permits the flexible use of the room when groups from different classes are working on their science and technology, with full teacher supervision whilst other pupils work in a different classroom with teacher support. The shared area has a variety of other advantages in terms of display, use of computers for data capture, data logging and control of other equipment in that such aspects can remain undisturbed for a longer period of time, but safe and accessible for children. Organizing pupils in classrooms refers back to the issues of group and individual working with which we opened this chapter.

Behaving safely in the classroom

However, there are other aspects which are of importance too. Classroom rules feature as one of these. In the Elton Report, 'Discipline in Schools'

(DES, 1989), teachers are urged to 'make the rules for classroom behaviour clear to pupils from the first lesson and explain why they are necessary'. This is a particularly teacher-driven approach. As several of our case studies (for example Sue Marran's Case Study 10 later in this chapter) shows, the pupils are more than capable of generating rules for themselves and including safety aspects of working in these. What is important is that the rules are known and owned by everyone in the class and the sanctions for transgression are clear. Clearly for young children, it is important that the classroom rules, particularly with reference to safety are made explicit by the teacher. For older ones though, a sense of ownership can be engendered by enabling the pupils to devise their own rules. Hunn (1993) has drawn up a set of questions which make a useful framework for a group activity on safety and result in a set of class rules which pupils can generate. Briefly his questions are:

- Can these materials or this situation damage my body on a large scale – fall on to me from a height, drown me, suffocate me?
- Can they burn me, scald me – heat, cooking, chemicals, electricity?
- Do I know how to use tools safely?
- Do I know that work with more resistant materials requires larger forces to bring about change and as a result there is more risk?
- Do I know how to deal with broken glass and how to handle glass so that it doesn't get broken?
- Do I understand that glue can stick to my body and do I always use a glue gun only under supervision?
- Do I avoid objects flicking or splashing into my eyes?
- Do I wear goggles when there are risks?
- Do I avoid touching my eyes when working with materials?
- Do I keep my hands away from my mouth when working with materials?

A set of agreed procedures can be generated from this list of questions by the class as an activity. The results of their discussions and agreements can then be word processed, displayed on the classroom wall in large print and kept in children's books.

Resource organization

In science and technology, a large part of the co-ordinator's job is concerned with resources, their acquisition and their organization. From knowing, for example, which of the local wood suppliers give free offcuts to schools to ordering the right choices of science measuring equipment, the science and technology co-ordinators are something of a cross between technical experts and scavengers. We address the issues of monitoring stock and organizing finance in Chapter 9 again as a part of the co-ordinator's role. So what basic equipment is needed if a science or technology area is being set up from scratch? The 20 day courses for co-ordinators funded by the DFE have yielded some excellent examples of such lists. We include an example of a technology list below.

This represents a baseline list which will enable getting started. It will need constant replenishing especially in the materials section.

Tools: for food

Whisk

Kitchen scales

Sieve

Tongs

Mixing bowl

Spatula

Rolling pin

Flexible working/chopping mat

Measuring jug and spoons

Tools: for materials

Hacksaw – try some with an easy blade removal

Bench hooks to hold work

Safety snips

G clamps

Screwdriver

Drill – try a pistol grip one

Hammer

Single hole punch

Scissors

Vice

Storage

Tool boards with silhouettes of tools and trolleys are a useful investment.

Materials

A variety of materials will be needed, and these will differ from project to project. Some essentials will be:

Wheels – wooden, card

PVC tubing – has many uses – acts as a washer, spacer for wheels and axles as well as ordinary uses

Fasteners – paperclips, bulldog clips, treasury tags, paper fasteners, double-sided tape, masking tape, PVA glue (water soluble)

Card of a variety of thickness and width

Gearing mechanisms of different kinds

As with any area of the curriculum which is taught within classrooms, the question of what is essential class equipment for science and technology and what is necessary but not stored within the class has to be addressed. A computer or access to one within the classroom or shared area is essential. Every class or year group base should have sets of plastic beakers, hand-lenses, balances or weighing machines, timers, running water, washing facilities, and a means of producing 12-volt electrical supplies. For technology, a range of materials for construction purposes, textiles, glue, scissors, cutting boards, and for older children some cutting mechanism, such as a fretsaw, G-clamps, a vice and staplegun.

Use of resources

This is an important issue and leads to a discussion of cost effectiveness. As more money continues to be devolved to schools, the role of the subject co-ordinator (for example, in ordering resources, monitoring their use and providing financial advice to the headteacher) now and in the future is crucial. Certainly in this area co-ordinators for science and technology have much to learn from their secondary colleagues and we discuss this in detail with practical advice in Chapter 9. Dealing with resources focuses on specialist provision of different kinds. So, it often means 'dedicated space' where science and technology activities alone are conducted. The tables, tools and materials are set there and the area not used for anything else. There needs to be separate storage for particular materials, and general classroom tables which allow maximum flexibility in use. In addition there needs to be specialist provision for:

- flammable substances
- a 'spill' kit
- fire extinguisher, fire blanket, sand bucket
- first-aid box and eyewash (quick access essential)
- bins for 'wet' and 'dry' waste
- tools (sharp cutters for example)
- aprons and plastic gloves

The co-ordinator will need to have some catalogue of materials and stock so that careful stock management can take place, and ordering can be effective. A 'paper-based' file or computer-based stock list will need updating at regular intervals, with a full stock-taking each year. However, classroom teachers too will need to address the issues of keeping track of what they use so that the co-ordinator is better informed and kept up to date.

Money allocation

Knight (1983) describes four approaches to internal school allocations:

1. *Benevolent despotism*: the Headteacher usually dispenses what is seen to be appropriate. It tends to revolve around individual discussions and special lobbying.
2. *Open market*: teachers produce estimates and are expected to justify their priorities. It tends to lead to overinflated 'wants' and 'needs', and is prey to the strategies and tactics of the wily or outspoken people on the staff.
3. *Creeping incrementation*: this assumes an increased allocation each year on what went before. It tends to simply perpetuate historical allocations and cannot deal with special circumstances.
4. *Formula*: based on a range of factors (number of pupils in the class, the time allocation for technology, requirements of the Programme of Study, etc.). It is not always fair and depends on the weightings given to various factors.

Whatever the system, the teachers in each class ought to be in the position to identify their financial needs each year and use this either to 'bid' for resources or to assess what has been given. Let us take stock first; if a detailed

Year group	Stationery	Books	Consumables	Audio visual	Major equip.	Minor equip.
Science AT1	4	2	3	2	3	3
Science AT2	4	2	3	2	3	3
Science AT3	3	1	3	3	4	3
Science AT4	3	3	3	2	1	3
Design and technology	4	5	2	4	1	5
Information technology	1	1	1	1	1	1

Figure 6.6 Stock card.

stock-take is not always possible then try an idea discussed in *Croner's Manual for Heads of Science* (1993). This uses a 1 to 5 scale to rate stock availability quickly:

5 Ample quantities and in very good condition
4 Reasonable numbers of essential items in fairly good condition
3 Most essential materials in workable condition though limited in number
2 Insufficient essential equipment and very lacking in support materials
1 Most essential materials not available and in poor condition.

This can then be used to rate main areas of stock, perhaps as in Figure 6.6.

There is probably a very carefully detailed procedure for ordering materials and equipment but responsible teachers will need to keep some log of:

• orders placed and goods received;
• guarantees and serial numbers of major items;
• some inventory of stock.

An easy proforma might look like that depicted in Figure 6.7.

As a rule of thumb, most 'heavy' items of equipment (like slide projectors, bandsaws, etc.) have a life expectancy of about seven years. They may well need repairs before that time but can be expected to be replaced after that sort of period. So, it is sometimes possible to predict what will be needed

Item	Cupboard no.	Bought from	Date bought	Cost	Last checked

Figure 6.7 Stock proforma.

(and when) and begin to budget in time. Hunn (1993) gives a fairly comprehensive run-down on the provision of resources for Science in primary schools.

Safety organization

We have already mentioned several aspects of safety within this chapter, but it is our intention here to draw out some detailed safety issues for classrooms. As our guidance for writing a policy statement states in Chapter 5, some good sources of safety help are to be found in the work of the Consortium of Local Education Authorities for the Provision of Science Services (CLEAPSS). However, in most primary schools, some of the more difficult chemical safety issues will not apply within science. Technology, however is fraught with many difficulties, as Catherine Ducheck's Case Study (below) points out. We drew up suggestions for generating pupil safety guidelines earlier in the chapter. Here below, we include a short checklist for *teachers* to ensure that they have made conditions as safe as possible before they start.

A safety checklist comprises the following questions:

- Is there a clearly defined place where tools must be returned that you can check at a glance?
- Are all saw blades securely fixed in hacksaws?
- Fine dust is hazardous if produced in large quantities – is there good ventilation in your technology area?
- Are hanging loads protected with a box underneath?
- Are stretch items (springs, etc.) only used with eye protection?
- Are all cooking surfaces clean before and after cooking?
- Do children wash their hands before and after cooking?
- Is there a special procedure for broken glass – such as a special box and an instruction to inform an adult?
- Is there newspaper readily available to wrap broken glass in?
- Is there a fire bucket with sand somewhere close when heaters are being used with older children?

- Do children know what to do if they burn or scald themselves – apart from inform an adult?
- Are sand trays available for candles and nightlights when heating?
- Do children obey good dress sense rules whenever they use equipment – tying back hair for example?
- Are safety spectacles available for older children?
- Do you know what the list of suitable chemicals for use at Key Stages 1 and 2 contains (Safe, 1990)?
- Do you know what chemicals are dangerous – particularly the household ones – have you checked your science stores recently for these?
- Do children always wash their hands after using chemicals?
- Is there an eye bath available in the first-aid kit?
- Do you check your batteries frequently to ensure they are not old and leaking?
- Are electrical leads safe – not frayed or exposing wire?
- Do children always wash their hands after handling plants – to avoid possible contamination from pesticides?

CASE STUDY 9

Making the classroom safer

Catherine Ducheck, Haverden Primary School

My class is Year 4/5. There were 33 children in it at the time of our work on classroom safety. The school is housed in a Victorian building with long cold corridors and high ceilings and the classroom itself is small, with barely enough room for the tables and chairs. Since technology came into the National Curriculum I had been struggling to find a way of teaching that allows me to allow the children the opportunity to learn skills as well as work at the design cycle. To learn the skills required time and space to practise such things as using a hacksaw, a glue gun and a hammer.

I teach my class mainly in both small groups and as a whole class. My history and geography work is in 'whole class' for some of the time, as is some language work. Science tends to start off in 'whole-class mode' and then move to small groups. Maths is in specific 'maths groups' but the whole class do maths at the same time. The flexibility for teaching technology comes from working in art and language with some history and geography. I tend to fit my technology around this. I have been concerned that children were getting a very patchy experience and, due to the room constraints, the working conditions were not helping to give good technology education.

There is a workbench in the school, but we do not use it because it is situated at the end of the corridor, near the technology store, and is a long way from our classroom. The support assistant who works with my class on Wednesday morning takes small groups down there to work on their technology. But even this is less than satisfactory since the workbench is small and with just two or three children at a time being allowed to use it. Thus, it is going to take a long time to give all of the class a turn on it.

The children, too, are frustrated by the overall lack of space. We have no shared area for storage of items or models in preparation and these are often placed on top of our 'paper cupboard'. When technology takes place for different groups, there is rarely a time when someone does not complain that their work has been bent or damaged since the last time they worked on it. The lack of general working space beyond their own tables proves an irritation as well. When a child gets to the point of wanting to use the glue gun, they have to go over to the class's own 'technology area' which, in reality, is a table at one side of the room with a pinboard behind it to house tools. Again, there is only room for three children round the table, which is against the wall. If others are working there, the next children in line often have to wait before they can complete what they are doing. This makes construction work very slow indeed.

One particular afternoon a small group of boys was working on a technology design. As part of a follow-up to a visit to London, they were making a cannon, which involved much wood, empty toilet rolls and glue. James wanted to build a support out of wood as well as a base for the body of the cannon. He used the hacksaw on several offcuts of wood without much success until eventually he had the shape he wanted. This took up much time during which others were not able to use the table or tools. Tony became very irritated by James and when he tried to move in beside him to use the hammer and a large nail, he missed the nail and ended up hitting James' hand by mistake.

I realized then that something needed to be done. This was a serious incident, but one that had the potential to be much worse. In maths later that morning, I suggested to the children that teaching technology safely was causing problems and asked them to design the arrangement of tables and furniture in the classroom in such a way that we could all work, have access to resources when we needed them, and still have space to carry out practical activities safely. They became very enthusiastic. One group in particular thought that part of the problem was the class safety rules above the window (a set from the Association for Science Education). They felt we needed a specific set that dealt with the special conditions in our classroom. They worked on a computer to design a list for everyone to talk about at the end of the day. Already I could feel my intended maths activity getting eroded!

The other groups however, worked hard at plans of the classroom, measuring everything from the sizes of cupboards, to desks, tables and bookcases. The activity fast began to take over. They wanted to move things, look into drawers and cupboards to see if they could fit things in better and organize things in a different way. By lunchtime, we were all exhausted! I decided over lunch that what was needed was to set aside a whole day for the work and make it into a mini-technology project. In the afternoon, I discussed this with the class and they agreed. On Friday, they started off by drawing up the plan of the classroom as it was at present then each small group drew their plans for how they thought it would be best arranged to be safe. The safety rules group, having finished their task the day before, set about trying to arrange things better in cupboards and taking responsibility for the better labelling of materials and equipment.

After break, we discussed the plans. Each group showed their plans to the class and said why they thought we should, in order to have a safer classroom choose their design. We decided to take our chairs and go to the hall for this activity so that we could sit in a large circle to see better and hear everyone clearly, since in our room there was not enough space to be comfortable and have presentations.

Of course it was difficult to get them to agree. They each wanted their own design to be the one chosen. In the end we agreed on some principles which we felt would ease the situation but were drawn from different plans. The children felt that our large storage cupboard would be better out in the corridor next to the classroom door. They wanted to store in it things that would be in use only infrequently or once or twice a week. We discussed the feasibility of this and decided that if the Headteacher would let us, it would provide more space. The next thing to go was my table! The children pointed out that I rarely sat at it, I only used it for putting things on and what I really needed was a set of trays to organize my work and a chair. I felt a little uncomfortable about this but agreed to give it a try.

They suggested different arrangements for the tables in the classroom and wanted to go back immediately and try them out to find the best arrangement. I had to remind them at this point that we wanted to find safer ways of working, not just rearrange their desks! Their solutions for safer working were interesting. Several of them felt that the safety situation would be eased if the tables for technology were not against the wall. They pointed out that more people could have access to the table if it were available to work at all the way round. They also suggested that a smaller table be set up in a different part of the room for use with the glue gun. We rejected ideas of putting the worktable in the corridor so that there would be more real space as this would not allow for safety to be watched over by me.

Finally, we got round to discussing the safety rules, and agreed some changes. The children printed out a large copy for the wall and we made our final plans for the classroom. The table for technology was to go next to the reading area – a small carpet square squeezed into a corner – so that there was more room for people to get round. The glue gun table doubled as the storage table for tape recorders and other electrical equipment in a box. The children reorganized the tables at which they worked and saved some further space in this way. Once my table was out of the room, and the storage cupboard was in the corridor, we had enough space to work in safer ways. The children also helped to make a pinboard for tools so that they were on display next to the safety rules, with hints for use of the equipment. The school caretaker was very helpful over the weekend at rearranging the room according to their specifications, so that when they arrived on Monday, it all looked different.

They were very pleased with the new look, and continued to make minor adjustments over time as they found some things working and others not. What was most interesting was the way they kept each other to safe working practices, pointing out their own rules to one another on use of equipment and space, whenever they thought someone was transgressing. They tried to amend the rules over time as well, when they saw someone trying a new way of working that looked better. In fact, they became so interested, that they asked for one of their fathers to come in – he had a fully equipped workshop in his garage – to check their rules and give them some advice, a month or two later. He had their final set of rules laminated for them, which seemed to set the end to this piece of work. There is no doubt that in terms of technology, the pupils, planned, designed a system and continuously evaluated it over time. It made technology come alive for them, and terms like 'planning' and 'evaluating' became really understood. They would remind each other what evaluating meant by referring back to their frequent refinements of the safety rules.

CASE STUDY 10

Pictures of olden days: information technology at Key Stage 1

Sue Marran, Rokesly Infants School

At Rokesly, our policy on information technology means that we design our Year 2 work to build, of course, on what happens at Year 1 – which in turn is preceded by our work in Nursery and Reception. When they come to me, my 'Red Class' of 6 and 7-year-olds have quite some experience in using computers and they are already familiar with creating pieces of work, saving and printing them. However, in Year 2 we move away from the BBC machines we have for the early classes and begin using an Apple Macintosh. Largely, I am working to National Curriculum Levels 2 and 3 so that, by the end of the year, children will know that they can 'store, modify and retrieve information', can organize and present their ideas by word processing, and can use a database confidently.

There have been three or four parts to this work which come together to enable the children to use the computer. For example, one part has been our topic called 'Schools in Olden Days'. It was a somewhat historical perspective on schooling in the locality – we needed to go beyond our own school since this is only fifty years old. The full topic meant children took photographs in black and white outside the front door of the school, made box models of different sections of the school, and made close observations of building materials and designs. They also talked to mums, dads and grandparents about what schooling was like in their days and made and displayed pen-and-ink drawings of children and teachers in classrooms. They were then asked to draft prose for their pictures and, when ready, to choose a script style from the menu and transfer their text to the screen. Funnily enough, the majority of them seemed to like a 'shadow style' since they thought this had an 'olde worlde' look about it (Figures 6.8 to 6.10). Given the current debate about formal and informal teaching methods, their pictures of Victorian classrooms have an eerie sense of prescience about them.

As usual, the real classroom management problem is one of organizing work for 26 pupils with only one machine in the room. First, I have to make sure that the spread of activities in the room allows me to teach some children individually – I have to organize their project work so that many of them are self-sustaining. I need this time because the Apple Macintosh is quite different to the BBC model and they often need some direct skill teaching, for example with the use of the mouse and the menu bar. I choose to teach children first who I know can work well with others. This is simply because I will then use them to help other children in the class. So, I deliberately pair children together so that there is a skill difference – a more able child partnering someone who is less confident on the computer. This is not so difficult to arrange because I know some have computers at home and – even at this age – are becoming used to using them. Together they take their turn at the keyboard and input, store and print their words.

One aspect of the partnership is that they must check each other for phrasing and spelling, and this means being able to use the backspace and delete keys. More important, it requires quite sophisticated use of the mouse to be able to position the cursor, and this is a set of manual and dexterous skills that takes time for children to develop. Small movements can be very sensitive and it is not always straightforward to move the cursor accurately, sometimes to lift the mouse and re-position

the children had school
uniform. They had benches
not chais. They did not have
electric litys instede they had
gasalitys. by Gino.

Figure 6.8 Examples of Olde Worlde printing.

it on the mouse pad and then continue with the positioning motion. In fact the children are often quite afraid of the mouse and worried that if it goes off the screen then they have done some irreparable damage and it 'won't come back again'. A second part of our work have been the processes of drafting and re-drafting. For example, when parents have come to class to talk about their own school days we have written to thank them, and the letter draft has taken time to accumulate (Figure 6.11).

Different pupils can contribute different parts to different letters – they can read what has already been written, add prose to it and then save it for a further time. This is a process we use quite a lot and so, for example, the children draft and re-draft stories and poems. In another context, throughout the year we have been building a set of rules for good communication. These are 'good behaviour' points that arise from time to time as we are working and we add them to the list when

In the olden days at school they
did~nt sit on chairs they sat on
benches.
by Leigh.

Figure 6.9 Examples of Olde Worlde printing.

they crop up (Figure 6.12). No doubt the next ones on the list are how to reduce stress on teacher and how to be kind to the mouse.

I finish with two more points. On the whole the children very much enjoy using the machine. Their favourite is to use MacPaint and to draw on screen as Nathaniel and Leigh have done in Figures 6.13 and 6.14.

In December, the class all made Christmas cards and drew angels, reindeer, Santas and Christmas trees. In the meantime, we are also beginning to use a database so that the cycle of development activity continues.

My final point is an equal opportunities' one. The school as a whole has an imbalance of boys to girls. In Red Class the ratio is 7 girls to 19 boys and there could be real problems of the girls being 'swamped' if there are no careful structures in place. With this in mind we organize 'girls-only' sessions each week where they have full access to construction toys, building blocks and the computer. We believe this has been very important in allowing them to develop positive relationships between themselves and become more confident in their technological skills.

In the old days the children sat on benchs but we sit on chairs and work in groups. The techr used to sit on a high chair so she could see all the children that sat in lins fasin the techr. by Coriene.

Figure 6.10 Examples of Olde Worlde printing.

Dear Mrs Hall
                thank you very much for coming to our class and thank you for answering our questions.
p

Figure 6.11 Draft letter.

Rules for Good Communication.

We have been thinking about why
we shouldn't all talk at once and
we have made a list.

It would be very NOISY!
No one would be able to listen
properly.
We wouldn't be able to
concentrate, so we wouldn't get
our work done.
Everyone should have a turn of
speaking or else it isn't fair.
It is important to listen.
We would all go home with a
headache!

We have also been thinking about
Good Classroom Behaviour and we
have made another list!

We should be kind to each other,
especially new children.
We should keep our classroom tidy.
If our teacher is busy we should
wait patiently.

We should be helpful to sad or hurt
children in the playground.
We should never run in the
corridor.
We should always try to do our
best!

If you can think of any more
suggestions please let us know
and we will add them to our lists.

Figure 6.12 List of rules.

I felt sad nervous and scared.
by Nathaniel.

Figure 6.13 Examples of children's pictures.

l felt sad and l felt nervous and l
felt scared. by Leigh

Figure 6.14 Examples of children's pictures.

Value arguments

We see these case studies as pinpointing a number of ,
classroom constructivism. Taken as a whole they illustrat\
tenets from Chapter 1 (see p. 10). While some cover all of t\
more specific in their focus.

All the case studies illustrate children being encouraged\
learners. In Case Study 7, Doreen Wootton refers to children developing
ideas in science and technology and being able to access the necessary resources to put these ideas into practice. The classroom environment is organized to support their autonomy. Similarly, Sue Marran in Case Study 10,
organized children to design their own list of computer manners. A second
feature of these studies is that they clearly show the practice of teachers-as-
facilitators. Sue Marran, for instance, scheduled children in pairs so that they
knew how and when to work on the computer. While she taught some
individually, her main concern was to enable the children to work independently. Catherine Ducheck, in Case Study 9, devolved considerable responsibility to the learners and facilitated their implementation of their own
designs for classroom safety. This fostered a growing understanding of the
process of evaluation in technology. In a more specific sense, both Jenny
McGivern and Sue Ducheck in Case Studies 8 and 10 show how they use
direct skill teaching to help build bridges between different tasks. They have
come to know their pupils sufficiently well to predict how and when they
need the particular skills before they can make the transition to a new more
open-ended task. In designing their task for individuals and groups they have
taken care to explore exactly what experiences the children bring to the
activity (for example about joiners, 'fasteners', and so on).

Both Jenny McGivern and Sue Ducheck use peers as a mechanism for
encouraging progression. These are good Vygotskian 'zone' points: older or
more able children problem-solving with younger or less-skilled children to
reach objectives they could not easily achieve on their own.

Organizing the classroom in order to facilitate active learning is premised
on collaborative activity, the talking, sharing and working together of the
class as they develop and implement ideas. In the next chapter we discuss
the role of language and focus specifically on its development through the
context of science and technology.

seven

Posing problems:
effective questioning

Introduction

'What is a question?' is not itself a trivial question. Just because we put a question mark at the end of a sentence does not mean the sentence is (or is not) a question – and many sentences can be statements, commands or other kinds of response just as easily as they can be questions – with or without a question mark. When someone says, for example: 'Who has left the door open?' or 'Whose pen is that on the floor?' they do not usually want to know the person's name ('John'; 'It's Mary's') but mean 'Whoever left the door open, would he or she please close it' or 'Whoever's pen it is on the floor, would she or he please pick it up'.

Some questions may sound like a command ('Hands up those who know what osmosis is') or be managerial ('Have you finished, Jane?'). Most commonly, it must be said, teachers rely upon questions to check that information they have given has been retained by the pupil. Similarly, they use them as a form of social control: they ask closed questions and use them tactically to maintain discipline. Not all questions need be like this, of course, and much, it seems, depends upon the questioner's intentions. Can we, then, discuss the whole process of questioning in terms of our four design questions? To do so might go something like the following.

Purpose

Why do teachers ask questions? Whether for short sharp answers or for maintaining tight control, they certainly rely upon questioning as a major tool in their box of teaching strategies. As Floyd (1976) points out, primary teachers in her sample asked an average of 348 questions during the day; while Moyer (1966) notes that, in science, teachers ask some 180 questions each lesson. Generally teachers seem to spend something like 30 per cent of their time asking questions. One classification of questions follows Bloom's (1956) taxonomy, and might be as follows:

1. Knowledge
2. Comprehension
3. Application
4. Analysis
5. Synthesis
6. Evaluation

This might help to determine purpose, so that testing straight recall of in.
mation might be a question of knowledge ('When did Columbus arrive first
in America?'); whereas an 'applications' question might explore ways of using
particular kinds of understanding ('Can you design a "squirrel scarer" to
keep squirrels off a bird table, without scaring away the birds?'). However,
some questions do not fall neatly into these kinds of categories, so that a
'knowledge' question can also call for analysis and evaluation.

'Why is the side of a mountain that faces the coast usually wetter than
the side facing the interior?' is a question which might prompt a range of
responses depending upon the context and the learners. For some it might
mean the recall of the facts just given in the lesson, for others it might mean
the restructuring of data from a range of sources, or the transfer of ideas
from geography into science, or the prelude to a problem-solving context in
technology. Biggs and Collis (1982) use this type of question to illustrate the
vast array of responses that pupils might generate as they are working. Some
questions, like the ubiquitous 'why?' questions, can result in a simple two-
turn exchange or a long protracted discussion. Young children know the
value of constantly asking 'why' in order to rattle even the most calm and
collected adult ('Why do I have to do that, Mummy?' 'Because I say so!').

Perrott (1982) distinguishes 'low-order' (recall) questions from 'high-order'
(conceptual) ones. The latter, she says, is where the child is asked to change
the form or organization of information to compare, contrast, summarize,
extend, apply, analyse, reorganize or evaluate ideas to resolve a problem.
While low-order questions can be dealt with easily, they are also of limited
value. High-order ones are much more complex to ask properly and to respond to, gauge and assess. In turn, Turvey's (1973) categorization is useful
because teachers ask questions which range from 'to arouse interest and
curiosity in a topic', through 'to diagnose specific learning difficulties', to
'developing reflection'.

In this text we are going to focus principally on the higher-order forms of
questioning. Our overriding purpose is that 'conceptual change teachers' ask
questions in order to challenge children's ideas and so enable and facilitate
conceptual development. Consequently questions in this kind of classroom
would be directed towards:

- determining what understanding the child might have of a particular part
  of science or topic in technology;
- making sense of insufficient data concerning learners' conceptions;
- reconciling conflicting evidence about their ideas;
- making value judgements about the quality of their constructions;

eking explanations for the links they make and the descriptions they use;
examining their general problem-solving strategies;
exploring the general state of their learning.

For us, this gives a very clear set of purposes for the use of questions in science and technology.

Structure

What sense does it make to consider the structure of questioning? Well, from what has been said, there are clearly different forms of questions and this may give some clue to the way we might then design good or effective questions. Let us say that one way to summarize our seven purposes above might be to 'help children give thoughtful responses about their ideas in science or technology'. In this case we might want to move between questions which require short answers and those which require extended responses; we might want to push for answers quickly to challenge ideas or allow time for reflection; we might want to shape key questions ourselves or prompt pupils to ask their own – and so on. In this sense, we might think about the design structure of questioning in terms of:

- providing an atmosphere of trust so that questions can be asked and answered without fear of ridicule;
- teaching pupils to ask questions of the teacher, each other and themselves;
- considering in advance the way prompts and pauses, open and closed questions, low and higher order questions might be used;
- planning how to re-direct questions to several pupils;
- thinking about how to restructure questions for different ability pupils;
- considering how to use questions to increase the participation and quality of response of some pupils in the class;
- framing questions to draw on children's own constructs, experiences, ideas, situations;
- directing children to respond clearly and appropriately where the context is complex;
- helping pupils to be original, inventive and creative;
- supporting pupils towards positive motivation and self-esteem as they work.

These ten pointers are not exhaustive but can be seen as a way we might structure questioning in the classroom and might be summarized broadly by a consideration of tactics, targets and sequencing.

Model cases

In Case Study 13, Virginia Whitby compares the classroom techniques of two teachers. They are teachers who commonly work closely together with very similar children, but nevertheless differ quite markedly in their approach. She uses Elstgeest's (1991) categorization of questions to comment on these differences, where distinction is made, for example, between questions for:

- attention-focusing;
- exploring 'how' and 'why';
- forging comparisons;
- problem-posing;
- prompting action.

The focus of the lesson is 'sinking and floating' and the two teachers come at this in distinctive ways – governed, says Virginia Whitby, by their respective levels of confidence in their own science knowledge. In Case Study 12, Steve Alsop looks at three classroom examples of ways to prompt children to ask questions. The context is electricity in science, and the life of Michael Faraday. He makes the good point that teachers' questions are too frequently used as a means of exerting classroom control. His examples are a clear indication that encouraging children to ask questions can be very structured and organized and mean no loss of classroom control at all. Steve Alsop's other assertion is that children's own questions provide a window on their thinking and can lead to conceptual change.

CASE STUDY 11

Encouraging the language of science

Pauline Prince, Foxes Piece Middle School

There are 22 children in my class from Years 4 and 5. Generally when I teach science I have the children working in four or five mixed-ability groups. I find that the mixing of the groups assists all the children. The language of the older children and their work and thinking assists the younger ones and those who are not as quick at understanding science. Our unit of work for this term has been on materials and I was particularly keen to use this topic to help the children improve their understanding of fair testing. So often when children use the word 'fair' they do not mean what a scientist would mean by a fair test. They are really just using it in a general sense – as a kind of justice type word. In order to ensure that they can achieve Levels 3 and above in Attainment Target 1, I need to be sure they really understand all the scientific ramifications of a fair test, and can grasp some ideas of variables and their control – even if those are not the words we use to describe what they are doing. This particular piece of work began with a discussion about materials – what they were, what we used them for, how many different kinds we knew about. I encouraged the children to bring examples of materials for a class display over a period of a week or so before the science lesson. By the time the first science lesson on the topic took place, the classroom closely resembled the council rubbish tip! We had empty washing-up liquid bottles, paper bags, plastic bags, envelopes, fabrics, plastic containers, shiny balloons, glassware, tin cans, aluminium cans, wooden toys and many other things that the children had brought in.

As many teachers do, I began by encouraging the children to classify the objects. They suggested the categories – some were very obvious – plastic, wood, glass, metal, etc. They also used colour, uses, flexibility – would it bend? – man-made, natural and so on. We had a wealth of suggestions, but I tried eventually to focus down on aspects of materials and the uses of the materials they had brought. This got us thinking eventually about materials and their function as objects for our use. We had a go at classifying the materials according to the function of them and began to think about the characteristics of materials from this.

For example, one group considered why most bags are made from plastic these days, not paper, when paper is clearly recyclable. They considered costs, durability, waterproofness and strength of plastic to be important characteristics of the materials that made it better as a bag than paper. In this way, during the first session, we considered a variety of characteristics of materials. By the end of the session we felt as a class that there were several characteristics that we could consider next time and test them out.

I chose to conduct the fair test session across a whole afternoon to give the children more time. Looking at their work from the earlier session, I realised that there were a whole range of facets they might investigate. However, if I was trying to enable them to understand fair testing thoroughly, it would be easier if they had a common experience, so I chose to concentrate on the durability of materials. I divided the children into their five groups and we discussed to start with what they needed to do. They decided that three-quarters of the materials would be sufficient for each group to test, if they all chose a different three-quarters. Since I wanted the test to reflect the kind of use that the material was put to, I asked them to consider the use before they devised a test for the material's durability. They soon realised that this might mean different tests for different materials. There was some involved discussion between them as to whether it was a fair test if the tests were different. However, in the interests of time, I asked them to start by devising the tests. Two children offered to put all the data from the class on the computer database so that we could see all the information before interpreting the results. I wanted the main processes of the lesson to concentrate on the problem of solving a method for fair testing and interpreting results so that they understood fair tests. I decided that writing up the experience should be an extension activity for a few children only and that I would concentrate on getting them to report back verbally to the class and discuss the results and their representation.

The activity could have taken far longer than a one-afternoon session. The children were enthusiastic at having to solve the problem of how they tested durability and at the same time making sure all their samples were treated in the same way. One group chose to rub their samples on wet and then dry concrete outside. They used a finger wrapped in the material to conduct the actual rubbing. Two members of the group were concerned that their fingers were not the same size as each other's and felt that this would affect the results. They were also worried that one member of the group seemed to be rubbing very hard. I was asked to adjudicate. Susan said: 'If he rubs harder than the rest of us, that can't be a fair test can it? – because his material's getting more rubbing every time he rubs.'

I introduced the word 'force' into the conversation and pointed out that perhaps one member was rubbing with more force than the others.

PAUL: Then they'll have to rub with the same force as me.
MICHELLE: But we don't know what force you're rubbing with. We don't know how hard you're pressing.

I left them with the challenge of working out how hard people pressed when they rubbed and trying to make the force a similar one.

Another group was concerned about the force as well. They decided that it would be better if they could make something that would rub for them instead of rubbing for themselves.

ROBIN: Then we can be sure that it rubs each one the same.

They decided on a pendulum approach. They set up a pendulum with a piece of string tied to a block of wood. The block of wood had sandpaper fastened round it with a rubber band. They placed the material beneath the pendulum and adjusted the length of the string so that the material was rubbed as the pendulum passed. They had some difficulty since the pendulum frequently stopped instead of swinging. They also realized that the pendulum was only ever applying one force. So they added weights to the bock of wood. This caused several initial problems because the weights fell off. Eventually they altered their design to a plastic margarine tub in which they could put the weights, with the sandpaper fastened on the bottom of the tub. This seemed to work much better, apart from the problem of the pendulum stopping.

Several other mechanisms were tried by the groups. They rubbed the materials on brick walls, used sandpaper – which wore out before the material! – and tried tying the material to their shoes and rubbing their feet (a bit like skating). The group who thought of this one had people in it who were of different builds. They decided amongst themselves that one solution would be to get the heaviest person to do all the testing, but since they all wanted to have a go – it was not fair to them if they just had to sit and watch – they would all try all the materials and compare the results to see if the heaviest person made a difference.

One group used the pendulum group's ideas, but adapted them. They decided that since the pendulum kept stopping it was not doing the job very well. Ideally I think they needed an electric motor-driven pendulum, but we had not done anything like that and they did not suggest it. What they did was to ask me if there was anything they could use that would tell them how hard they were pulling or pushing something. I suggested a newton-meter and helped them to read and understand one. They then used the margarine tub idea, but dragged it with a newton-meter to measure the force being applied.

Eventually, I gathered them together for the feedback. They had been told that they must all present their results to the class, say what they did and explain which of their test methods was the fairest and why. It was at this point that the language development really began to take off. When they heard the pendulum group's results, they were impressed by the ideas and thought it a better method than rubbing with a finger, even the same person's finger, because the results got over the problem of the force. But Jenny had some interesting thoughts.

JENNY: Did you alter the length of the string every time you put a new piece of material underneath?
ROBIN: Sometimes.
JENNY: Then it's not really fair. Because if the string wasn't tight then the weight of the tub would be different.
ROBIN: How can the weight be different? It's still the same tub.

Jenny could not explain what she meant in terms of the mass of the tub and its contact with the material, but the children became very interested in the idea. They explored the notion of weight and rubbing, and I introduced the word 'friction' to them. They wanted to know how they could measure the friction. Was there always friction? We talked about winter weather, and ice and making slides and if they thought there was as much friction then. They soon began to get the idea that some conditions and surfaces have less friction than others, and that some substances – like oil – can reduce friction. This led to a discussion about oil in car engines and oiling your bike chain.

I had real difficulty in bringing them back to ideas about fair testing – the object of the exercise. They eagerly listened to words like 'control' and 'variables' because they were searching for something to describe accurately what they had done. Their own words were things like: 'We kept them all the same.' 'What things', I asked? 'The things we were testing.' I suggested variables and we looked at what these might be for the different tests that had been conducted. Not only did the session bring real enthusiasm, it also progressed their scientific language and conceptual understanding of ideas about force, such as friction, and mass and measurement.

One unexpected spin-off was the interest displayed by parents. Many of the children went home and talked about their afternoon's science. At a parents' evening some two weeks later several parents came to me and said how much the children enjoyed the science they did. Several parents got involved too. The group where the sandpaper wore out before the material had one dad who in his workshop produced a testing bed for us – a block with several different grades of sandpaper fastened in so that we could test with different grades and see the effect all at the same time. Other small 'inventions' like this kept coming in – either from the children themselves or with their parents' ideas and help over the next few weeks. I was almost at the stage of having to offer a prize for the best invention for fair testing. The essential parts for me were that through the problem-solving, experimentation and evaluative explanation to their peers, the children's language and concepts of science developed.

CASE STUDY 12

Questioning

Steve Alsop, Roehampton Institute

'What's the average weight of a badger?' is one of the worst questions I have ever heard a teacher ask. It came out of the blue; quite how a group of 11-year-olds were expected to know the answer, I am not at all sure. Another question, 'What are we all doing now?' gave the children few hints since the required answer was 'breathing'! Although these are extreme examples, I can look back over my own classroom teaching and cite a number of examples where the questions I asked were poorly phrased and in some instances wholly misleading. Asking good questions is an art, it is often not as straightforward as many teachers assume.

One of the most comforting feelings when starting teaching is when children have the confidence to respond to questions and exchange views with each other. Children are used to asking questions. It is their way of finding out about the world around them and communicating their findings to peers. In the classroom children's questions can embarrassingly reveal gaping holes in the teacher's understanding. 'Why doesn't the Earth stop moving?', 'What causes electricity?', are just two examples of questions I have been asked by inquiring 9- and 10-year-olds. The explanations are far from simple, but the pupils' curiosity is laudable. Asking questions is a measure of self-direction and personal involvement. Many educators (for example,

Rogers, 1969) identify such personal involvement as being the essential conditions for children to learn.

Most (if not all) teachers use 'question-and-answer sessions' as a major teaching strategy. White (1988) differentiates between the majority of questions asked outside school (which are to obtain information) and teachers' questions. Teachers' questions serve purposes of control: control of behaviour, control of learning and control of the pace of the lesson. Kyriacou (1989) highlights higher-order questions which involve reasoning, and lower-order questions which involve recall. An example of a lower-order question would be, 'Where did we find the birds nest?', 'What shape is it?' These types of questions fail to set up scientific explorations. Higher-order questions, 'What holds the nest together?', 'Why do birds build nests?', 'Do all birds make nests?' are questions which require investigating which involves research and reasoning. Different questions require different investigations – an important point for children to realize. The question, 'What holds the nest together' would require pupils making careful observation, whereas, a reference study would be more appropriate for discovering birds which do *not* build nests.

The National Curriculum for science (1991) is clear. It expects teachers to develop in children the ability to 'ask questions such as "how . . .?", "why . . .?" and "what will happen if?"; encourage pupils to question what they have done and suggest improvements'. All teachers would agree that pupils need a sense of enquiry. The central component of enquiry is asking questions and setting up testable hypotheses. The ability of children to ask questions is a fundamental skill in a science curriculum.

Children's questions are central to scientific enquiry and conceptual change and need to feature greatly in the primary classroom. Scientific investigations stem from higher-order questions and children need experiences of questions that require scientific reasoning and investigation. They need to be able to identify different questions in order to plan scientific explorations. Although children's questions form the foundation of conceptual change, teachers provide few opportunities for children to ask them. White (1988) explains this in terms of the control role that teachers questions serve: 'Teachers find it hard to separate control of behaviour from control of the course of a lesson, and treat the rare questions from students as attempts to side-track the direction . . . which the teacher is determined it shall go.' Teachers need to listen to children's questions and provide opportunities for children to ask them. Too often they see themselves as controlling the flow of the lesson and might not think of the types of questions which *children* would ask. 'Why doesn't the Earth stop moving?', 'What causes electricity?' are not the sort of questions which teachers might consider with a group of 9- and 10-year olds.

Children need to be encouraged to phrase, answer, discuss and investigate different questions and the following three classroom activities were devised with this in mind.

Example 1

It was the bicentenary of the birth of Michael Faraday and my school was planning a project on the life and science of Michael Faraday. This was a cross-curriculum activity. The starting point was a question: 'If Michael Faraday was alive today what questions would you want to ask him?' Groups of children were given time to construct five questions which formed the basis of their topic work. Each group was encouraged to share their questions with the rest of the class. My colleague teaching the class asked them to explain how they could find out the answers to these questions themselves. This helped emphasize that different questions required different kinds of solution. Our role was to act as facilitators to discuss the questions asked and then suggest follow-up activities giving encouragement and guidance where necessary.

Example 2
Rather than providing an explanation for a puzzling phenomenon or observation, it is revealing to ask groups of children to come up with questions themselves. Groups can be given the brief to think up five questions to discover the explanation. Each group asks a question in turn to attempt to solve the problem. This gives opportunities to discuss the virtues of different questions and pupils are forced to adapt their questions depending on what has already been asked. For example, children were presented with two electrical circuits containing a single battery, wires, a bulb and a switch. The paradoxical situation is that one of the circuits does not work! There were a host of reasons for this: in some cases it was not a complete circuit; the bulb was blown; the battery was flat; the battery was incorrectly connected.

The children were asked to explore the reasons for this through their questions. Not only does this kind of activity provide an opportunity for children to ask questions; it also reveals a lot about the children's preconceptions of simple electrical circuits, essential as a starting point in learning. White (1988) quotes Suchman who devised a technique very similar to this one. The teacher would demonstrate a puzzling paradoxical situation. The children have to form an explanation by asking questions to which the teacher can only respond by 'Yes' or 'No'.

Example 3
During a class discussion children are expected to ask a question immediately after they have answered one. This results in questions being passed around the classroom. For example, after the children have finished their projects on Michael Faraday, we asked one child a question. When the child had answered, she or he was expected to ask another question to another child in the class. This enabled the children to find out about the other topics and helped them to phrase questions for their peers to answer.

Children asking questions should be viewed as a fundamental process of scientific enquiry and a fundamental tenet of conceptual change. The ability to reflect is the ability to ask questions to oneself. Teachers need to provide more opportunities for children to discuss different types of question and how they can be answered. Most importantly, providing children with the opportunity to ask questions, provides them with the freedom to explore their own ideas.

CASE STUDY 13

Effective questioning for developing concepts

Virginia Whitby, Roehampton Institute

In a recent study (Whitby, 1991) I was keen to discover the questioning techniques teachers were actually using in the classroom. I worked with two teachers with *one year* classes, both of whom were regarded by the head as good primary practitioners. One of the teachers had a science degree and felt confident in teaching science to young children. I shall refer to her as Mrs Clark. The other felt her scientific knowledge and understanding was very limited. Although she lacked confidence, she regarded science as an essential part of the primary school curriculum. I shall refer to her as Ms Scarlet.

Both teachers worked in a large open-plan setting which was well resourced. They worked very closely together, planning collaboratively to ensure all the children had access to the same activities. They had recently been providing the children with experience of the concept of water. Therefore the activity chosen for investigation was: 'How can we make a plastic lemonade bottle sink and a stone float?'

Each teacher worked with a small group of six children. The questions asked by both teachers enabled the children to become engaged in first-hand investigation, during which the children were able to draw some conclusions about the behaviour of the bottle and stone in the water. However, the questioning technique used by the teachers varied greatly. Parts of the lesson were tape-recorded and when analysing the transcript I have been able to explore the difference between the two teachers.

Broadly speaking, Mrs Clark encouraged the children to spend time exploring both their own ideas and the materials with which they were going to work. It was some time before she set the actual task. When she did so she only referred to the first part of the problem: 'How can we make a plastic lemonade bottle sink?'

This gave the children the opportunity to focus on one aspect of the activity. She made the task very clear, and gave the children her definition of 'sink', the bottle was to end up on the bottom of the water tray. Ms Scarlet, on the other hand, was more limited in her range of questions and presented all of the problem at once. If we examine further how both teachers introduced the activity we can see these very clear differences.

Transcript of Mrs Clark

TEACHER: [to the group] I've got a special job for you. I want you to make the bottle sink to the bottom of the water tray. How can you do that?
JENNIFER: Take the top off the bottle.
TEACHER: What will happen then?
MARK: It might sink.
TEACHER: What do the rest of you think?
[Children call out a mixture of responses 'sink', 'float', 'stay on top'; children push the neck of the bottle into the water and a small amount of water goes in; the children put the top back on]
TEACHER: What is happening?
[No response as the bottle is partially submerged]
TEACHER: Is it floating or sinking? Look through the side of the water tray.
[Children again call out mixed responses 'floating' or 'sinking']
TEACHER: Has it gone right to the bottom of the water tray?
ANNYA: No.
TEACHER: What can you do?
DAVID: Put more water in.
[Children push the whole bottle under water with the top off to fill it up]
TEACHER: What is coming out?
JENNIFER: Bubbles!
TEACHER: Where have they come from?
MARK: The bottle.
[The children continued to fill the bottle until it was on the bottom of the water tray]

She then encouraged the children to predict what they thought would happen next throughout the activity. She helped the children to develop their ideas and their thinking through her questioning. For example, she encouraged their observations, when bubbles came out of the bottle, and asked: 'What is coming out of the bottle?' and 'Where have they come from?' She was also careful not to allow any one child to dominate and after one child had made a suggestion she asked: 'What do the rest of you think?'

The questions she used to help the children were well matched to their ability; therefore, the children felt their contributions were valued and they were confident in making suggestions. Mrs Clark appeared confident in her questioning and was able to respond well to the children. Her questioning helped the children to solve the problem.

Ms Scarlet, did not ask as many questions as Mrs Clark and the activity was introduced in a different way. The whole problem was set initially and she was not very encouraging of the children in examining the materials they would be working with prior to starting the activity.

Transcript of Ms Scarlet

TEACHER: (to the group) How can we make the stone float and the bottle sink?
[*The teacher was holding the stone in one hand and the bottle in the other*]
EVELYN: Put the stone on top of the bottle.
MATHEW: Fill the bottle with Plasticine.
TEACHER: What do the rest of you think?
[*At this point, though, she did not give the children time to respond before she asked:*]
TEACHER: Will the stone stay on top of the bottle?
NAOMI: It might fall off.
TEACHER: How could we make the stone stay on top of the bottle?
[*This led the children to believe the only way to make the bottle sink was to place the stone on top*]

Ms Scarlet did not encourage the children to explore their ideas but seemed to rush them into the activity. She did not define for the children what she meant by 'sink' and the young children became very confused as to exactly what was meant by the terms 'floating' and 'sinking', since the vocabulary was new to them.

Overall, the questions asked by Ms Scarlet were closed and generally unproductive. She did not allow time for the children to explore their own ideas. Her interactions with the children were limited and she appeared to lack confidence. For example, when one child suggested putting the stone on top of the bottle the teacher's response assumed the child knew the stone would sink. Did the other children know? Another child had suggested filling the bottle with Plasticine, yet this idea was completely ignored by the teacher. Why then was there such a difference between the two teachers, both of whom are regarded as competent and effective class teachers? Did Ms Scarlet simply lack confidence in her questioning technique, or does her lack of scientific knowledge encourage her to ask only closed questions?

In discussion with Ms Scarlet after the activity, she stated she rushed the activity because she did not want the children to ask *her* questions, for fear she may not have the 'right' answer. This has been a cause for concern for primary teachers for several years. It is interesting to consider the questions used by both teachers in the light of the categories used by Elstgeest (1991).

Mrs Clark began by using what Elstgeest refers to as attention-focusing questions. She drew the children's attention to the bottle and stone. She then used comparison questions. Next she set the problem-posing question. This led back to the attention-focusing questions, to ensure all the children were aware of the problem set. Only then were action questions used to enable the children to solve the problem. The children then predicted that if the plastic bottle was filled with water it would sink; this prediction was correct. However, the children had been involved in several processes in reaching their conclusion.

The approach of Ms Scarlet was very different. She began by using a problem-posing question, and set the whole problem at the start. She then used a mixture of attention-focusing questions and what Elstgeest refers to as teachers' 'how' and 'why' questions. She did not use any action questions of the 'what happens if . . .' type. She could have enriched the activity for the children by doing so. Instead of asking the children, 'Will the stone stay on top of the bottle?', she could have asked, 'What will happen if we put the stone on top of the bottle?' This would have given the children the opportunity to respond.

In summary, it is important for teachers to make an effort to change their questioning technique particularly in the light of the National Curriculum which has identified questioning as being of great importance. From this kind of evidence it would seem that questioning in primary school science has a profound effect on children's learning. As teachers, we all need to ask productive questions to help children formulate and develop their own ideas in science.

Argument and value

What can we say of the value of this way of working? There is no doubt that careful and effective questions can promote conceptual change, and that is the central purpose behind our writing here. To establish this set of values we end this chapter with three activities for classwork adapted from the work of B. Bell (1992). Some, like 'Twenty Questions', are well known, others more unusual.

Twenty questions

The object of the game is well known – to home in on an item that teacher or one of the class has thought of and written down. In this context, the item might best occur in a science lesson, or as part of a design session where the focus might, for example, be guessing the purpose of an unusual piece of apparatus or a mechanism. The class or the group then have twenty questions only in which to arrive at the name or purpose of the item. The teaching point is to encourage broad questions at the start but funnelling these down to specific questions as time goes by.

Interviews

These can be real or pretend. There are sometimes when real data can be collected and used to put into a database, for instance. The children can work in pairs or as small groups, deciding the questions beforehand and judging the best way to record their results. They will need to be schooled in ways of interviewing so that they know not to interrupt, to prompt for more information at points, and so on.

Fish bowl

This is where a question or issue is posed to a small group of pupils and the rest of the class observe and support the group's discussions as they take place. If the discussion group is three or four members strong, the rest of the class can be divided so that they are the support team for one of the participants. So, before the discussion begins, they can help to draft questions, help to think through the possible answers and act generally as the research team. They then follow the discussion in silence while it is played out.

Of course there are many other ways to prompt questions and pose problems and some are discussed, for example, by Watts (1991) and Bentley and Watts (1992). No doubt readers will have their favourite approaches – we hope they are used to good effect.

eight
Solving problems in science and technology

Introduction

Invention, design, and creativity always seem such risky activities – it seems difficult to imagine an inventor or designer actually sitting down and, say, creating ten new things before breakfast each day. Our purpose in this chapter is to explore some of the features of problem solving and we begin with a look at the inventive process.

Purpose

No doubt chance plays a part in every scientific and technological activity. It may be a small or large part, although each new invention that comes along must be subject to the full measure of deliberation, structure and polish as well. Let us take two examples for a moment, from an excellent compendium of scientific and technological discoveries (Roberts, 1989).

The first concerns a chemist working in a laboratory in USA and who was trying to produce an insulating material for electrical wire that would not deteriorate in high temperatures or in high humidity. During a conversation with a colleague he remembered a particular chemical composition from his PhD research days and went off to recreate some of the chemical reactions he remembered from this work. He went to the storeroom to get a chemical which he thought would produce the desired polyester. Fortunately, as things turned out, the necessary chemical was out of stock and he chose to use a related substance instead – one which was cheap and easily available. After a couple of tries he heated a particular combination and noticed that the resulting compound in his glass flask became thicker and thicker all the time – so viscous, in fact, that the mechanical stirrer eventually refused to turn and gave up on the job. Because he could not actually pour it out he left the mixture in the flask to cool. As this happened, the product shrank away from the insides of the flask and solidified. The chemist broke the glass flask away and was left with a blob stuck on the end of the mechanical stirrer. He said:

'This [blob] was pounded and thrown on the concrete floor without much effect. It was even used to drive in some nails in a pine block. Eventually pieces were sawn off...'

Developing the new plastic was not straightforward but eventually became commercially successful. Polycarbonates are transparent, very tough and useful over a wide temperature range and are now used for bullet-proof shields for VIP cars, bank windows, canopies for supersonic aircraft, scuba masks, police riot shields, headlight and tail light covers for cars, etc. The chemist added this to his story: 'It's been a lot of fun and a great source of personal satisfaction to see how far the glob on the end of the stirrer has gone and the lives which have been touched.'

The second example centres on an employee of 3M Company who make a wide range of products. He was a chorister whose Sunday choir book was marked in the usual way with slips of paper so that he could find the right page at the right time, when he wanted. Naturally, the paper slipped out at annoying times. During a dull moment in the church service he remembered a glue product discovered a few years earlier by a colleague – a glue which was not used because it was not strong enough to glue things permanently. The inspiration of the moment was that this glue might serve to keep the slips of paper in his choir book without them being stuck in permanently. The following Monday he set to work and soon realized the potential of note making of all sorts – though the glue needed quite a lot of developmental work to make it both sufficiently 'temporary but permanent'. And so 'Post-its' came on to the market and are now sold all over the world and an indispensable aid to all teachers!

These are not the only examples by any stretch – Velcro fasteners were designed by an inventor who constantly had to remove cockleburs from his clothes after walking out in the countryside. He noticed that the burs had hooks which had entangled in the fabric loops of his jacket and set about trying to recreate this effect with tiny nylon hooks and loops.

But what do such stories tell us about teaching and learning in science and technology in primary classrooms?

Inquisitiveness

The first point to make concerns inquisitiveness: some people are naturally inquisitive and seem to leap at the chance to play and experiment with things. This is easily apparent when children want to 'see how it works' or 'find out what it does'. It can be an irritating disposition, and many adults want to keep children 'out of mischief' and to stop them meddling with things. However, there is good evidence to support the idea that it is this kind of playing that allows problem-solvers to get a 'feel' for the problem, to help conceptualize what needs to be done. Being inventive in science and technology means having the opportunity to explore playfully. The stories highlight, too, the ways in which people draw upon that they already know in order to shape their understanding of a new phenomenon. In this way, problem-solving is a

way of developing children's 'prior experience', those expe\
call on to provide context and significance. This context hel\
of the problem and leads (hopefully) towards a solution. So,\
children are making something which needs to be supported\
then they need some appreciation of the strength of materia\
might be appropriate in the circumstances. Some of this appr_____ comes
from direct experience of using, say, a range of domestic materials, building
blocks or construction toys, while some comes from tests and trials in the
problem-solving situation. Prior experience also involves other kinds of knowledge, such as an understanding of situations (what is likely to happen in
certain circumstances) and relationships between materials (like card and
glue, or Blu Tack and plastic).

Transferring contexts

The Post-it and Velcro anecdotes also indicate the importance of being able
to switch from one context to another. In classroom terms, this simply means
that if children can see the solution to a problem in one situation then they
are more able to transfer this understanding to a slightly different problem
in another context. This is a vital feature of problem-solving – using knowledge in maths, for instance, in the context of a technology problem; using
construction skills from one project to another. There are several ways in
which transfer of learning can be eased and we discuss some of these further
into the chapter.

Investigative skills

Clearly, too, these kinds of stories highlight investigative skills in both science
and technology. These skills are pretty much the same in both areas, those
of conducting tests and trials, studies and explorations of how and why
things work. Children need to understand the parameters (and/or variables)
associated with problems, selecting the appropriate or manageable ones,
exploring how they relate to each other and to the central purpose involved,
and how they can be quantified and measured. They need also to appreciate
how the results of their tests can be best communicated to others: adults and
peers.

Motivation

The next key word is motivation. Most scientists and engineers are likely to
be motivated by their jobs and lifestyles in order to produce the products they
do. In the classroom there is no doubt that the activity of problem-solving
itself is highly motivating – a feature that has been noted time and again.
Children enjoy the relative freedom and autonomy of making their own
decisions, correcting their own mistakes and reaching their own solutions. As
Simon and Jones (1992) note, problem-solving develops broader capabilities

d, in doing so, encourages interest and motivation: children enjoy the sense of ownership and responsibility that comes with this way of working.

Self-directed learning

Finally, for our purposes here, these tales of invention illustrate the primacy of both self-reliance and good group work. Being both scientific and technological involves moving between acting as a self-directed individual and a good member of a team. Whether the person is a specialist or a more general organizer, manager, or 'people's person', there is need for a combination of individual flair and joint collective activity. This, too, needs to be developed in the classroom. Elsewhere (Bentley and Watts, 1992) we have detailed a range of ways in which we think group work can be achieved through problem-solving in primary classrooms. Suffice to say that many of the case studies in this book illustrate how this works in practice. One of us (M.W.) discusses some of this in Case Study 15 below.

Structure

Here we use Juniper's (1989) framework for structuring thoughts about problem-solving. We have adapted this framework and, for us, it consists of being:

- *decisional* – taking account of the issues to be separated and compared;
- *procedural* – establishing priorities in amongst all the organizational details to be considered;
- *solutional* – seeking some precision in solutions and choosing clear objectives to be achieved;
- *generative* – developing materials or outcomes which will carry over to other problem-solving sessions.

Let us take these one at a time.

Decisions about problem-solving

The kinds of decisions that need to be taken are:

- How open will the problems be – carefully structured and constrained or wide open to a range of solutions?
- Are all the children tackling the same problem or different ones? If they are tackling the same problem, can it be divided into related sub-problems or will all pupils undertake exactly the same task?
- If the problems are different, or are sub-problems of a main theme, will these all be at the same level of difficulty?
- Who chooses the problems – are they teacher-provided, or can the children choose and generate their own problems?
- If they are teacher-provided, how much can the children negotiate variations on the theme?

- How long do they have for the problem – is the timing appropriate?
- How can the materials and equipment be constrained – are they free to find specialist items from sources outside the classroom? From outside the school?
- What distinctive skills are likely to be needed? Can these be taught as a whole class? Will they derive naturally from the problem itself or will they need to be taught directly before or during the sessions?
- What level of intervention will the teacher use? Will s(he) throw questions back to the children, point to resource material or feed in information in small packages?
- What kind of outcomes are expected? Will the children report their outcomes verbally, through prose, through role-play and drama, in verse or song?
- How will the groups be chosen? Will there be roles to play in the group?
- What forms of assessment are appropriate?

Of course there are many other decisional choices to be made (what ways do the problems cater for progression, for example) and our list is not meant to be exhaustive. However, it can help to give some indication of the kinds of decision that need to be made. There are no hard and fast rules on what to do, of course, and there are many examples in the case studies here of what paths our teachers have trodden. Along with many other authors we have explored some of the approaches to problem-solving, sources where there may be concrete advice to be had (see, for instance, Fisher, 1987; Watts, 1991; Bentley and Watts, 1992; Jones *et al.*, 1992).

Procedures and priorities

Within both science and technology, the National Curriculum has been instrumental in shaping priorities. So, for instance, any form of classroom work must entail the provision of learning opportunities which:

- set clear aims and objectives for the activities and their outcomes;
- ensure progression in both knowledge and understanding;
- enhance skill learning, the core skills of the National Curriculum, in terms of manipulative, numeric, communicative, social, economic and process skills;
- differentiate tasks and outcomes for different purposes;
- meet the requirements of cross-curricular themes and dimensions;
- enables the provision of equal opportunities in the school.

Problem-solving, too, must satisfy teachers that these sorts of opportunities are forthcoming. Again there are no straightforward ways of shaping priorities here – these will be influenced by the class, the teacher, school, development plan, and so on. It might help, though, to go through an example.

The point arrives when a Key Stage 2 teacher wants to work within the National Curriculum Science Programme of Study for Attainment Target 4, in particular that pupils should be introduced to:

'the idea that energy sources may be renewable or non-renewable and consider the implications of limited global energy resources. They should be introduced to the idea of energy transfer' (DES, 1991).

The Attainment Target for this part of the programme requires that pupils should:

'understand that energy is transferred in any process and recognise transfers in a range of devices;
understand the difference between renewable and non-renewable energy resources and the need for fuel economy.'

There is no doubt that this kind of work can lead to the design and making of some 'energy conscious' devices which would involve some environmental dimension and raise issues of social responsibility and economic awareness. A good example of this in practice is the work of Gollitt (1993) who describes an energy project which made use of the hot water from the school dishwasher outflow to heat a seed propagator made by the children. The hot water from the machine could not be used directly since it was under quite high pressure and was full of detergent and particles of food. Instead, this was all re-directed into a large dustbin before being sent back into the drain, and a heat exchanger put into the bin to service the seed propagator. This heat exchanger was really an old radiator which heated its own supply of clean water and which then circulated in copper piping under the seed beds. It all proved very successful and enabled seedlings to be grown even during a cold winter. There were clear energy lessons for the children, about heating as a mechanism for energy transfer, issues about care for the environment, the cost of the wasteful discharge of hot water (money 'down the drain') and the enhancement of skills for designing and making the system.

There are, though, many other ways in which this kind of work could be realized – the energy transfer does not have to be through hot water – it could be a solar-heating device which will heat water on a sunny day, a windmill to light a small bulb in windy weather, or a model waterwheel in a local stream. All have the same capacity to meet the kinds of priorities implied through the National Curriculum science and technology. Jane Eaton's case study below is a good example of how problem-solving is built into everyday classroom life. It is only one part of the work she is doing with the class and she manages to incorporate several other objectives within the work as it progresses. So, for instance, she realizes some of the attainment targets for information technology; she develops a list of 'safe working' and this is kept on the computer; she has children drafting and re-drafting prose through the keyboard, and they are constantly learning new skills as they work.

Reaching solutions

There is no doubt that planning and preparing for problem-solving means driving through a sometimes messy approach to arrive at some outcomes for

Type of material	Magnetic	Non-magnetic	Current	Number of coils	Number of pins
String			3	5	6
Paper			3	10	12
Pencil			3	15	16
Paper clip			3	20	28
Book			1	10	4
Wood shavings			2	10	6
Ruler			3	10	14
Drinks can			4	10	22
Keys					
. . .					
. . .					
. . .					

Figure 8.1 Magnetic table.

both individuals, small groups and the whole class. In this context youngsters need to know what the requirements are for the project – the time, the possible resources, the menu of possible strategies to be used, the broad range of acceptable outcomes, the nature and level of negotiation possible for the task, the form of the recording and communication of results, the mode of assessment and the overall pattern of work. These are all decisions teachers need to make before they begin so that, conceptually, the members of the class reach their goals while, managerially, the teacher reaches hers. Another example might help.

The topic is about magnetism. Here, the National Curriculum science says that pupils should:

'know that magnets attract some materials and not others and can repel each other.'

If we look at the first part, we can make a device for transferring energy from electricity to magnetism (an electromagnet) and use this to sort different materials according to their magnetic properties. In science this could take the shape of an investigation into the factors which affect the strength of an electromagnet and how well this can be used to sort materials. The technological perspective could be the design of a database to tabulate and represent these factors graphically, which itself then allows assessment to take place on the outcomes of the pupil's work. Both these aspects are well within the reach of children at Levels 2, 3 and 4 of the National Curriculum.

A computer-based chart for an investigation might look like the one in Figure 8.1. The materials can be common classroom ones; the number of turns of wire, the current and the number of pins it can then pick up can be tabulated.

Generating materials

There is no doubt that as teachers we need to generate and collect good materials that we know will work. Some of this is simply a collection of ideas, hints and suggestions and the storage and production of these through word processing is now becoming commonplace. It is a trend to be encouraged, since it allows the use of attractive materials and support resources very easily, and a bank of – say – problem-solving ideas can be built up in short time. For the non-computer literate, there are many good books with lots of ideas around and there is no substitute for the school or the individual teacher having a good stock of contemporary reading on the shelf. Useful examples are Browne (1991) and Makiya and Rogers (1992).

Equipment and resources

Many of the physical materials for problem-solving revolve around household packaging and waste. This approach has been disparaged as 'yoghurt-pot technology' or 'Blue Peter' work. Such materials, though, are cheap or free, easily available, versatile, safe to work with, quickly bonded, recyclable and familiar. They should not be a substitute for 'high tech' materials like commercial construction kits, computer-driven models, electrical circuit components and the like, but they are a highly useful format for introducing children to simple construction modes with the minimum of expenditure and teacher demand. The models in Jane Eaton's work below were built this way, though the electrical circuits were developed from kits and components. In Mike Watts' study, the children worked both with common household materials, off-cuts of carpet, copious amounts of polystyrene packaging, as well as a signal generator, oscilloscope, noise meter, and so on. We have discussed the planning, financing, management and storage of materials in Chapters 2 and 3.

CASE STUDY 14

The lighthouse keeper's lunch: pictures and stories on the computer

Jane Eaton, Rokesly Infants School

The story is about trying to get lunch each day to the lighthouse keeper at the top of the lighthouse. The main problems are how to get the lunch basket to go uphill to the lighthouse and then how to prevent the seagulls eating it all on the way up. The tale is very popular with my Year 2 class of 6 and 7-year-olds and we have used it to set the scene for some model-making and problem-solving. So, for instance, we made a large model of the lighthouse and we needed to design a 'carry

Figure 8.2 Lighthouse keeper's lunch.

mechanism' for the basket. I then further complicated this by asking the children to solve the problem of how one might free the basket if it got stuck on the way up: the mid-point of the basket's travel is supposedly high up, out of reach and directly over rocks and rough seas. For the model we also designed a circuit for the lighthouse lamp and met some good technological problems along the way in trying to make and support a battery holder within the size and shape of the model (Figure 8.2).

Apart from the obvious creative designing and making work in a model like this, the children used the Apple Macintosh in the class to recreate the story in their own words. The children normally work in mixed-ability pairs – deliberately chosen so that a 'computer-confident' child will work with one who is less skilled. Where possible, I mix gender, too, so that boys work with girls in pairs. Each pair takes it in turn to work on the computer so that the first pair start the introduction to a story, the second pair read what is written and carry it on, the third take it further, and so on. They work in quite tight time slots so that they all get to use the machine within a reasonable period of time. This process works for 'free flow' story writing, too, and three examples here are 'The Princess' Chocolate Cake Food Fight', 'The Dragon and the Witch and the Cat' and 'The Three Frogs' (Figures 8.3 to 8.5).

In fact, time on the keyboard is one part of a set of 'good computer manners' we have been developing so that children learn that, for example, they:

The princesses chocolate cake food
fight.
A history ago princesses lived
there was a couple. Carol the princess
threw a chocolate cake at David the
prince the cake knocked him out flat
and he had to put ice bag on his head
the ice bag had 100 tons weight in it
and he turned into a square flat man
OOOOOOOOOO! that hurt. Then he
went
up to prince heaven. The prince had a
harp bing bong! The End.

Figure 8.3 Examples of children's work.

The dragon and the witch and the cat.
Once upon a time there was a dragon
he comes out at night . One
night a witch came out with her cat
and the dragon saw the witch broom
and the witch saw the dragon tail.

Figure 8.4 Examples of children's work.

The three frogs was having a
party. They had a good time with some
good friends and a theif came then the
frogs saw the theif then the thief ran
home happly.

Figure 8.5 Examples of children's work.

- must never switch the machine off at the wall;
- always save their work (especially at playtime and lunch);
- must not interfere with others as they are working, in case they make a mistake or lose their work;
- never delete anything without checking carefully first;
- always be patient and be willing to take turns;
- must remember their time limits as they work.

We build this list as we go along and – on the whole – it works well in regulating the way the children work. One of the real virtues of word-processing stories like

Krishen

Figure 8.6 Examples of children's work.

this is that it can very much appeal to children who do not like the mechanics of writing – they can correct and re-draft without the chore of re-writing. There is a wide spread of abilities in the class and I like the way that, while some work much more intensely than others, everyone can contribute to story telling of this kind in their own way.

But story telling is just one part of the information technology work we do. The bulk of the class are working towards National Curriculum Level 2, and some of the most enjoyable work has been using the drawing facilities on the machine to 'make and retrieve pictures'. Some, like Krishen and Glenroy made pictures of hedgehogs (Figures 8.6 and 8.7) while Yanti, Kate and Felicity undertook pictures of the front of (and an airship ride over) Alexandra Palace, a landmark local to the school (Figures 8.8 to 8.10). Tessa did Famous Teddy Bear Nelson and Sam's picture shows people ice skating (Figures 8.11 and 8.12). Here again the machine can come into its own and the programme KIDSPIX allows them to take a symbol or an initial and move this around like a rubber stamp to create a picture (Figure 8.13).

There are some in the class who are at Level 3. Amongst other things, this means providing opportunities for work which involves 'locating information stored in database, retrieve information and add to it, checking the accuracy of entries'.

Here I have been using a program called MY DATA and have been able to log various physical attributes, such as eye colour (Figure 8.14).

On the whole, my main problem has been trying to keep up with being able to use the machine myself, let alone teaching the children what to do. My sources of support tend to be colleagues in other classes, though I am also lucky to be able to make use of an experienced 'computer-expert' teacher in our adjacent junior school. Actually, one good source of help and guidance proved to be a local computer dealer who was both very friendly and obliging. Unfortunately, that came to an end when I also inherited a virus from the shop that took an unhealthy amount of time and 'disinfecting' to get rid of.

Glenroy

Figure 8.7 Examples of children's work.

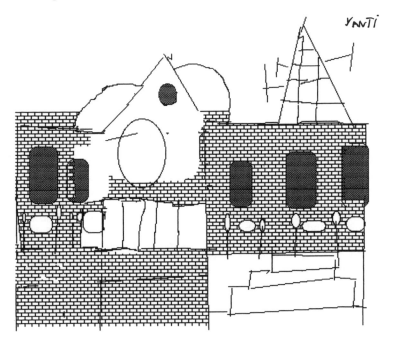

This is The Front of Alexander Poloce.

Figure 8.8 Examples of children's work.

This airship's only flight was in 1905. It was built at

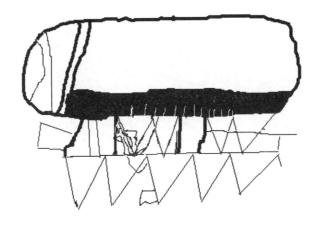

Kate

Alexandra Palace

Figure 8.9 Examples of children's work.

tLis is a picture of the front of the palace.

feliciity

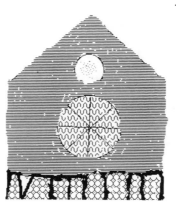

Figure 8.10 Examples of children's work.

This is the Famous Teddy Bear Nelson   Tessa

Figure 8.11 Examples of children's work.

Sam

ice Skating

Figure 8.12 Examples of children's work.

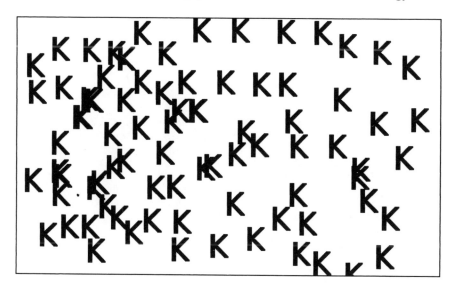

Figure 8.13 Examples of children's work.

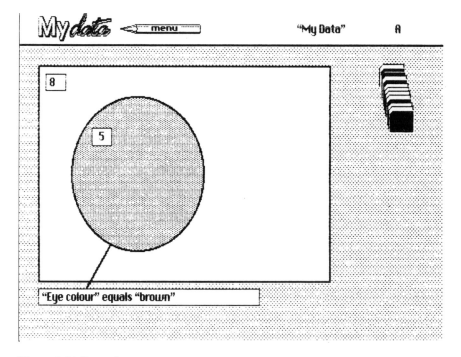

Figure 8.14 Eye colour.

CASE STUDY 15

Sound constructions

Mike Watts, Roehampton Institute

The context and some of the planning for this work are discussed in Case Study 1 in Chapter 1. Here I describe the way the work developed and the kinds of outcomes reached by the pupils. During the seven sessions available we constructed our version of a Vygotskian 'zone' with a class of 11-year-olds. In this time we (the class teacher and I) moved between whole-class teaching and small-group science teams. The first session was given over to exploring the children's ideas of what sound is and how it works, and the results were fairly predictably in line with research findings, so that few children

- understood that sound is the vibration of materials;
- appreciated that sound travels as a wave through materials;
- knew that air is needed for sound to reach the ear;
- understood the difference between listening and hearing.

This 'diagnostic' session used a 'fun session' of pre-recorded sounds which the children had to identify, along with a range of questions to be answered about various phenomena in sound. This gave us the opportunity to establish our starting position – the 'where they're at' point. And this then allowed us to sort out how we wanted to approach the next six lessons. The class of thirty were divided into their regular five science teams of six members each. For this work we tried a new tack and gave each person a role, which were:

- team leader (arbiter of disputes, maintainer of group purposes);
- manager (site-manager, quantity surveyor, safety officer);
- go-getter 1 (fetch and carrier);
- go-getter 2 (fetch and carrier);
- writer (scribe, recorder of results);
- reporter (end-of-session class reporter).

These roles changed each week so that each pupil had an opportunity to lead, report, organize, etc. Sessions were all led from the front but then moved quickly to group and team work. Some demonstrations were teacher-led – for example, the actions of long spring 'slinkies' to illustrate wave motion, a signal generator and oscilloscope to show 'pictures' of sounds as they are made; models of the ear; role-playing the movement of air molecules, and a class game to demonstrate the acuity of hearing.

The general problem of noise in the school hall gave the overall context for the sub-problems we then devised. Different teams worked on different aspects so that, for example, when we looked at vibration through various materials, it was possible to ensure that the groups all had different combinations of materials with which to work. In other cases the problems were quite different but had to be at roughly the same level. This became difficult to sustain when – in transferring the responsibility to the pupils – some teams re-interpreted the problems and changed their shape. For example, a problem for one team was to explore how sounds can help or hinder concentration and conversation. The team were given tape recorders with ear-phones, various tapes of noise or music, and they then needed to test out on each

Figure 8.15 Spinfield pupils' problem-solving.

other how much the sounds became a distracter and hindered mental processes. The problem was all about the difference between sounds (say, like music) and noise (a nuisance) and the type of noise that made concentration difficult, as part of the overall problem concerned with the effects of noise in the general environment. They were then free to devise what variables to explore and to set their own parameters. In the end they changed some of the problems so that they focused mainly on memory tasks and general knowledge questions and simply varied the volume.

The sub-problems consisted of:

- modelling the school hall both roughly and with scale models;
- exploring sound insulation through designing industrial earmuffs;
- the design and efficacy of 'string telephones';
- studying the effects of sound on concentration and memory;
- marking and measuring a 'noise trail' through the school using a calibrated noise meter;
- constructing novel percussion and string instruments.

I need some evaluative comment here to finish. First, the role-play in the teams was not always a success. They were very used to working in teams but the added layer of having roles was new. So, normally extrovert and outgoing individuals found difficulties in preventing the 'playground dispositions' of older, larger, noisier characters taking over the teams. Even quieter and more thoughtful individuals found even greater difficulties in realizing their managerial roles. That said, some unusual 'conversions' took place so that seemingly timid personalities seemed to blossom given the task of leading the team during their turn. Second, one or two pupils took some advantage of the greater freedom to be unproductive, but this was unusual within the normal brisk and ebullient swarm of classroom activity. Third, we varied the nature of the feedback at the end of each session and gave teams the freedom to report in whatever form took their fancy. They entered into this with great spirit and, since the role of reporter changed each week, each pupil knew that their turn would come and they needed to choose how they would present their activities to the whole class. They took pains to vary the style and approach to their reports (Figure 8.15).

The final accolade came when – some time after the work was finished – the class were asked to describe in an assembly for the whole school some of the work they had been doing. They chose their work on sound and mounted a montage of presentations that included a group mime of the way the ear works. Altogether the work was greeted with generous applause.

Value arguments

Problem-solving is quintessential constructivism. The task is open, learning starts with the learner's own experiences, the learner is responsible for how he or she works, it is rooted in relevant activities and contexts, it is motivating and encouraging of language development and conceptual shift, it is skill based and the teacher is facilitator all through the activity. The zone of development can be very clear with the stated objectives and the support mechanisms in place. The story from Jane Eaton and Mike Watts is that this can work at either end of the primary age range, can be very productive and fun.

nine

Working for equal opportunities

Introduction

In a recent survey (Nott *et al.*, 1992), teachers seemed to be put off by some discussions concerning equal opportunities. For example, those professional training days that dwelt on these sorts of issues were, on the whole, seen to be 'irrelevant', 'theoretical' and 'idealistic'. One can only imagine that – for some teachers – such topics have been 'done to death' while, perhaps for others, they have been tackled in a way that is removed from the general swim of school activity. It is hugely important that concerns like these do not become side-lined for the need of direct classroom exemplars and model ways of working, and part of our purpose here is to keep equal opportunities clearly on the agenda for school science and technology.

Purpose

Ours is a very positive view of equality of opportunity and our cases are drawn from work current in the field. We draw on classroom-based enquiry and research without, we hope, driving too far into the theoretical and idealistic to lose sight of pragmatism.

In our view, teachers in all phases of the professional arena work within a series of moral and ethical dilemmas. So, for example, we teach groups and whole classes but must assess individuals; we want children to control their own learning but need to closely direct them through our teaching, we are concerned with the 'whole child' but must deal largely with only that part accessible through the classroom. Similarly, we want to treat each child as equal but know that many suffer social deprivation and need extra help and attention. This is the 'equal opportunities' tightrope we all walk: how to *be* equal, be *seen* to be equal, while at the same time discriminating positively for those in greatest need? And, in some cases, be *seen* to be positively discriminating for those pupils. It all hinges on our interpretations of justice and being 'fair': being fair in meeting some children's needs is sometimes at the expense of not being fair to others. If this seems to be an impossible task (and therefore one to be shelved) it is no more difficult than the many other tensions teachers deal with every working hour, and so can be – and must be – drawn into the general ambit of professional life. Nor are there any clear-cut answers and so this continues, and always will continue, to be a persistent dilemma in professional life.

A common response in schools is that 'I do not discriminate – for me every child is the same' or 'I treat every child on their merits – they all have the same opportunities'. It is extremely difficult for many teachers to view themselves as 'social engineers' and would sometimes reject the notion that they are instrumental in shaping societal values at all. The home influence, peer pressure, television, the educational system are commonly seen to be much more influential than the lone teacher with a class of thirty children. However, we must also recognize the power and potency of a close adult, structured classroom activities and of valued role models in helping to shape children's perceptions. They can serve to either perpetuate or challenge particular perspectives, stereotypic thoughts and actions. What 'Miss' says and does is clearly influential on young children.

So what does contemporary research tell us? Any review of research is bound to be selective and our one is no different: we want to use research findings to foster our own perspective, that – generally speaking – life in classrooms is *not* equal for some and we need to redress this through clear, purposive and deliberate actions. In broad terms ours is a complex picture, and there are no simple lines to take. Where to start? First, with gender differences. We know that such differences manifest themselves at a very early age and that, as we have already noted, they are bound up with aspects of socialization, parental attitude and teacher expectation. For example, Davies and Brember (1991) have investigated the effects of gender on children's adjustment to nursery classes. They found that, while there is a difference in adjustment between children who attend nursery school in the morning compared to those who attend in the afternoon (afternoon attenders being less well adjusted) girls are always better adjusted than boys whenever they attend. They point out that teacher attitude may well have an effect here. Children are judged to be less well adjusted if they are aggressive and their behaviours take up much of the teacher's time. Teachers judged boys to be in this category. They described them as more anxious, aggressive and with more learning difficulties.

If we continue this thread by taking the nature of bullying as a further indicator, then boys tend to bully both other boys and girls in their vicinity. Generally speaking, girls will report bullying more than will boys and, while some girls will bully both other girls and some boys, it is far more common that it is the boys who do the bullying. Figures for this can come from a number of sources – from the kind of 'Childline' statistics where young girls' reports of physical abuse outnumber boys' by four to one, alongside short case studies as reported in Smith (1992). The message here is that, while schools differ greatly in their tackling and tolerance of aggressive and hurtful

behaviour of young boys to girls, teachers are in the front line o
actions and values within the school environment. They must lea.
entiate better between taking reports of incidents and dismissing 't
between recognizing signs of distress and overlooking certain ;   .. the
robust atmosphere of the classroom.

We noted some issues of language in Chapters 4 and 5. Here we can note
that gender differences in children's talk has also featured in research. French
and French (1984), for example, looked at pupil interaction in public talk
with the teacher and found that on average, boys had nearly four times as
many turns at this than girls. Hammersley (1990) has been critical both of
this finding and the explanations given by the researchers for their results.
Although there is some substance in what he says, nevertheless, other studies
have supported the work of French and French. In primary and secondary
classrooms, girls come up against teachers' attitudes, boys' attitudes, their
own socialization and parental expectations, all of which influence teacher
time and modes of play, and this can mitigate against the kind of fair treatment discussed earlier. Not because any teacher deliberately wishes this to be
so, arranges it so, or simply lets it happen, but because it is an insidious
aspect often forgotten in the complex matrix of classroom life.

Gender, science and technology

Moving particularly to issues of gender in science and technology we can take
the point that teachers commonly rate girls to be 'more academic' than boys
but still value the creativity and spontaneity of boys' rough-and-ready work.
They say they prefer the acquiescence, conformity and greater social skills of
girls in the classroom but consistently concede to boys' greater insistence on
teacher attention as they exploit their 'nuisance value'. So, Crossman (1987)
found that in general, science teachers interact more with boys than girls.
Even female teachers were more biased towards boys than girls in classroom
interactions – more biased even than their male colleagues. In fact, there is
some research to suggest that, given a preference, both male and female
teachers would *prefer* to teach science to boys (Goddard-Spear, 1989).

While on the one hand teachers feel the National Curriculum will be
important in changing gender stereotyping in science and technology, they
also recognize that the volume of administration, lack of support, poor
resourcing through cash and staff, means that any attempt to redress im-
balances in the classroom must take a back seat while 'implementation' and
'accountability' rule the fore. Smithers and Zientek (1991), for example,
report research in this vein.

Referring again to Davies and Brember (1991), they point out that these
judgements may well influence (and be influenced by) the type of play which
the different genders choose. Girls tended to choose

> the quieter activities of painting, bead threading or table top games,
> which are done with or near the teacher or the domestic role-play of the

home corner. Boys, on the other hand tend to choose play with construction toys, vigorous physical activities and rough and tumble play.

The very clear point to be made here is that boys and girls react very differently to construction activities in the classroom. As Beat (1991) says:

Boys tended to make models that move and were part of an imaginative scene they had created. They made such things as cars, fire engines and space ships which they talked about in great detail as they were making them and they almost always played with them when they were complete and would go to the teacher for praise and approval. Girls tended to make non-moving models such as houses or gardens and when making them were usually talking about something quite different. When models were finished they were left – sometimes not even in a place where they would be safe.

Davies and Brember's work suggests that teachers should encourage children to play in ways they would not normally choose at this early age (rather than giving totally free choice) and that this might go some way towards counteracting any imbalance. This is not always a clear-cut way forward, however, as Browne (1991) points out: 'Girls were very adept at sabotaging teachers efforts to ensure that they engage in activity they would not normally choose.' Their strategies included moving to another area of the classroom where the teacher could not see them, or sitting near the activity, keeping a low profile and then moving away. The most successful strategy was for a girl to produce a model which involved little effort and was simple and then to show it to the teacher to receive praise. Browne comments that 'this would suggest that at a very young age the girls concerned had worked out that not much was expected of them in the field of constructional activity and that minimal effort resulted in praise.'

Smail (1993) points out that girls' inexperience with construction toys in their childhood may well act as a disadvantage in later school life. This is particularly so for children within whose cultural background toys and play are not as firmly rooted as they are in Western culture. When it comes to dealing with materials as in science and technology activities, these children may be seen to have some 'catching up' to do.

This is one disadvantage which could be added to many others. Spear (1987) found, for example, that science teachers marked boys' work higher for richness of ideas, scientific accuracy, organization of ideas and conciseness. The only characteristic for which girls received higher marks was that of neatness. Our point is that by the time children arrive in school, girls are already behaving in ways that reinforce the teacher's attitudes about what constitutes work, what constitutes expectations, conformity, effort, praise, aggression and that they expect to counterbalance their actions with those of boys. It confirms the notion that boys take up more of the teacher's time and – where possible – girls work quietly close by.

Before we leave this section we need to note data about the relative achievement in science. We can more easily explore gender issues here because results from SAT testing is available in this form and not by ethnic group. SAT testing at Key Stage 1 (5–7-year-olds) is particularly interesting because it is a national test which examines the performance of all children at one point in time regardless of relative age or gender. So, though there is ample work to suggest that – at this age – girls' cognitive development outstrips that of boys' it is also clear that, since children are born throughout the year and yet are tested all at one time, there will be clear advantage to those who are older and disadvantage to the youngest. This is the complex kind of formula that needs to be teased out from the early results. Copeland (1992), for instance, concludes that at Level 2, the 'average' level for this age range, the girls outperform boys and that time at school makes no difference. However, at the higher attainment level (Level 3) then boys outperform girls and here length of schooling shows. He notes that, in science and mathematics, three-quarters of all the girls attained Level 2 but only a little over half the boys. The bulk of these boys and girls, paradoxically, is drawn from the younger age groups. Hence, experience of school does not appear to be an important factor (Figure 9.1). At Level 3, twice the proportion of boys gained this level compared with girls: one-third contrasted to one-sixth. Three-quarters of these boys came from the older groups with the longest experience in school so, at this level, age and experience for both girls and boys in school seem important factors.

Anti-racism and multi-culturalism

Let us talk briefly now about culture and racism. Neither science nor technology are removed from the culture in which they exist – in fact, they are both created by it and inseparable from it. This is a difficult idea perhaps because we are often given the impression that both science and technology can be objective, neutral and value-free. However, this is clearly not the case – both are fully embedded within culture and reflect its values and norms.

It is hard to take a look at science and technology in our own culture when we are so close to it; it is difficult to see what values and value assumptions are being made and what is taken for granted. Layton (1992) has pointed out that education in technology is about making these values and assumptions 'visible': 'In order to "see" the values embedded in artefacts, systems and environments we need to view here, as it were, through special spectacles.'

He goes on to suggest that unless we are aware of these sometimes hidden values, we may not understand the clashes and conflict that may arise when an artefact or system is out of keeping with the prevailing culture, for example when a 'high-tech' solution is introduced into a culture where this is wholly inappropriate. Budgett-Meakin (1992) uses this telling quote from an agriculturist from Ghana:

> When I first went to a supermarket in Europe they gave me two plastic carrier bags to carry home my groceries. I folded them carefully and put

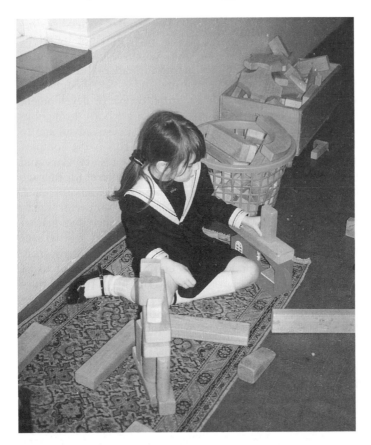

Figure 9.1 Constructing with blocks.

them under my bed to take the next time I went. But when I did they gave me two more. It was only then I realised I was supposed to throw them away. But I couldn't bear to ... by the time I came to go home at the end of the year I had a whole pile of bags under my bed to take with me.

This is the way you live ... a throwaway life. In the Third World we use something until it is destroyed. We use old cans to carry water; when they get a hole we patch it. You create waste. You make rubbish and pollute the environment. One day I went to a rubbish tip here in England; I saw all kinds of things which at home I could have fixed and used to furnish my house. Many of them were not even broken. They were just out of fashion.

This leads to the notion of appropriate technology. Webster (1992) describes this as a 'technology which recognises and accepts that human needs are complex'. Such a technology does not accept that just because something *can* be done that it necessarily *should* be done, or that any technology is necessarily transferable from one context to another: 'Appropriate technology is often specifically local, needs-orientated, resource-efficient and flexible.'

How might we explore this with young children? Clearly, one way to get children to see the effects of our own culture is to look at the science and technology of others. This is a sensitive process that must be done with openness but without denigration. We address some of the issues below and point the reader at other texts like Peacock (1991).

Structure

How can we talk about the structure of equal opportunities teaching in the classroom? We use here a series of five sub-headings to structure our ideas on awareness:

(i)   consciousness of systems;
(ii) consciousness of perspectives;
(iii) choice and responsibility;
(iv) actionable knowledge;
(v)   the medium and the message.

Consciousness of systems

It is our experience that most primary teachers are careful about how they work, and how they operate systems within their own classes and the school in general. For example, they understand about grouping children in their classrooms and have organized strategies for their groupings, such as age (mixed- or single-age groups) or by ability (in reading, or mathematics). It is very rare to find a primary classroom in which children can be clearly seen to be sitting in single gender or race groups. However, perhaps because primary teachers are so used to taking the gender of pupils into account and ensuring that mixed-gender groups are arranged so that children have 'equal' experiences, some of the research into gender issues in science and technology may have passed them by.

Indeed the problem lies deeper than just a lack of familiarity with the research. The busy nature of primary classrooms and the need for teachers to operate at a variety of levels of analysis at any one time means that the subtleties of gender bias in children's behaviour is not the first priority of classroom life upon which teachers concentrate. The opportunity to stand back and observe the dynamics of the small group, the behaviour between individuals in the group is a rare event in most primary classrooms. While many teachers can describe minute and carefully analysed information about every individual in their class, about each group and how it behaves as a group, there is a missing layer of within-group observations. Di Bentley explores some of these in her case study below.

Consciousness of perspectives

And how does the research into children's behaviour translate into the structure of work within science and technology classrooms? Commonly, girls and boys express differences in their areas of interest as early as eight (Smail, 1993). They are aware of gender differences in the roles adults play even earlier and this gender-role perception extends firmly into the area of scientific activity by the time they are five or six. Smithers and Zeintek (1991) investigated views of young children about gender perceptions of role. All the children firmly viewed scientific type activities as being something men did.

Choice and responsibility

There are some useful pointers to be set out here, though more come through the case studies a little later:

- Choose artefacts, plants and foods from other cultures for scientific investigations. There are a number of plants and vegetables, materials or musical instruments that can be used to familiarize children with different cultures.
- Encourage children to choose from home objects with which they are familiar, so that, for example, a science or technological activity might start through the use of toys or music from other parts of the world.
- Let festivals and celebrations be a starting point for scientific and technological activities.

Actionable knowledge

The central point here is the need to start science as soon as possible. Actionable knowledge implies that children can reach a level of scientific literacy or technological fluency to enable them to use their knowledge in the course of everyday life, in the solution of everyday problems. It is a kind of immersion in science and technology that leaves the learner comfortable with ideas and theories, designs and actions. It is appropriate science as well as being appropriate technology.

Part of this is the encouragement of children to talk about their scientific and technological ideas and activities. The more they are able to feel confident in their articulation of design and principles then the sooner they will feel they own and can use their knowledge. And while neither science nor technology can be the panacea for all global and human problems, there can be few solutions to these kinds of problems that have no scientific or technological input.

The medium and the message

Again, a few pointers might be:

- challenge racism and sexism at all points in school life;
- avoid material and work cards that are offensive or which will not be understood by the pupils you want to use them;
- allow children to use their mother tongue when discussing their design or scientific ideas;
- value non-verbal communication of scientific or technological solutions, as a vehicle for the expression of difficult ideas;
- inviting scientists and engineers from different cultures to talk to children;
- ensure good multi-cultural display in classrooms and throughout the school.

As before, these are simply indicators and food for thought. The case studies exemplify some of the ways in which these 'starters' might be turned into action.

Cases and models

Let us move now to some exemplars and models of work in this area. In the first study (Case Study 16) Di Bentley picks up some of the issues about teacher awareness of grouping; Liz Whitelegg describes a research project, and then Di Bentley returns to describe some interactions between girls and boys.

CASE STUDY 16

Teaching for equality

Di Bentley, Roehampton Institute

This case study looks at work with primary teachers, helping them to observe equality of opportunity in the work of children in their classes within science. I begin with some examples gathered while I was a local education adviser and the observations I made in primary classrooms of children as they worked together – most often in mixed-gender groups.

In one classroom of 7-year-olds the teacher arranged a science experience on corals and sponges in 'observation' and 'experiment' for pupils. The pupils were in mixed-gender groups and at the time, two of the groups in the class were working on the investigation whilst others were conducting other activities unconnected to science. The investigative work was largely open-ended and pupils had been asked to find the name of the sponge/coral by using a key to identify it. They were then encouraged to find out as much about their specific sponge and coral as they could. The teacher made suggestions as to what they might find out, and asked them to observe structure very carefully and record this by drawing. Since both corals and sponges live in water the children suggested that they might find out how they behaved in water. The teacher provided them with some key questions to help their investigations and reminded them of the apparatus such as scales, magnifying glasses, tanks of water, rulers, and stop clocks on which they might draw. She pointed out that they could use other things too, that were available in the room and encouraged them to ask for unusual items. At this point, none of the children suggested any further items of apparatus that they might want.

The boys in both groups immediately sought out the tanks of water, stop clocks and scales. They squeezed out the sponges, put them in water, timed how long it took for water to be absorbed, weighed the sponges and corals and, in general, conducted several investigations which were determined in large part by the available apparatus. The girls, on the other hand, observed the structure of the corals and sponges, drew them in detail and spent considerable time identifying them from the books available. A familiar pattern, you might say. Part of the issue for me was that the teacher was clearly busy with several activities going on at the same time. She was unaware of any differences in the response of the girls and boys within the groups. It was obvious too, that within the small groups – of four and five in each case – the children had divided themselves into smaller working units along gender lines.

When I offered to take over her role with the whole class and when she could then observe the small groups working on the science investigation, she immediately identified the differences in the work of the children. She was concerned that she had not identified this earlier in the session, this or any other, and yet, as she discussed it later, she said she realized that she knew the children had chosen to work in small gender-based units within the class. She had, however, attached no great significance to this.

Nor was she alone in this. In a second school I watched a teacher undertake technology with a class of 9-year-olds. Their class project had been to look at the playground as a play environment for young children (younger than themselves). They had been to other classes in the school and asked the reception and first class (Year 1) what they most liked to play with, what they played on or with in the playground and what other things they would like to have in their playground. Different groups had also gone to the same classes during part of the afternoon sessions when the children were engaged in play activities of their choice, and which included opportunities to play in the 'wet play' area immediately outside the class. They had observed the children for a short time and recorded what equipment was played with most and seemed to keep children happy longest. From this they had, as a class, drawn a plan of the playground with part designated a 'young children's' area. When I joined the lesson they were making the playground plan and constructing the equipment the young children wanted. Two groups were engaged in making a map some 3 m × 4 m for display in the front entrance of the school. The other four groups in the class were constructing apparatus, or in the case of one sub-group, drawing and describing the garden part of the playground which their research had shown was something the young children enjoyed very much – playing between the shrubs and having the opportunity to grow things. When I observed them, the two groups making the map had chosen to operate as one larger group and had decided on tasks between them. The boys had completed the measuring, using a measuring wheel and the girls were busy sticking together pieces of paper to make the correct size. The boys on the whole stood back from this part of the activity, giving advice about the sticking, handing out the Sellotape and cutting off strips, whilst the girls moved around on hands and knees getting the pieces stuck together. The construction groups too were similarly disposed. The garden drawing group was exclusively girls. The boys who were members of that group were making the shrubs for the garden. When I asked why they had chosen to do this part of the work they said it was because they had sets at home that contained these shrubs, and they knew how they should be made. The girls in the group said they liked painting and drawing. One said that she knew making the shrubs would mean using the glue gun because ordinary glue would not be good enough. She did not like using the glue gun – why, she did not say.

Only one group was working as a mixed gender group as the teacher had intended. They were making a 'house' because they had seen children enjoying themselves in the home corner and thought that a building children could adapt for their own games would be a good idea. They had chosen to make it out of balsa wood and in this case the girls had cut up the wood to a size decided by the boys who had drawn the template for them. All were engaged in trying to make it fit together and stand up. The discussion was fully engaging, both boys and girls made suggestions and both tried the ordinary glue, Sellotape and the glue gun as an adhesive. When I asked the teacher for her observations, she had noticed the integrated group but had not spotted all the variations in the others. No surprise in this. With the need to look at safety issues, resources availability, manage groups and having an observer present, she was more than busy! When we talked later, she too expressed frustration at not being able to address her time to finding out the details and dynamics of behaviour within working groups and not being sure, anyway, what to do about it if she knew the detail.

As a result of this and in response to requests from other teachers, we organized an equal opportunities evening for local schools. During the evening, we looked at some of the research findings mentioned earlier, for example NUT (1983) and Whyte (1983). We also examined specific parts of the science education literature (Brighton Group, 1980) and talked through the experiences of the teachers of their own science education.

As a result of this reading and discussion, several teachers agreed to set up some co-observations in science and technology. They felt that, given the hard work that needed to be done by most of them in organizing their own classrooms, an observer could offer a better view. The observers were to concentrate on three aspects of observation:

1. Girls' and boys' use of equipment.
2. Teachers' use of questions – directed and undirected and the type of question.
3. Use of any sexist behaviour by girls or boys – taking over equipment, specific roles developing when children were sharing a task, etc.

After some six weeks, the initial observations were complete and the group met to compare notes. The findings again were unsurprising. Everyone found that, in general, boys gravitated towards the equipment quicker than girls when a choice was available to them. Teachers tended to use a variety of questions, some open-ended, some directed, some undirected. In general, in science the undirected questions were answered by boys, as were the more difficult open-ended questions. Sexist behaviour was observed in some instances when boys and girls were working together and often tended to be of the 'passive girl'/'active boy' nature, so that boys would operate apparatus and girls would let them.

These findings, as the group admitted, mirrored fairly accurately the findings in the research which they had been reading. What surprised them most was that, since much of the research dated from the early 1980s, things had not changed much and that the National Curriculum for science for both boys and girls did not seem to be making much difference to the chances of girls in science. Exactly the same kind of problems being recorded in secondary schools were now manifesting themselves in primary science classrooms. The group decided that solutions, such as there were lay in their own hands. As a group they agreed to do things such as:

1. To bring their observations to the attention of other colleagues in their own schools.
2. To use directed questions, wherever possible, so that girls were given an even chance of answering and could be pushed out of a passive role.
3. To make a conscious effort to work at asking girls more open-ended questions.
4. To continue their good practice in having mixed-gender groupings, but to develop this further by organizing equipment rotas or sessions that ensured girls used the equipment fully, in the same way as many of the participants already did with the use of the computer.

Several of the teachers went further than this and began to look in more detail at the other aspects of classroom life, the stories read to the children, directing girls' reading towards science fiction and science books, setting up of a 'bring-and-show' session especially directed at a piece of mechanical equipment or toy so that girls and boys could explain how it worked. In general, the teachers valued the opportunities to be exposed, busy though they were, to research that they had not read, or only heard about vaguely. They appreciated the observations by colleagues and all declared that they now saw things happening in their own classrooms which they had never seen before – despite the fact that they agreed it must always have been there.

CASE STUDY 17

Group work in science investigations – do boys and girls do it differently?

Elizabeth Whitelegg, P. Murphy, E. Scanlon and B. Hodgson, The Open University

Group work has been a feature of primary classrooms since the time of the Plowden Report (DES, 1967) although the ORACLE survey (Galton, *et al.*, 1980) doubted the quality of some of this group work and felt that it was not as extensive as Plowden suggested it should be. Research by Howe (1990) suggests that mixed-ability groupings of children on science investigations promotes effective learning, but a random allocation of children to groups does not take account of the gender dimensions of the groups which may inhibit learning for some members. This project looks at the gender dimensions of group work in primary classrooms on science investigations.

Current research indicates links between gender differences in:

• children's cognitive response to science investigations, i.e. the variables they consider relevant and the solutions they judge appropriate (Murphy, 1991);
• children's affective response to science tasks, for example girls' learned helplessness (Licht and Dweck, 1983; Smail and Kelly, 1984);
• children's involvement in problem solving in groups leading to achievement (Kempa and Aminah, 1991);
• teachers' response to mixed groups according to the teacher's own awareness of gender issues (Renee and Parker, 1987).

The study
We set out to investigate two types of collaboration. Firstly, collaboration amongst pupils engaged in some 'formal' set tasks using established methodology designed by the Assessment of Performance Unit (APU) in science and secondly, pupils undertaking 'authentic' tasks that arose from pupils' present learning.
   We were concerned to explore within our work:

• the selection of science tasks to investigate;
• ways of grouping pupils;
• aspects of collaboration worth pursuing;
• presentation and administration of tasks to enhance collaboration;
• resourcing of tasks;
• data-collection methods;
• data analysis.

The 'formal' task
This task was based on an established APU investigation. The APU research showed that children performed at a higher level when in a practical situation because of the direct feedback they received about the consequences of their actions and the decision making (Russell *et al.*, 1988). When the pupils were allowed to work together in pairs in a practical situation and to discuss their ideas and ways of working, their performance improved (Whyte, 1988).
   The task required the children to test different sorts of papers to find out which one would be the best for covering a book. The children were given samples of four different types of paper – brown paper, wallpaper, writing paper and sugar paper. They were also supplied with items to test the papers' durability. These were sandpaper, a stone, erasers, scissors, water and a water dropper. This task was set out in a standard way by the teacher/researcher and the children were then left to discuss and carry out the investigation.

The 'authentic' task
This task developed from classwork that the children were currently doing. The class topic was set around one of their reading books and the science focus of the topic was sound. The first stage of the study was to elicit the children's ideas about sound and then to discuss these ideas with them. The teacher/researcher (herself a very experienced primary teacher and science specialist) then spent three mornings, at weekly intervals, working with the group of four pupils. Her brief was to guide the pupils in their investigation, but to let the pupils decide which aspects of sound were to be investigated. The children investigated various ways of preventing sound travelling and also collecting sound by making ear trumpets.
   The data for the study were collected by video and audio recordings of all the groups as they worked. The tapes were transcribed for detailed analysis. The pupils' written report of their investigations is also available and the teacher/researcher compiled a report of her observations. The video recordings provided the most detailed data for our analysis.

Carrying out the investigation
The two tasks took place in different schools. In Fairlawn School, where the 'formal' task took place, the children normally do science as a whole class, working in groups on the same aspect of a topic, but at different levels. The children are used to investigating to find answers to open-ended questions; however, teacher support in the form of a structured plan or discussion of the next steps in an experiment are usually provided. This was therefore the first time that the pupils were asked to

carry out an investigation without their usual level of support. Three groups were established in a Year 3 class. These were: Group 1 – a group of four boys; Group 2 – a group of four girls; and Group 3 – a group of two boys and two girls. The teacher selected the pupils in each group on the basis that most of them were already used to working together.

We found that there was a marked difference between the two single-sex groups and the outcome of the investigation on the formal task. Both groups appeared to collaborate and the boys' collaboration helped their progress significantly. The boys all offered individual contributions but different roles were clearly established and accepted by members of the group early on. The girls were 'on task' for the investigation, but easily lost sight of what they were testing and why. Although they were better than the boys at articulating fair test procedures, they did not then use them. For example, aesthetic qualities of the paper and its suitability for writing on took over from the paper's durability as the focus of the investigation. The girls also got side-tracked by discussions of who should record the results and what should be recorded and this took time away from the investigation. If the girls had been assessed on their written results or on the quality of the paper as a book covering from its aesthetic point of view, then they would have achieved at a higher level than the boys. There was also little evidence to show that these girls had collaborated before and they were relatively hostile to each other.

In Ryehatch First School, the 'authentic' task took place in Year 3. Three boys and one girl were chosen to participate in this part of the study. The group of four was chosen by the class teacher because she felt that they would work well together and that within this grouping each child would benefit from the others in different ways. In the more open-ended authentic tasks, the nature of the task is vital in encouraging an atmosphere that is conducive to collaborative working. Even though many of the activities were suitable for collaboration, it did not occur as frequently as it might have. When it did occur, it most often excluded the girl. As with the 'formal' tasks, the girl was anxious to help the teacher/researcher and exhibited characteristics which can hinder pupils' progress in science investigations by looking for the answer that she thought the teacher/researcher wanted rather than investigating from her own ideas. She also paid more attention to the decorative properties of her ear trumpet than to its effectiveness for collecting sound.

Observations from the study

- A single girl in a mixed-sex group will end up working on her own.
- Girls' enthusiasm and skill in writing gets in the way of collaboration.
- Girls' perception of the aesthetic qualities in an investigation obscure/confuse the ultimate goal of the investigation.
- Boys find it easier than girls to collaborate in a mixed-sex grouping.
- Single girls in a mixed-sex group suffer more 'put-downs' from boys (leading to an undermining of their confidence).
- Girls' desire to 'please Miss' gets in the way of effective collaboration – they are looking for the teacher's agenda, not their own.
- Girls need an audience to provide information/results for.
- Boys are more comfortable with measuring instruments.

A quotation we like that seems to encapsulate much of our opinion is the following (Morgan, 1989):

Early socialisation of girls and boys seems to produce a situation where boys find it easier to handle the teaching and learning styles frequently employed in primary science, particularly group work and open-ended discussion. Recognition of this will allow us to plan teaching strategies which actively encourage girls to participate more fully in groups and discuss their ideas freely . . . Development of science skills (observing leading to hypothesis formulation, co-operative working, experimenting and predicting) are ones in which girls can experience particular problems. Often a level of confidence in putting forward ideas and participating in group discussions is required. Girls find active participation difficult; boys are more assertive.

This study has been taken from a longer paper which can be found in volume 1 of the contributions to the GASAT East and West European Conference held in Eindhoven, The Netherlands, in October 1992

CASE STUDY 18

Watching girls working with girls and boys

Di Bentley, Roehampton Institute

The cases reported here are drawn from work in an infant school with Year 2 pupils working in technology to follow up a history project, and Year 6 pupils in a primary school who were looking at science investigations on 'shape and movement'.

In the infant school, the children had been undertaking project work on castles. The session started with the teacher reading a story to the children about a siege of a castle. He showed pictures of siege machines and discussed ideas for how to get over the castle walls using the technology and materials that might have been available in the 10th and 11th centuries. The children suggested different materials for making towers and mangonels and then groups split up to develop some of the different machines in detail. It quickly became clear that building the tower from wood was not going to work easily, and the teacher suggested to this group that rolled paper tubes would be easier to manage. He had provided a variety of other equipment, such as wooden blocks to form the basis for a mangonel, nails, rubber bands, balsa wood, card, hammers, glue, newsprint and scissors. The children were free to choose whatever suited their purpose best or to ask for other things, but the supply of these was fairly restricted.

The tower builders were all boys. They began, under the encouragement of the teacher with a plan, which they drew on a large sheet of paper in the middle of the reading area whilst seated on the carpet. The discussion was fairly conflictual, with one boy being very sure that he knew best:

SIMON: You're doing it wrong.
PAUL: No it should look like this . . .
SIMON: I saw my dad draw one like this. His looked better than that.
ANDREW: You're very bossy, Simon. I think if we make it that long, the side bit won't stick on.
ANWAR: We'll need lots of Sellotape to hold it on . . . will that make it too heavy?
SIMON: Yes, it might fall down. Shall we use two rolls to support it there?

In two other groups, where mangonels were being made, two girls and a boy were working together. The boy had taken charge of the hammer and was hammering two large nails into a block of wood to provide supports for the rubber band which would provide the force to propel the missile. In the next group, however, two girls working together were successfully completing their own hammering. In fact when the boy failed to get one nail to stay in, one of the girls took over from him and completed the task.

Whilst girls passed to and fro in the classroom, they would stop and look at the tower builders whose efforts were becoming larger and more complex and by now taking up a large amount of the reading area. Two girls proffered advice at different points, but were resolutely ignored. Others, wiser, looked but said nothing. It was very clear that the boys' group had, by virtue of their noise and the size of their project, become the dominant group in the room.

One quiet group of girls, building a mangonel, speculated about how long the arm had to be, helped by suggestions from the teacher.

SOPHIE: I'm not really sure – was it as long as the base of the machine thing in the picture? [The story book had contained a drawing of a mangonel which the teacher had shown the class]
ANN: What difference does it make how long it is?
SOPHIE: None I suppose – shall we just guess?
RACHEL: No let's make two or three – they're only made from card. I'll do three then we can try different ones; it might make a difference. I mean, if the arm was very heavy it might break the band.
ANN: Do we need a thicker band then?

The final piece of work for the mangonel groups was to test their catapults. The group of three girls were delighted that their tests with the different rubber band and length of arms had resulted in a good match that made their catapult launch an object the furthest.

In the junior school, pupils were working on open investigations around shape and motion. Two groups were making a windmill and in the process were testing out how many blades a windmill needed to spin fastest and what angle they had to be relevant to the wind. One group of boys worked very quickly and in an organized way. They selected a particular size and shape of blade, made them from card, stuck onto cocktail sticks and pushed them into a cork. The other small groups around them quickly learnt from this experience. The two girls who were tackling the same problem began to work at a plan on paper first. They spent quite some time watching the group of boys develop their work and eventually shyly ventured out to use a similar model but with four blades instead of the eight the boys had worked up to. When the girls tried to make their first attempt work, the boys were on model number 3. The girls spent some two or three minutes blowing their blades, trying to get them to revolve. The boys became impatient for the use of the fan which produced the air stream to make the windmill turn. They eventually asked the girls, 'Have you finished? We want to get on.' The girls immediately moved away. They then watched the boys and stayed on the periphery of the area when the teacher arrived to see how work was progressing. The boys immediately announced that they found eight blades best tilted at a particular angle. It was noticeable that after this the girls made a new model with eight blades, which they shaped carefully before they stuck them onto the cocktail sticks. They then returned carefully to painting their windmill, having learned from the work of the boys but with minimum investment from themselves.

Another two groups in the room were testing boat shapes for speed of travel in an open water pipe. They chose the size of the hull as a whole group, but in this discussion period, the girls in the group stayed very quiet and let the boys make the decisions. The group agreed to make different shapes of hull as pairs. Two girls in particular were very careful about their use of tools. They used a fretsaw well and produced a very competent boat that at the end trial proved to be the most successful shape. In some respects, considering the time spent on meticulously making the shape designated to them this was not surprising. What was interesting however, was the point at which the boys began to use the vice and fretsaw. One of the girls watched his efforts for a while, as he systematically destroyed two pieces of wood and then quietly took over and finished the task. Not a word was exchanged between them. She simply handed him his finished hull and walked back to her partner.

Value arguments

Here constructivism meets a real challenge. It may well be that boys and girls arrive at science and technology with very different start points – the 'where they are at' might be very different. Society influences gender and cultural learning in many ways and here there is a distinct message we would want them to learn. Working for equal opportunities means working for prejudice reduction, greater tolerance and confidence in plurality. The case studies certainly highlight some of the problems of encouraging the girls to be more confident in their work, and of asking the boys to be more tolerant in theirs. Teachers are good at structuring classes to facilitate equal opportunities though clearly lack the opportunities sometimes to see this through. Conceptual change – change towards a different conception of role and relationship will be a lifelong task for many – teachers and taught.

ten

Teacher assessment

Introduction

Much experience has now been gained of assessment within the National Curriculum at Key Stage 1. In this chapter we are not concerned with the administration of summative tests, their marking nor the compilation of the scores. We are concerned, instead, with the crucial issues of informing children, their parents and other teachers about progress on a regular basis. This means that we see formalized assessment to be an essential and integral part of the curriculum and of every learning experience. At an informal level, all teachers assess children every day.

Purpose

The National Curriculum requires assessment against a clearly defined and explicit framework. When pupil activities are planned, so Attainment Targets need to be planned. This planning has a dual function: not only does it aid teachers in pinpointing pupil progress, it is also – and most importantly – a tool for pupils. Continual exposure to feedback about their progress helps learners take ownership and control that progress for themselves.

Because teachers assess children informally every day they are very skilled at it. It is an everyday occurrence, probably for most of the day, as they make judgements about when to intervene in an activity, which type of question is the most appropriate, how pupils are progressing, when they need help and when they are best left to persevere. This is a simple matter of professional judgement. Although this appears simple at face value it is not to demean the complexity of the process nor the large amount of skill displayed by teachers in using it. In managing their classrooms, teachers make complex assessments of pupils and groups involving many variables and make considered judgements about how best to deal with a situation or learning experience in seconds. They 'weigh it up' and make a decision – each decision an act of assessment in its own right. In this chapter it is our intention to help readers to see how that skill can be used in more formal ways. The National Curriculum makes explicit a framework for formal judgements and in this respect would appear to make the judgements easier. It does however beg two very important questions. First, how well do the levels in individual Attainment Targets reflect any of the realities of classroom life or of children's learning? Second, how much interpretation is placed on the Statements of Attainment so that the judgements made by two teachers of the same work can in fact can be quite different. We have strong views about the first of these questions, but it is not our task to re-address the National Curriculum here. It is the second of those questions which the chapter will address in more detail.

Structure

Here we consider three levels of organization:

1. Classroom assessment.
2. Whole-school assessment.
3. Between-schools assessment.

Classroom assessment

If classroom assessment is to be successful there are several aspects to consider. Those teachers who trialled their way through the first set of SATs will remember very clearly how important aspects like classroom organization were in ensuring a peaceful existence for themselves and the children being tested. It is classroom organization which we consider first.

Classroom organization
We have already said that if assessment is to fulfil its potential as a feedback mechanism, it needs to be planned into the programme of work every time activities are undertaken, particularly for Attainment Target 1 in science. Since a normal part of classroom routine and organization is group work in primary schools, this gives primary teachers a distinct advantage. Flexibility in choosing children and tasks for assessment purposes is helped by the normal organizational characteristics of the work. Successful assessment that entails the minimum amount of disruption to class life and teacher workload is best assisted by assessing small groups. Since, in our view, the point of assessment is to enhance pupil achievement and progress, then the degree of pupil autonomy the classroom offers is paramount. This implies some of the organizational strategies outlined in Chapter 3. To assist readers we have produced a checklist to determine if a classroom learning environment is at a state of readiness for assessment.

Readiness for assessment. Do the classroom conditions give you time to spend working with particular small groups when they are completing their science and technology tasks?

Checking for working conditions.   Do the physical arrangements enable group work? For instance:

- Does the arrangement of tables facilitate pupils holding discussions in groups?
- Are basic science and technology materials and equipment clearly labelled for pupils and accessible to them?
- Are there areas of the room where different activities can take place, such as reading, writing up an activity, getting on with a technology project, etc?
- Can all the areas of the room be seen wherever the teacher is standing so that safety aspects are always under control?

Checking for autonomous working.   Do pupils operate autonomously?

- What is your response when you are asked for equipment or materials which are easily accessible in the room?
- How often do you use other pupils as 'experts' who can help their peers solve a problem?
- Are sources of information (dictionaries, reference books) easily available in the classroom?
- Do pupils have responsibilities to the whole group for – say – putting away equipment, storing tools, correctly?
- Is there one pupil designated to take responsibility for technology tools? What is your expectation for pupils who finish a piece of work? To read? To talk to friends, complete other unfinished tasks? How do you prepare them for this expectation?
- How do pupils decide when to move on to a new activity? Do they ask you, does the group decide?
- How often do pupils go out of the room to use other parts of the school environment (the library, the grounds, the computer) as a normal part of what they are doing? How do they seek permission for this?
- What expectations do pupils have of helping peers who are having difficulty with a particular idea?

Checking planning and its relationship to assessment.   Does the curriculum preparation draw on pupils' autonomy?

- Do pupils know what they have to achieve in the time span and what the goals of the work are?
- How often are different types of work planned to take place in a session (discussion, planning, evaluating, conducting a practical experiment, writing up results, surveys, library work, preparing a report)?
- What role does pupil self-assessment and peer assessment play in your teaching?
- What role does peer teaching have in the classroom?
- How do pupils record their own progress through tasks over time?

- How often do you prepare practice exercises for pupils who feel that they lack confidence in aspects of skills such as hypothesizing, reading instruments, using tools?
- Can pupils practise areas of self-assessed weakness easily and frequently?
- How often is marking used to direct pupils towards practising particular aspects of work, and what check is made to ensure they do this?

Planning for assessment

Most teachers are familiar with the idea of a 'planning unit' as far as the curriculum is concerned. When planning themes or topics, this 'planning unit' usually represents a half-term period. In terms of assessment too, the planning unit needs to be carefully defined and may not be a half term. What skills in science AT1 will be acquired and practised during the planning unit? Can time be deliberately built in for practising skills such as hypothesizing, interpreting data, using particular kinds of measuring instruments, for example, as spin-offs from a piece of experimentation. Groups of pupils might be directed – through a teacher's marking – to undertake different tasks which help them to practise skills.

Whole-school assessment

Although classroom processes are the crux of assessment, they rest on a good organizational structure at whole-school level. This involves communication with colleagues and pupils about assessment. This needs to be done within an agreed framework for the whole school, so that consistency of approach, agreement about methods and interpretation of statements is a part of whole-school working. There are mundane parts to this, such as agreed dates for completing assessments and the compilation of marks for handing on, dates of moderation meetings, etc. but in general, the framework needs to be at policy level.

Establishing a policy

The essential first step is the agreement of a whole-school assessment policy. In their teacher assessment packs, SEAC (1989) have some advice for the major areas that such a policy might cover. These are:

- Planning
  - progression in schemes of work
- Management
  - how continuous assessment is monitored
  - who has responsibility for monitoring assessment
  - arrangements for ensuring consistency of interpretation through moderation
- Recording and reporting
  - organizing records of achievement
  - recording and storing evidence of pupil achievement

- reporting evidence of achievement to other teachers
- reporting evidence of achievement to parents and the LEA
• Special educational needs
  - dealing with pupils with a Statement of Special Educational Needs
  - dealing with the disapplication of pupils

One other area mentioned by SEAC in its paper is the process of sharing the assessment with the child. In the light of our earlier views concerning the role of self- and peer assessment by pupils, we feel that aspects of pupil responsibility for their own assessment, not just sharing teachers' assessments, should be included in any policy document. We have suggested some guidelines for this part of assessment below.

Encouraging pupil responsibility for assessment
We believe that the following aspects need to be in place in every school. That is, if staff are fully committed to the idea that pupils have a legitimate role in assessing and recording their progress in aspects of the National Curriculum.

• Recording progress
  - pupil-friendly statements of the attainment levels in science and technology need to be prepared by subject coordinators
  - self-assessment records of progress and practice of science and technology skills need to be prepared for pupils to use
• Process of assessment
  - the first half-term should be free of assessment to allow pupils and teachers to get to know one another
  - every pupil should be assessed in some aspect of science and technology at least once a fortnight
  - sufficient time for progress should be allowed before the same area is reassessed
  - pupils should also be encouraged to assess themselves once a fortnight on an aspect of science or technology where they are working to improve
  - peer assessment should take place regularly to expose pupils to other expertise
  - half-termly discussions of progress should take place between teacher and pupils
  - decisions about retention of evidence of attainment should be a joint one between pupil and teacher

A framework for drawing up an assessment policy from the work of the assessment team in Buckinghamshire is included in Appendix 6.

Moderation
As the SEAC information pointed out, one of the essential features in managing assessment is moderation. Moderation means ensuring that the interpretations placed upon criteria for attainment are similar. This is obviously

important as far as year teams are concerned so that pupils are all treated in a similar way, and 'levelness' is the same within each class of a year group. Similarly, if the information passed on to other teachers in the school is to be regarded as valid and accurate, then discussions between teachers in different years are important so that consistency of interpretation is maintained throughout the school. At present, much of the work of moderation takes place between groups of schools and is organized by assessment coordinators who work at LEA level. With the demise of these posts over time, the onus will be thrown back on schools to arrange their own moderation both inside the school and with other schools.

How is moderation organized? In one school of our acquaintance, the school assessment coordinator told us of her experiences:

> We spend INSET funding on releasing myself and the deputy head. Over a term, we manage between us to work, once a term, with every teacher in joint assessment tasks in the classroom. This helps us to see how people are interpreting evidence and also to look at evidence that is ephemeral – like watching children when they make observations during an experiment or read a thermometer. We also organize moderation meetings about every half term. These involve usually year teams and some members of the Governors' working group on assessment. All the members of the year team bring work from pupils and we all have to award a level in the specified Attainment Target and discuss our findings. For example, the one for last term was on Attainment Target 3 in technology. Teachers brought the watermills pupils had made and their written accounts of what they did and we marked them – without knowing what level the teacher had awarded. Usually we just talk about those marks that are very much out of line. It took us a while to train Governors to look for particular things, especially in technology, but they really appreciate how difficult the task is now. My worry is that if there is a discrepancy of one level, we don't tend to discuss the marks, but one level is quite an important step for some children, since they may not progress more than this in some areas over two years. The deputy head collects examples of tasks set by staff, and the assessments agreed by the moderation meeting on pieces of work. This all goes in the assessment bank that we've set up. It provides a good resource and also a record of agreed standards. Everyone is free to use the bank regularly for help in assessing.

Collecting evidence

The first question with regard to evidence is, who is the evidence for? If the evidence is for the teacher doing the assessing, then almost anything counts as evidence – conversations with the pupil about their experiment or plan for an artefact for example. All, and any, observations, conversations and experimental situations are available as the basis of professional judgement.

If the evidence is for others, or needs to be moderated, the preservation of the evidence needs consideration. This is obviously not a problem where written work or drawings, diagrams or other two-dimensional aspects are the basis for judgements. Where more ephemeral evidence is used, such as a conversation, then recording in some way will be necessary. At this point tapes, photographs and other means may have to be considered. Often however, it is sufficient to log the child's comment on a record sheet of progress and date it. It is self-evident that certain kinds of evidence lend themselves best to the assessment of certain kinds of attainment levels. Certain scientific skills, for example can only be assessed by means of observation on behalf of the teacher as the experimentation takes place. Clearly-written evidence is the most easily accessible for teachers in terms of preservation of judgement for consideration by others. In Bentley and Watts (1992) we suggested that recording levels attained by various writings or drawings as work was marked and dating it was a helpful practice that achieved several things.

1. It allows the teacher to check her judgements again later. For example, does she still agree that the statement in the child's work is indicative of that level?
2. It allows the teacher to check her judgements against those of colleagues easily.
3. It saves time. Marking is an important feedback activity for pupils. It can now be a feedback activity for teachers as well.
4. It makes assessment part of the everyday processes of teaching.
5. It helps to keep an easy record of children's progress.
6. It can be used to show where help was needed to achieve the level – recording with a comment the teacher's question which helped the child to understand.

Whilst the recording of ephemeral evidence through audio and video tape is possible, the question always has to be, is it feasible – or necessary? Where teachers are unsure of their judgements and feel the need for checking with colleagues, then if it is not possible to invite a colleague to the class to assess the real evidence, recording by such means may be necessary. However, this is likely to be very rare. Some teachers have found it useful to create a checklist made for a specific piece of work, or experiment to show how they made their judgements at the time of observation, and to record this as an annotated account.

Collecting and storing work

The building up of portfolios requires a variety of decisions at whole-school level, not the least of which are resource ones in terms of storage of collections or portfolios. Such portfolios of work should aim to provide direct evidence of progress and thereby enhance dialogue between the child and all the other partners in the assessment process such as teachers and parents. The type of questions schools will need to address in this area include:

- What is the purpose of a collection of work?
- What types of work should be stored?
- How are items entered into the collection?
- Who puts them in?
- How often should the collection of work be reviewed?
- What is the role of pupils in choosing items for the collection?
- How is the collection kept current?
- Where is it stored?
- Who has access to it?
- When are items replaced or removed?

A collection of work should serve two purposes. It should act as a record of evidence for teachers about progress through the National Curriculum and provide examples of the quality of work which an individual child wishes to retain. Both the child and the teacher should have the right to enter work into a collection by negotiation; however, only the teacher should have the right to permanently remove work from a collection. This should apply only if the work is to be replaced because the child has progressed to a higher level of attainment and thus the original has been superseded. Removal of work designated as quality by the child should not be removed by the teacher. Only the child has that right. Technology poses special problems here. Pupil work cannot be stored for any length of time and quite rightly pupils are proud of it and want to take it home. Therefore, if the final artefact is to be preserved, photographic evidence is needed. However, this can be very expensive for schools. One school of our acquaintance had a good idea in this respect. They organized half-termly technology evenings for parents and put the children's plans and work on display at each child's desk. They explained to parents the need for evidence and many parents took photographs of their children's work and sent them to school. One local photographer put up a photographic exhibition of pupils' work in his studio and sent the photographs to the school after the exhibition had finished.

It will be important to annotate any collection of pupils' work. For example each piece of work could have written on the back the context of the work recorded (done in a group, as an individual, as a result of a particular idea, etc.), the level of attainment, the reasons for selection (a good example of a particular level of attainment) and the date of selection.

Between-schools assessment

This area of work has two dimensions. First, there is the work associated with schools of the same phase, to ensure that standards are similar from school to school. Second, there is cross-phase work to ensure that interpretations of Statements of Attainment are being made in similar ways from first to middle and from primary to secondary schools. At first glance, both of these look straightforward even if time-consuming. However, some problems have emerged in the INSET which teachers have been organizing for Key

Stage 3 SAT operation. This is the issue of 'levelness'. The Statements of Attainment in the National Curriculum science and technology are far from clear; indeed, many are very ambiguous. Teachers from different phases who moderate their work have found that when making judgements about the levelness of a piece of work, their judgement is affected by the knowledge of the age of the child so that a piece of work that is, for example, from a 7-year-old can comfortably be judged at Level 4 will receive a different treatment when teachers know that it is from an older child. The judgements against the statements are meant to be criterion referenced. The truth of the matter is that one of the implicit criteria appears to be age. Older children as judged as being expected to attain higher levels, so when work is compared later, because language and sentiments are expressed in a more sophisticated way, the science and technology becomes clouded by the sophistication. In part, careful moderation will sort this out, but at present, what is Level 4 at Key Stage 1 may not appear to be Level 4 work from a child in Key Stage 3, even though the concepts expressed are very similar.

When schools of the same phase put teachers together to moderate work, this is always a difficult process. Everyone has heard the horror tales of judgements being changed when staff returned from moderation meetings because they had been too generous in their marking and thus lowering the school levels in a particular subject. Most, if not all, these tales are apocryphal. However, you cannot get past the idea that staff have genuinely put hard work and effort into working at their marking and their judgements. Any finding themselves out of line with colleagues from other schools may well be difficult to come to terms with and there may be reluctance to change – if your marks are not over-generous, there is always the temptation to say that this is because standards are high in your school. It is important then to establish some prior conditions before staff meet from each other's schools for moderation purposes.

The prior conditions, then, in putting schools together for moderating purposes would be comprised something like:

- Always have, whenever possible, people paired from a school so that one person does not feel under threat.
- Agree from the beginning of the meeting that one person's judgement will be final in deciding levelness of work, especially where disagreements arise.
- Ensure that a record of judgements is kept so that they can be referred to later by interested parties and also as a standard against which schools can judge future assessments.
- Agree to share-assessment tasks with each other so that at the end of the meeting people go away with more than just a list of assessment agreements – they have less work next term.
- Ask colleagues attending not just to bring a range of assessments but also to bring any they cannot decide, so that others can help.
- Ask staff to bring all the essential documentation – annotated notes saying what was written on the board, worksheets, etc.

Most schools are familiar with the format of moderation meetings now – work is brought, everyone has a marking session, making the judgements about levels. Usually staff quite rightly complain that without annotated notes saying – for example, what was written on the board or on a worksheet – it is difficult for others to decide what is the child's own work and what help was received. So some work remains unmoderated. After the marking session, judgements are compared and discussions about meaning begin. These are usually enlightened by the teacher concerned making their own feelings and judgements known to colleagues. These are invaluable parts of the pen portrait of a piece of work. In time they will come to be annotated detail on a piece of work, but at present, there is simply too much to do to write everything down. Once judgements are agreed, staff can return to school with a set of standard markers against which to make future judgements.

Across-phase meetings are always more difficult. There is a tendency for primary colleagues to assume that secondary subject teachers automatically know better what the level of a piece of work is and to draw back from sharing those important pieces of information about the child and her progress that illuminate the judgements. The work can only get better for sharing such information. It is helpful too, to secondary colleagues, to see the range of pupils entering the school and to have some ideas of the different judgements different feeder schools are making. Ideally, all feeder primary schools to any one secondary school would be part of the moderation meetings. In fact, this is not possible.

Values and arguments

Our five tenets outlined in Chapter 1 (p. 10) have been explored to some extent in this chapter. We have looked at the continuation of autonomy for the learner through the sharing of assessments, and enabled the facilitative role of the teacher in negotiating progress and diagnostic information with pupils. Assessment, of its very nature, starts where the learner is. It is the process which helps to inform us *where* the learner is, even when that is not as sanguine an experience as teachers would like, since it also tells them how effective a piece of teaching was for that particular individual. Assessment has the power to be a very useful tool in progression, since it can help pupils, if information is properly communicated, in a way which encourages understanding, take their own progress on board and work at it as a partnership with the teacher.

eleven

Being a co-ordinator

Introduction

The role of the curriculum primary school co-ordinator has become pivotal in recent years. In this chapter we look carefully at that role and its many facets, and give some advice on the way it might be further developed in the future. That is, with one eye on the needs looming from the publication of the NCC advice to the Secretary of State for Education for Key Stages 1 and 2 (NCC, 1993).

Purpose

In the chapter we present some models for the roles and responsibilities of the co-ordinator, and look at the skills involved in different aspects of the role. We use a typical co-ordinator's job description for work in science and technology and then look forward to address underdeveloped aspects of the present role. Part of our exemplar cases in this chapter derive from interviews with two co-ordinators, one science and one in technology, in order to examine their views and their emphases for the future.

The need for a curriculum co-ordinator

As we noted in earlier chapters, there has been a shift in emphasis in primary schools away from a fully-integrated approach towards a curriculum in which subject areas are more clearly defined. This has inevitable consequences for the work needed to maintain curriculum subjects. Ideally, of course, each teacher would be a teacher of *all* subjects in the best primary tradition. But this is clearly seen to be inefficient and, in truth, probably an unreasonable expectation given the 'content knowledge' requirements of the National Curriculum. While every teacher needs to understand both science and technology, they will still need help in translating that understanding into suitable curriculum experiences for pupils. Indeed many will continue to need help in developing their own understandings of science and technology. The co-ordinator has an essential 'expert's' role to play in terms of working with colleagues to provide, manage and deliver INSET. They will need also to monitor resources across the school each term, advise the Headteacher on new developments, INSET needs, equipment and materials and deal with the large amounts of bureaucracy relating to assessment.

Structure

The role of the curriculum co-ordinator is not new but has, in many schools, been underdeveloped until recent years. Indeed in 1978, the HMI reported that only 17 per cent of primary schools had a science co-ordinator (DES, 1977). Technology co-ordinators were of course, non-existent then. In 1987, Barber and Michell were advocating the use of 'posts of responsibility' in science, and drew out some of work that such a post-holder might do:

- create resources for science;
- store, repair, maintain and check stock;
- formulate a school policy for science;
- keep staff up to date with new acquisitions;
- be responsible for science-related safety matters;
- generally advise and help other staff on matters scientific.

This was written well before the National Curriculum and for many schools the role advocated by Barber and Michell was merely a faint hope. Many did no science at all, or little that would be recognized in terms of today's curriculum. In the interim, there has been a marked change in the role of what has now become a curriculum co-ordinator post, a change which has taken place even in the short time since the National Curriculum Council published their statement of the role of a curriculum co-ordinator (NCC, 1989a): Where possible, teachers should share responsibility for curriculum leadership to include:

- detailing schemes of work in the light of the Programmes of Study;
- working alongside colleagues;
- arranging school-based INSET;
- evaluating curriculum development;
- liaising with other schools;
- keeping 'up to date' in the particular subject;
- managing resources.

Increased government funding has ensured that the role of co-ordinator is being seen as a key to the development of the curriculum in primary schools. At one time the Headteacher was the one expected to have the major curriculum role in the school. Now this is no longer possible given that Heads are expected to have total 'curriculum vision' – seeing where the whole curriculum might be going in three or four years time – rather than having specific and detailed knowledge about the latest resources and developments in any one area.

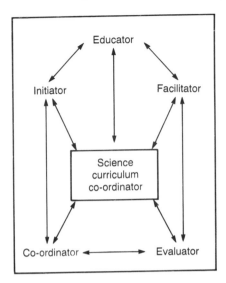

Figure 11.1 Bell's model.

The role of the co-ordinator

Some models

D. Bell (1992) has drawn a model for the role of the science co-ordinator, although this has wider implications for co-ordinator's roles generally (Figure 11.1).

Bell rightly points out that some aspects of the role are at present under-developed and require expansion. In developing Bell's model further, we would suggest there are three major features to the role. Each of these is associated with specific skills required of co-ordinators.

Skills
These are:

- communication – pertaining to other individuals in facilitating school;
- researching – pertains to the curriculum subject in reflecting the school;
- evaluating – pertaining to the school as a whole;
- planning;
- managing;
- analysing;
- reporting.

Our model, developed from Bell's, would appear something like the one in Figure 11.2, taking into account the skills outlined above and the areas to

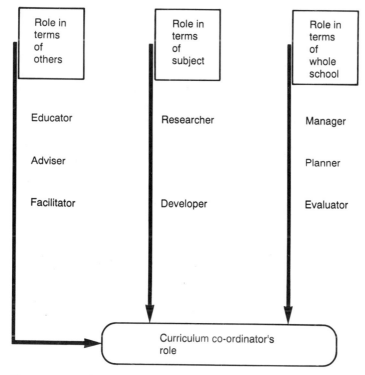

Figure 11.2 Role of curriculum co-ordinator.

which those skills now pertain. We deal in some detail with each aspect of our model further on.

Other individuals

The role involves communicating with others, whether at the level of INSET for colleagues, informal conversations at breaktime, or discussion with the Headteacher, Governors and parents to inform and persuade them about new directions and developments.

Educator

As Bell (1993) points out, this involves:

> helping colleagues with their knowledge and understanding of [the subject], running workshops, working alongside colleagues in classrooms and disseminating information to keep staff up to date with developments ... nationally and locally.

It also includes educating parents and Governors of what is expected of pupils and what assessment information in each subject actually means. The role also means disseminating the work of the school to other primary schools.

Adviser

This is a very specific but important part of the role. It involves giving advice about future directions, resources, funding and developments. It means assisting the Headteacher and the curriculum sub-committee of the governing body to maintain a future curriculum vision and the co-ordinator needs to be able to report annually on the role of his/her subject in the school development plan, the future resource needs, changes in direction that will need careful planning. Although this also involves good communication skills, it requires the co-ordinator to have a carefully-developed sense of audience in reporting information and planning future strategies and we see it as being significantly different to that of the 'educator' part of the role.

Facilitator

While some of this depends on the provision of information and resources, it is actually much more subtle. To ensure that developments are taken forward, the co-ordinator needs to engender a spirit of trust and goodwill so that colleagues feel they can ask for help, admit when things are not working and receive non-judgemental assistance. This has potential role conflict with some of the aspects of being an evaluator and requires careful role definition by the Headteacher and the co-ordinator so that colleagues do not feel threatened.

The curriculum subject

This is really a part of the role which looks at the professional development of the co-ordinator within the subject. It involves the co-ordinator researching aspects of his or her own practice as an 'action researcher', researching aspects of subject knowledge (in terms of their own and others' concept development) and taking this further so that work done in school involves others in the process of evaluation.

Researcher

Seeking information about the subject and ensuring that other teachers understand it too. Predominantly, the co-ordinator is using their own practice as a mechanism for evaluation. They are observing themselves teaching, perhaps keeping a diary of events, changing their practice and recording the changes. They are also examining their own concept development, perhaps as a result of INSET training they have received.

Developer

Taking ideas from curriculum materials, or that discussed with colleagues in other schools and making them feasible within their subject in the school.

The whole school

There is a variety of skills associated with developing a subject area within whole-school work. These include the management of resources and time, the monitoring and evaluation of the curriculum, evaluation of progress by pupils, the analysis and reporting of information on future needs and the planning of future curriculum work.

Manager

This involves the management of resources, finance and professional development for colleagues, keeping them informed of opportunities, seeking collaboration between colleagues and their work, providing materials for curriculum development and ensuring that teachers' and team plans are in line with school policy statements. It also means working on policy documents and providing schemes of work that enable continuity and progression.

Planner

This entails organizing future developments, looking forward to examine how plans, themes and topics relate to cross-curricular areas and the work of other subjects. It means working collaboratively with other co-ordinators so that, for example, assessment time for staff is maximized.

Evaluator

Here, this means reviewing progress and matching teacher's classroom activities with schemes of work. It means ensuring pupils make progress and experience continuity year by year, and checking the progress of pupils with special educational needs and helping staff to moderate assessments and work. It includes evaluating the place of the subject within the whole curriculum and analysing future needs on this basis. It means encouraging staff to evaluate formally and to observe each other's teaching.

The role of the co-ordinator is clearly a complex one, requiring particular skills. A job description for a technology co-ordinator, for example, might look like the following.

Primary technology co-ordinator

Job description

1. To be responsible for a class.
2. To be responsible for the development of the technology curriculum and ensure the appropriate integration of work throughout the school.
3. In liaison with Headteacher, staff and Governors where appropriate, to prepare guidelines and schemes of work and to identify and give advice on current needs in technology.
4. To keep abreast of current thinking by attending courses, reading and sharing with staff all significant developments.
5. To liaise with colleagues with like responsibilities in other contributory schools and the secondary school in the area, and participate in national and county initiatives as and when appropriate.

6. In liaison with the Headteacher to convene meetings for staff to discuss, plan and agree work in technology. This will involve drawing up agendas, keeping minutes and notes of actions to be taken.
7. To be responsible for the purchasing and management of resources which relate to technology and to be aware of the potential of further resources, for instance the school library.
8. To support and implement school policies and curriculum statements.

In cooperation with senior members of staff

9. To monitor work and evaluate and review progress of all pupils.
10. To support colleagues in all aspects of their work in technology:
    • teaching approaches;
    • progression of ideas;
    • first-hand experiences;
    • resource use and management, including the school library;
    • children experiencing difficulty, etc.;
    • methods of review and assessment.
11. To co-ordinate the work of staff and work collaboratively with colleagues in the support of a curriculum-based school library and information service both centrally and throughout the school.
12. To be prepared to lead school-based INSET in technology and support local liaison initiatives.
13. To ensure continuity and progression in technology throughout the school.
14. To encourage the involvement and support of parents, community and other agencies for the benefit of pupils and the school.
15. Further, to undertake other duties as may be required in consultation with the Headteacher.

The role in practice

What, in practice, are the tasks co-ordinators need to do? To reach into this, we first provide an overview by Brenda Barber (Case Study 19) and then interview two co-ordinators – Pauline and Angela – and use their responses to frame a set of practical suggestions for managing the job. Brenda shows how the role has developed through teaching co-ordinators as part of an INSET course.

CASE STUDY 19

Science co-ordination in the primary school – an overview

Brenda Barber, Roehampton Institute

The National Curriculum has revolutionized the place of science in the primary curriculum, from a minority enthusiasm avoided by many teachers, to one of the 'core' subjects on equal footing with English and mathematics. The role of the co-ordinator for science has consequently developed, taking an important part in the senior management of the school. That being said, the actual role played tends to be idiosyncratic to the school concerned.

Many science co-ordinators are also responsible for other areas of the curriculum, such as technology, games and PE, and the humanities. This is inevitable in small schools, but also in not so small schools where the teaching force is stretched to breaking point in the effort to cover all curricular areas.

Much has been written about the role of the co-ordinator, and a comprehensive job description would include such broad areas of responsibility as resourcing for science, developing school policy and schemes of work for science, assessment and record-keeping, SATs, keeping up to date with courses, literature, etc., attending to safety matters, helping colleagues, 'fronting' for science at Governors and PTA meetings, and most important, *being the enthusiast*!

At the start of term 20 science co-ordinators joined us for a 20 Day Science Course. Our pre-course survey showed that they had been in post for between three months and six years, some with experience co-ordinating in more than one school, and many with responsibility for other subjects as well as science. As we have got to know each other, we have spent some time discussing the role of the co-ordinator, initially from their own experiences and then from an ideological standpoint: 'This is how it is in my school – but this is what we think it ought to be'.

All the co-ordinators had some responsibility for resources, what we might look upon as the housekeeping part of the job. The storage aspect of resourcing varied from, on the one hand setting up a resources room, to actually finding some storage space to start with. The range of facilities include a cardboard box under the teacher's desk, a cupboard in the co-ordinators classroom, and a whole room for resources shared with maths. One co-ordinator reported with some pride that science had been allocated two alcoves for storage, a 100 per cent increase on the previous year! The rationale behind the organization of resources, and their maintenance also falls to the co-ordinator and may be topic-based, alphabetic or pragmatic . . . these things need to be locked away, these do not, although supporting teachers teaching science is always the underlying aim.

Updating, repairing and replacing lost or broken items is a perennial task, solved in a variety of ways. The caretaker or the PTA sometimes help with maintenance and even making things, but at the bottom line funds are needed. Some co-ordinators have an annual budget which they have authority to spend to support their curriculum area, others have to negotiate with other curriculum leaders for a division of available funds. Yet, others have to approach the Headteacher cap-in-hand for every purchase. Many co-ordinators report difficulty in getting cash for local purchases, an essential part of any co-ordinator's budget.

Whole-school resourcing is still a problem for many co-ordinators, but some schools are well resourced overall and are now looking to service the needs of the individual classroom or teacher. If we are to promote the development of investigative work led by children required in AT1, then the means need to be readily available, preferably in the classroom. As one of the tasks they undertake on the school-based days of the course, many of our co-ordinators take a close look at resourcing. Some have conducted questionnaires to identify what resources staff would like to have available in the classroom, and predictably these include magnifiers, magnets, torches, batteries, bulbs and wires and often a tank for small creatures and pots and tools for growing things. Co-ordinators report that ideally they would like to have a reasonable amount of money, allocated annually to be spent at their discretion, after consultation with staff and the Headteacher's seal of approval. Contrary to popular belief, primary science cannot be supported in school without spending money.

Most of the co-ordinators on the course have written, or have led the school working party who have constructed the school's policy for science. Such documentation is often regarded as of secondary importance, now with greater emphasis being given to the construction of schemes of work, the sharp end of implementing science in the National Curriculum. Headteachers are passing the responsibility for the production of schemes of work to the co-ordinators, who may not have the breadth of experience to cater for the needs of R–Year 6, a marathon task indeed! Such writing tasks are ideally undertaken by small focused groups, presented to the whole staff, and modified so that a sense of ownership is achieved by all. There are, of course, a variety of approaches to schemes of work; in the experience of my co-ordinators, topic-based planning is the most common. In tandem with organizing resources and supporting staff with written policy statements and schemes of work, co-ordinators would like to offer support to colleagues in the classroom. This would, of course, give them the breadth of experience and understanding of both the learning and teaching needs across the schools' age range, as well as the individual needs of the teachers. However, many primary schools seem to be unable to provide this sort of time for their co-ordinators.

An hour a week, carefully planned, can help the nervous colleague to venture into science investigations. Ideally, such support must be timetabled, jointly planned by the teachers concerned, and evaluated afterwards. The co-ordinator also needs to evaluate her own success in supporting and encouraging her colleagues, and will need to feedback to the Headteacher on the use of her time. One of our school-based assignments on the course requires work with children across the age range of the school, and can provide an excuse for venturing into another teacher's classroom, which can be a difficulty in some schools.

The co-ordinator is also expected to act as a channel for all information which comes into the school about science. This will include INSET provision both by the school, the LEA and other bodies such as HE, ASE, etc., updates on National Curriculum matters, changes to the orders, SATs, etc. Catalogues for resources and books, the development of new schemes were all felt to be part of the job. A universal complaint by the co-ordinators I work with, is that information fails to reach them. The Headteacher, deputy or the school secretary all have access to the mail before the co-ordinator, as I have found to my cost. Perhaps those who wish to communicate with the science co-ordinator in a school should recognize the failure of schools to identify the correct resting place for information, unless separately mailed, named if possible, and clearly labelled for the science co-ordinator. The other side of this coin is time at staff meetings to inform staff of new developments, to show new materials, to discuss purchases; these slots need to be reserved in good time.

Groups of co-ordinators rank enthusiasm for the subject as an essential part of their role if they are to encourage other colleagues in their science teaching. This enthusiasm is shown far more easily by those who have been in post for some time, but is much more difficult for the new co-ordinator who has taken on the role because no-one else in the school wants to do it. The developing knowledge base that 20 Day Science Courses provide helps to give the co-ordinator the confidence and the enthusiasm to develop their co-ordinating role in school. Our school-based assignments also allow co-ordinators to venture into areas not always open to them, in order to cover the requirements of the course.

Interviews with co-ordinators

Pauline and Angela are co-ordinators in science and technology in schools in the South of England and describe the many features of their roles in practice. We have subdivided and commented on their work under separate headings relating to our model above.

Dealing with other individuals

PAULINE: I find it best to have regular team meetings each half-term. Part of the problem in our school is that people have to work very closely together if we are to keep to the whole-school themes that have been devised. Everyone needs to be following the scheme and organizing themselves at the same kind of rate. That's difficult for some people and it makes the co-ordinator's life difficult.

INTERVIEWER: How?

PAULINE: Well when resources are being used, for example, we don't always have enough. It's very difficult if someone is out of phase. They find the resources are scant when they come to use them. Also it's important when you are team teaching as we do in our school that everyone pulls together – then one or two don't end up teaching the majority of the children or coping with the resource and organization problems.

Angela's experience, as a technology co-ordinator was different. In her school they did not team teach.

ANGELA: I find the most difficult thing is being treated as the expert. I mean, for example, now that the technology orders are changing, people expect me to know what is coming. I've asked the technology advisory team, but even they don't know – how can I be expected to? I try to reassure staff that all the hard work we've done won't be wasted, but it's difficult. Then again, there's my own feelings. I knew very little about technology when I started as the co-ordinator, but I've learnt a lot. I feel as though I can give advice in some areas to staff, but now they're changing everything; what will happen to my understanding – will I have to learn it all over again?

INTERVIEWER: How do you cope with staff needing to ask for help? Is this done informally or formally?

PAULINE: We have organized several sessions where staff come and share my lessons. In order not to set myself up as 'super-teach' I've always asked them to evaluate and be critical of what they see so that I can improve. I find this works well, so that they can point out things I haven't noticed.

It helps them to feel better when they ask why I did something a particular way, or why something works the way it does.

ANGELA: Most of my advice is given in the staff room informally. In my school, we have a separate technology base, so I have sessions with all the upper school classes in there at some point in the week. The class teacher teaches my class. I like this system as far as my role as a co-ordinator is concerned, because I feel I really know what is happening with the subject, but as far as other staff learning and asking advice, it tends to keep the expertise mainly with me. Other staff do use the separate technology base when they carry on the work with their class but it's not quite the same.

INTERVIEWER: How do you avoid the conflict between evaluating what is happening and advising staff?

ANGELA: I've been here quite a while and staff trust me. I don't find that it's a problem, but then I suppose I don't know the extent of the times they don't come and ask. Since many lunchtimes are filled with discussions on technology in the staff room, I think they ask quite a lot.

INTERVIEWER: What role do you play in educating or advising Governors?

PAULINE: I think that's an important part of the role. They need to understand what the National Curriculum demands of teachers and pupils, especially in terms of assessment. I've organized evening sessions for Governors and invited parents to see the work, explained the National Curriculum and in some cases, let them have a go at the kind of work the children do.

INTERVIEWER: What about your own and subject knowledge of the other staff?

PAULINE: That's quite difficult. I never pretend I know when I don't. I always say that I can find out, and they know that I will come back to them with an explanation.

ANGELA: I think that's one of the main problems in being a co-ordinator. I'm not qualified to help the understanding of difficult ideas by staff and I wonder often if the children are missing out. I'd really like the school to have some kind of link with a higher education institution so that I or staff could update our knowledge, or just explore ideas when we don't understand. Not a course, but the opportunity to ask questions about the subject.

INTERVIEWER: Do you get the opportunity to advise the head about future developments, new curricula, new ways of working?

PAULINE: Yes, and I find that very satisfying. The role has some power to bring about change in the whole school. It's good to be able to influence work and future directions. I also control the budget, so that helps.

ANGELA: I'm not sure how much of that I do. I suppose I shall be expected to do more now that the technology curriculum is changing, but I don't really feel that I have a grasp of this area of my work.

Commentary

The experiences of our two co-ordinators are obviously different. For one, the advisory part of the role is underdeveloped and the educator is kept largely at the level of informality. For the other, 'the adviser' is a full and satisfying part of the role, and the educator role takes place with team teaching and evaluative comment of her own teaching of the subject. What has not been an apparent part of their role here is the work in promoting their school outside with other schools or finding out what is going on elsewhere, although Angela mentions some of this in the next section. What is still problematic is the role of co-ordinators in the informing of subject knowledge of other staff. Angela is clearly feeling apprehensive about this and although Pauline admits when she does not know, it may not always be the case that her explanation can relieve their lack of understanding or lack of confidence.

To summarize their advice then:

As educators they have
- organized Governors and parents' evenings to keep information up to date;
- through team teaching, permitted the spread of good practice;
- kept a clippings' file of new developments, resources and texts.

As advisers they have:
- controlled the budget for their subject;
- been involved in developing the four-yearly curriculum plan and advising on new schemes and courses arriving in the school.

As facilitators they have:
- encouraged the trust of other staff so that informal questions can take place;
- shared their own teaching so that staff can evaluate and at the same time share where they feel a need for advice.

Subject role

Here we explore Pauline's and Angela's opportunities to research and develop the subject and their own and others ideas and practices in the classroom.

INTERVIEWER: Are you able to devote much time to finding out new things about the subject or looking in detail at your own practice?

PAULINE: Most of my work for the co-ordinator takes place at home. With a full teaching load, there is little time to develop any areas during the school day. I do get the opportunity to reflect on my own practice by having colleagues in my class and asking them to evaluate. I also visit them, which provides another opportunity for evaluation.

ANGELA: I do reflect on my practice and I try to read new information that comes out but I manage this very rarely. I miss the opportunities to talk with the advisory teams that we used to have. They are in a position to keep us updated so much better, but with the new arrangements we have to pay for their advice and we can't afford it in all subjects. It's only those subjects that are being developed in the development plan that get the money. We do still hold co-ordinator's meetings between our school clusters though. That helps me to share other colleagues' practice and that's good. But I don't have time to write anything down about my own practice to see how it is changing. I'm not sure I'm a good developer, although I do pass on ideas to staff about new ways of teaching and projects they can do.

Commentary

Time is the issue for our co-ordinators here. The bulk of their time as co-ordinators is taken up with working to teach the subject and their own class. The non-contact time they have is small and often taken up with other things. Their capacity to research their own practice and the concepts of the subject is limited by the resources to which they have access – such as local advisory teachers and the opportunity to think about and study new writing and resources. The future development of the subject within the curriculum of their schools is at the mercy of their time, their own personal resources and their access to new thinking. Neither of them had ever attended a national conference in their subject area to update their thinking, mostly because the money was unavailable in the school INSET budget. So what had they been able to do in this area?

As researchers they had:
• observed others' practice and been observed;
• shared ideas with staff from other schools from time to time;
• reflected informally on their own practice and had evaluative comments from other staff.

As developers they had:
• made some opportunity to read up about the subject.

Whole-school role

In this section we explore the co-ordinators' views then proffer some advice of our own on the matter of managing resources.

INTERVIEWER: In terms of your whole-school role, how do you feel that this is progressing? Have you been involved in writing policies, looking at pupil progress, and so on?

PAULINE: I've been involved in updating policies. We already had a policy, but it needed changing in the light of the National Curriculum and its changes. I've involved all the staff in that. In terms of pupil progress, I've organized an informal INSET session for staff after school in which we assessed children's work that the staff brought along so we could agree what levels they were and this gave me a much better picture of the kinds of work that children were being asked to do. It also gave me some better understanding of the issues of continuity and progression in the subject.

ANGELA: I've re-written the technology guidelines and the safety rules for using the technology area for teaching and non-teaching staff. I also now manage the resources for technology. I keep the stock, order consumables, and generally ferret around local suppliers for off-cuts of wood, plastics, paper, card and anything else. I've been surprised what people throw away or are prepared to give you especially if you agree to collect it.

INTERVIEWER: Do you have a large monitoring role in the school in terms of your subject?

PAULINE: I monitor in a variety of ways. I use my non-contact time to spend time in classes with other staff and I look at children's progress and the teaching in this way. We team teach, so that gives me the opportunity in the lower part of the school to see how children from other classes are getting on and decide if the work is challenging enough. I also use team meetings to get informal feedback from staff about their teaching of the subject. This helps me in the future planning. For example, although we use a particular set of books for our teaching, this feedback has helped me to focus what extra resources are needed and I provide these as well as new materials for staff. I've also issued a questionnaire for staff to use relating to the scheme of work we use so that I can amend things. Oh, and I have asked staff to join in a book search – we collect the work of four pupils in each class and look at continuity, progression, challenge and marking across all these children on a regular basis. It's very helpful when we plan for the next year. Finally, there is the curriculum record sheet. Because children are taught in mixed-age groups and team teaching occurs, it is important to have a record of what is actually taught to each child. Not what they have achieved or know, but what has been taught. So I've set up this kind of record system now for future tracking.

ANGELA: I don't monitor children except through the teaching that I do. Since I teach most classes, this is in fact quite easy and allows me to be sure of what is needed. I also monitor resources better in this way, although I need a more formal system to do this better. I always seem to be running round because things are running out.

Commentary

One of the co-ordinators obviously had a sophisticated monitoring and evaluation function as part of her role and has developed this very fully. The elements that seem to be missing here are those of the overall contribution to the curriculum planning for the school and the provision of advice to the Head for change in the light of evaluations, such as the time for the subject to be taught in the curriculum. Curriculum analysis did not seem to be a part of their role. Their development of their role was that of managers and evaluators.

As managers they had:
- monitored pupil progress through a book search;
- written policy statements, guidelines and safety rules;
- organized methods of tracking resource use.

As evaluators they had:
- monitored teaching and resource use through team teaching and class visits;
- taken informal feedback at staff meetings;
- compiled a curriculum record sheet to track the delivery of the curriculum.

Dealing with resources

We turn now to flesh out in detail one of the most important areas of the co-ordinator's whole-school role – that of dealing with resources. In Chapter 3 we suggested some mechanisms for keeping control of stock and managing consumable items. Here we deal with the essential features of stock control and budgeting through the work of the co-ordinator.

In any school, the co-ordinators need to know what consumables are required, as well as what capital equipment is needed. Controlling stock is important. Hunn (1993) has suggested that each teacher be given a stock sheet. Whilst this can be useful, we would suggest that Year team leaders are better control points than individual teachers. They can monitor resource use on behalf of the co-ordinator and link future use clearly to the schemes of work for the year group. What co-ordinators need to know is rate of consumption and new requirements. It is essential therefore for the co-ordinator to meet regularly with Year team leaders to ascertain their needs, the stock levels and requirements being generated by teaching and by changes to the plans as they progress. We have already given an example in Chapter 3 of a stock sheet which the co-ordinator might give to year team leaders. Such a stock sheet does not need updating very often, but is a valuable source of information for co-ordinators who are trying to plan the resources for the school and manage the requirements of several year teams. It provides information on the use of consumables and capital equipment needed. It is also important for the co-ordinator to work out a resource development plan for larger items of capital equipment, so that the ratio between consumables and capital items can be maintained over a period of time. Obviously, this is a matter which needs drawing to the attention of the governing body, since it may involve virement of funds, from year to year if a specific item is being saved for. Alternatively, some governing bodies create a special fund for non-consumable items for science and technology. The management of the capital equipment fund should lie, with due accountability, in the hands of the co-ordinator. If there is a resource-development plan for capital items, then accountability is a simple issue. It does mean, however, that the resource budget generally, both consumable and capital, is in the hands of the science and technology co-ordinators.

Some terms need to be sorted out if a resource-development plan is to be drawn up by co-ordinators and is to be realistic. Guidance is needed from the governing body as to their views of particular aspects of the budgeting. The co-ordinator would need to ask the governing body for guidance in the following areas:

- On what basis are the science and technology budgets allocated?
- Is there a formula?
- How are the needs of practical subjects built into the formula?
- What in the view of the Governors represents capital equipment?
- What is the write-down factor for items of capital equipment on an annual basis?

- What is the depreciation built in for renewal?
- What is the viability line under which capital equipment cannot be bought because it is cheaper to hire/borrow?
- What degree of use do Governors expect from capital equipment – must it be used by all classes in the school every year to be a viable proposition?
- What arrangements are the Governors making for consumables?
- Is there to be an annual automatic ordering on particular consumable items such as iron filings, plastic beakers, glue, nails, sandpaper, etc. as there is for paper and exercise books?
- Is there a petty cash flow for perishable consumables that can only be bought fresh or a few days before?

Evaluation

The complexity of the co-ordinator's role involves a range of different skills, as the earlier part of the chapter explores. Some of these are new, others less so, but still in our view in need of further development in most schools. One co-ordinator in our interviews clearly had a well-developed role in evaluation, which is the area we tackle first. We draw on some of Pauline's experiences in making our suggestions.

In many schools, evaluation of the curriculum is often an informal undertaking. Teachers discuss the development of work at team or staff meetings and plan changes for the future. This is a useful mechanism for sharing ideas, but lacks an evidence base. Co-ordinators need a more formal and explicit base for their judgements if they are to advise the Headteacher and Governors about future developments and needs, and explain pupil progress.

So what can co-ordinators do to help produce an evidence base that is useful without being overwhelmed by the task and making staff feel threatened? Being an effective evaluator means working in a systematic way, being clear about what needs to be known, and what judgements will be made. To evaluate systematically means to gather evidence so that decisions and opinions can be presented in a way that is supported by evidence. The methods used to collect the evidence need to fit with what needs to be found out. The reports – either verbal or written – will need to show how evidence has been derived and how this led to the conclusions made. Evaluation means being careful of ideas, methods and people. There are six steps to effective evaluation (see Bentley and Watts, 1992 for details).

Step 1. Deciding on the purpose

Co-ordinators need to decide on the purpose of the evaluation – is it to inform teachers, Governors, the parents, to help change things as a formative exercise, or to make some final decisions, for example about a change of text support? There are several possible purposes for evaluation. In general, for co-ordinators the main purposes are:

- formative evaluation, for example to improve on-going work as it is developing;
- evaluation for policy-making, for example to help develop a new science or technology policy;
- evaluation for pupil progress, for example to help show which parts of the planned work are producing the best match with pupil needs.

Step 2. What will be evaluated?

This may arise through the demands of others, such as the governing body in drawing up a school development plan. It may also arise naturally through the work of a particular year team. Generally, the questions which give rise to evaluation are of two types – of 'why' and 'what'.

- Am I using an effective range of teaching and learning strategies?
- Am I meeting the needs of all my pupils?
- Does the current scheme of work meet the Programmes of Study?
- Is the policy for the subject being implemented effectively?
- Is communication between the co-ordinator and teachers effective?

Step 3. Preparing evaluation plans

Once the 'what' has been decided, the 'who' will do it, and 'how' will they go about it are the next steps. Making decisions about the 'who' will be influenced by the purposes of the evaluation. Is it just for personal development, or will the evaluation report be used to influence others about a series of decisions to be taken?

Who should evaluate?

Although this is a part of the co-ordinator's role, it is usually much more effective if several staff are involved as a team. Having a member of the governing body on the team can often be helpful, if the object is to influence decision-making. There can be a more subtle reason for including Governors in an evaluation too. If they are likely to be in a position of making a judgement about the subject in another context, it may be important to help them be as well informed as possible. Being part of an evaluation assists them in having this information and access to understanding and judgements too.

Drawing up the plans

Once the evaluation team has been decided upon, plans can go ahead. These plans need to be drawn up with the members of the evaluation team. These plans should include:

- discussions on the purpose of the evaluation;
- methods of information gathering being used;
- any observation visits the team want to make to particular classes;
- documents to be read and analysed;

- people (pupils, parents, teachers) with whom discussions might take place;
- a timetable for collecting information, analysis and writing;
- ways of reporting results.

Planning resources
It is important to allocate time resources to each part of the plan and leave plenty of time for the analysis and reporting stages. This is often much more time consuming than is imagined – too much information and not enough time to analyse and report it. Other resources are skills, materials, opportunity and access. Time, materials and access are issues to be negotiated in the context in which evaluating is taking place, since they may be outside the evaluator's control.

Reporting the results
Who receives the report will depend on the reasons for the evaluation. On the whole, be very parsimonious with release unless the documentation has been cleared for more open discussion.

Drawing up operational guidelines for an evaluation
The guidelines are mostly commonsense ones, though they can involve some hard work. They are, however, crucial in terms of keeping the trust of staff with whom the work is taking place, and helping to preserve good working relationships so that staff are assured that the curriculum and not their specific work is the subject of evaluation.

- *Be tactful.* Take care to ensure that you observe protocols with individuals.
- *Be explicit.* Talk to people about what you are doing and report on progress. Allow people to make comment about the evaluation.
- *Be correct.* Do not examine files, documents, books or correspondence unless you have clear permission to do so.
- *Be confidential.* Control what you say and how, take responsibility for information in your possession and observe the wishes of others. You will need to be clear whether comments are made 'on' or 'off' the record and make sure people know what responsibilities you have for reporting.

Step 4. Collecting evidence

Wherever possible, information should be collected in several different ways. This helps to provide a variety of viewpoints and can act to check against obvious bias, a process sometimes referred to as triangulation. For example, if a year team had recently been teaching a new theme which they wanted to evaluate in terms of their teaching approaches they might collect pupils' opinions (depending on the age of the pupils), ask a colleague from another year team to join the group to observe teaching (using an agreed observation schedule).

It is important not to forget the value of documentation when evaluations take place. 'Statistics' such as test scores, policy statements, teachers' plans may all have bearing on the information you collect by interviewing or observing teaching. Knowing that a class has 25 per cent of the pupils within Warnock Stages 1–3 will affect the observations made of that class and thus the judgements which result from the observations.

What is acceptable evidence?

Two broad types of information are quantitative and qualitative data. Quantitative methods are based on counting and measuring what is taking place. This is sometimes considered to be 'objective' data and more reliable than qualitative or 'subjective' data. Qualitative methods are based on listening to reports of people's experiences. Thoughts, impressions, values, ideas, policy and principles are vital ingredients in judging the quality of teaching and learning.

Both kinds of data have their uses and neither is better or worse than the other – they simply tell different parts of the story and provide different information drawn from different data. Some methods can combine both, so that a questionnaire, for instance, can be used to collect feedback from pupils on the quality of a topic or theme and provide statistics. Both approaches can lead to a better understanding of what is taking place and it is often helpful to use a combination to achieve a broad picture.

So, acceptable evidence depends on:

- *the questions asked* – if you want different information you must ask different questions;
- *the context* – both how you ask the question, and where; if an interview takes place in the Head's office the answers may be different than if it happens in the staffroom;
- *the methods used* – different methods generate different information.

Clear evidence can be difficult to collect for some issues. For example, 'staff awareness' after an INSET session, can defy sharp definition and no one method alone can give acceptable evidence for (or against) such an idea. In making decisions about the method to be used to collect evidence, it is important to remember the following advice. Any method of evidence collection should:

- be appropriate for the situation being investigated;
- be sensitive to the questions you want to ask;
- be quick to prepare;
- be simple to carry out;
- cost as little as possible in materials and time;
- give data which is straightforward to interpret;
- be able to capture complex processes;
- not require high levels of skill to use;
- be reliable;
- provide strong data, i.e. evidence which can be linked directly to what is being evaluated and can be seen by others to be valid.

Step 5. Carrying out the evaluation

Once all the planning has been done, the action needs to begin. Part of this action involves choosing the correct methods to evaluate. A summary of the pros and cons of the commonest methods is included below to help.

Questionnaires and checklists

These can provide very specific information though they are not usually able to deal with very sensitive issues. They can be difficult to design but easy to administer. They commonly have a poor rate of return, are time-consuming to analyse and suffer from problems of constrained answers.

Classroom observation

This can provide very rich data, be simple and can detail on-going action. It is very time-consuming and can be difficult to construct to give meaningful categories. It can be both sensitive to complex interactions and yet threatening to the participants.

Structured interviews

These can be used with many participants of different types and ages and can capture very in-depth and complex information. They are time-consuming, expensive of people, and can be awkward to analyse. They are good for specific, detailed information, impressions and opinions. They need skill to manage well.

Personal documents and diaries

These can be illuminative and provide novel and unusual perspectives. They are useful (and sometimes contentious) because they provide very subjective information. They are diagnostic of classroom issues and are very useful in triangulation.

Content analysis

This can provide a range of performance indicators against which a co-ordinator can measure progress towards implementing a policy. The analysis of the policy is not sufficient on its own; it provides a framework of questions through which practices can be examined.

Step 6: Using the information to make judgements

Judgements are made against criteria agreed at the outset of the evaluation when drawing up evaluation plans. For most of the evaluation issues co-ordinators will want to explore, the criteria against which judgements are made are left with colleagues. The process of judgement is a difficult and complex one. It relies on drawing together of all the strands of information outlined from the variety of methods and sources above, and making sense for the evaluators out of all the possible conflicts contained therein.

Value arguments

Much of the co-ordinator's role hinges on her work with colleagues in the school. She is every bit the facilitator with them as she would be with the children in class. She needs to start where her colleagues begin, in terms of their experiences in science and technology. She needs to think of how she will structure encounters and learning experiences for her peers – often a much more demanding job than that of organizing learning for children. She must look to forms of active learning and choose approaches from strategies for teaching adults on how to manage their science and technology work. Brenda Barber's case study above illustrates some of these kinds of techniques. The value messages are clear: constructivist approaches are as valuable to the teachers of teachers as they are to the teachers of children.

twelve

Teacher knowledge and teacher education

Introduction

While this chapter is a short summary of some of the many discussions we have already generated, we also take time to visit other issues. For example, we discuss aspects of teacher education and professional development through in-service training. To some extent this arises naturally from the features of classroom work we have described and prompts the question: How can teachers grow in confidence in the work they do? One way forward is to promote that skilled confidence both through initial teacher education (ITE) and through in-service training (INSET). Before we do this, though, we want to revisit a core issue.

Purpose

We hope it has not escaped readers' notice that this book has been premised on a particular theoretical perspective. We have brought constructivism to the fore at every opportunity and have tried to show how it fits with the normal everyday features of classroom science and technology. Not all of our contributors would describe themselves as constructivists, but that seems a moot point – we have taken leave to interpret their work through our own constructivist spectacles. So, for example, having explored some of the principles of constructivism in Chapters 1 and 2, we then discussed how we construct concepts, language and meanings and we rounded this by focusing on a range of language-based activities in Chapter 3. We discussed ways in which we could – pragmatically – plan for this way of working in the school and its classrooms. We needed at this point, too, to refute some of the prevailing opinions which try to discredit child-centred learning. In Chapter 6 we looked at ways in which learning can be organized and our case studies illustrate some excellent practice. We then took a specialist look at two features of science and technology so that, in Chapter 7, we considered the posing and answering of questions and, in Chapter 8, the development of problem-solving skills. At no point can we ignore or take matters of equality for granted and Chapter 9 brought these vital issues into the frame. Chapter 10 considered teacher assessment and Chapter 11 the role of the lynch-pin co-ordinator.

Prevailing moods: back to basics

We have mentioned the ways in which prevailing moods influence the shape and direction of work in school and its seems timely that we should explore some of the issues now. Where to start? Without doubt, one place is with the advice of the National Curriculum Council to the Secretary of State for Education (1993). Here the NCC ask the question:

> Is classroom organisation, planning, teacher knowledge and support adequate to deliver the National Curriculum (at Key Stages 1 and 2)? The short answer to this question is no.

Of course, this is a loaded question – who decides what is adequate, for instance? In the report the NCC consulted and researched widely and have suggested that teachers consider the National Curriculum too complex and overprescriptive and that the collective load of content is leading to curriculum overload and superficial teaching:

> As a consequence depth of learning is being sacrificed in pursuit of breadth and the lack of rigour and challenge is not resulting in the necessary improvement in standards [. . .] At Key Stage 1 teachers are concerned that the scope of content [. . .] is resulting in insufficient time and emphasis being given to the basics of reading, writing, spelling and arithmetic upon which all future learning depends.

Our disagreement with this line of argument is twofold. First, the 'basics' are still seen to consist solely of 'reading', 'writing' and 'arithmetic' without the acknowledgement that science is – and has been for some years – a core subject in the curriculum. It is still not seen to be fundamental, a basic aspect of knowing upon which 'future learning depends'. Clearly, as we write, we think very differently. We believe that the development of logical argument, reasoned discussion, developing rationale, intuition, creative construction, design, an understanding of relationships between changing variables, thought experiments, hypothesis testing, inferring, scrutinizing evidence, making fair tests, closely observing, experimenting, asking 'what if . . . ?', 'If this happens then what . . . ?' and 'Why?' questions are all fundamental and basic to future learning.

The usual response to this is that all the skills and competencies we list here depend themselves on literacy and numeracy and so these are more basic. This is a fairly obvious *non sequitur*, since the development of both numeracy and literacy itself depends on increasing linguistic competence. It might be difficult to learn how to 'do fractions' without being able to read

– unless, that is, one argues that a fraction can be entirely a non-verbal concept. But then the conservation of volume and mass lie at the heart of science and one could make a similar case for these kinds of concepts. No. Scientific concepts are vital to an integrated understanding of the physical world in which we all live and need continually to be emphasized as part of the fundamental core of learning.

So, our main objection to the NCC's general tack is that educators still do not see this to be the case. The reasons remain speculation. Perhaps, in the case of many primary teachers, science is still very new and alien and their feel for the depth and meaning of the subject may still be tenuous and fleeting. Their familiarity with maths and English will be much stronger and so these are seen to be much more fundamental and basic. This is understandable but – in our view – needs to change. And change implies a renewed onslaught on teacher education.

But our second objection is that science and technology provide such wonderful contexts for the development of literacy and numeracy. The case studies here so easily demonstrate that children are keenly motivated to read, write, spell, and count when they have real contexts in which to achieve this. If they read stories, then some of this can be the kind that Jane Eaton uses – 'The Lighthouse Keeper's Lunch', for instance. While not all their reading should be chosen simply on the basis of its 'technical merit', there is no doubt that good science and technology can develop good reading and arithmetic. The same can be said of the two 'historical' case studies in the book: Sue Marran's look at schools in olden days and Rosemary Denman's at old waterwheels and mines. Both provided exciting contexts within which to draw out a wide variety of skills and competencies. At this stage let us open the discussion to involve the general area of teacher education and consider some of the ways forward – given more of the current and prevailing moods.

Teacher knowledge

One of the ways we can look at the different forms of teacher knowledge is to think of two people separated by a ten-year age gap. The first (person A) is 18 years old and entering teacher education straight from school in order to do a degree – a BA (QTS) course (BA with Qualified Teacher Status). The second (person B) is a 28-year-old teacher who has been through the system and now has five or six years experience in the job. There's no doubt that person B is more qualified and experienced than teacher A – and the question is: what are the forms of knowledge that B has that A needs? Some of what A needs, of course, comes from their initial teacher education (ITE) when they do their degree and their teaching practice in schools. Some comes from watching and listening to other teachers as they are working, and some comes from 'learning from experience'. Moreover, there are further inputs as the growing experience of teachers happens through in-service training and professional days. This 'knowledge gap' can be described in six ways:

(i)   Content knowledge.
(ii)   Pedagogic knowledge.
(iii) Strategic knowledge.
(iv)   Professional knowledge.
(v)   Situational knowledge.
(vi)   Personal knowledge.

We deal below with four of these as being the most relevant to our work.

Teachers' content knowledge

This normally means the subject base expertise that teachers have. Since 1974 teaching has been designated an all-graduate profession requiring a degree for entry. And each graduate has to be a graduate of something. Few, though, have been graduates of science (even fewer in technology) and many chose to leave science behind in the middle parts of their secondary education. This clearly creates a problem in terms of teaching. In Key Stage 1 it is not unreasonable to suppose that some children will be operating at Level 4 and a very few at Level 5. As we point out later in this chapter, in order to be able to teach children at these levels and ensure a thorough understanding by the pupils, it is necessary that teachers themselves understand the concepts being explored. One of the major difficulties which teachers without a scientific background have experienced is the lack of confidence which comes from an insecure content base. It is knowing which crucial question to ask next to help the child progress that is one of the essential tools of the primary teacher. Without a firm foundation the teacher may well not know where 'next' is.

In several chapters of the book we have tried to bring to the fore and explain scientific concepts such as energy and sound. We have done this through the framework of what it is children need to know, but have painted a picture which we hope will assist the understanding by readers of concepts which traditionally have proved difficult to understand.

The Open University has addressed this matter in some depth since the national curriculum became statutory, producing some excellent distance-learning materials for teachers. However, as with the youngsters in the classrooms, teachers need to talk and share ideas if they are to deconstruct and reconstruct. The distance learning materials cannot always be successful in these terms.

Teachers' pedagogic knowledge

This covers a wide area. It includes how children learn, how to start and end lessons, and what to do in the bits in between. It includes all those aspects of planning, differentiation, curriculum and assessment tasks that we have discussed in earlier chapters. Each one of these areas needs to have as a foundation, we believe – a set of theories which underpin it. The current trends away from theory, showing an indication that all pedagogic knowledge can be learnt by being a practitioner may have something to offer in value for money terms. However, this begs the question of how people learn. We have made our assumptions about this clear in the book. We are not for a moment saying that if all teachers ever did was teach and had no access to theory they could not discover for themselves ideas very like constructivism. After all, the theory itself designs its own continual reconstruction as people work with it. But this seems to be a monumental waste of time: rather like the curriculum development of the late 1960s when everyone reinvented all the wheels. Our point is this. Teachers acquire pedagogic knowledge by two means – working with children and sharing with other teachers. The sharing with other teachers may not always be at the level of theoretical sharing, but there is no doubt that everyone has their own theories, implicit though they are, that gear the way they approach their teaching. They know how children learn in their class. The theoretical base to pedagogy that is to be found in ITE, and in INSET, through the route of Master's degrees, is respected and sought out by teachers. Teachers want to discuss theories and ideas at a deeper level than is provided by the everyday opportunities of the classroom.

We are in danger in the teaching profession, it seems to us, of becoming de-professionalised. The continual eroding of the idea that theories are important concomitants to ways of working in education is leading to our pedagogic knowledge being devalued. It can now be acquired simply by being in a classroom. It has no importance of its own. We would strongly resist this argument. Time and reflection need to be provided for teachers if pedagogic knowledge is to be assisted to gain its own place of importance. Unlike current trends, we believe it is an essential part of teaching and if it is learnt only from working in classrooms, then classrooms will be the poorer for it. Reconstruction needs to take place in teachers' thinking all the time. Experience will bring some of this about, but teachers need to be exposed to the thoughts and ideas of good thinkers. These may not necessarily be found in the next-door classroom.

Teachers' professional knowledge

This is usually the knowledge that teachers have about their role in the profession. It includes understanding the ethics and morals of teaching – what can, should or could be done and not done with the children under their care of the school, the personal and social education aspects of a school and how it operates. Also, the understanding of the profession in the eyes of society in general – how teachers are perceived by the public is part of this knowledge. This is an area which recently has undergone much change. The eroding of the professional status by the media and the Government, through headlines such as falling standards ('a quarter of children in England and Wales cannot read' is an example) has had a very detrimental effect on the profession.

Teachers' strategic knowledge

This includes the ways of handling pupils – what to do in terms of getting pupils working together, sitting quiet in assembly, organizing themselves around the school, knowing when a pupil needs time to calm down, and so on. It too has a set of theories which underpin the work and are an essential part of the way in which schools run. Teachers' understanding of their place in the school, how the management system operates, how the day-to-day running of the systems and structures work are all part of this strategic knowledge.

What role does all of this knowledge have in teaching science and technology? The first two types of knowledge explored here are self-evident. The work that teachers do in terms of their pedagogic and content knowledge is what gears the curriculum for the school and classroom. Without professional and strategic knowledge, the running of schools would break down. So how do teachers acquire this knowledge? As we have said, experience must play a large part, certainly in professional and strategic knowledge. But what of content and pedagogy? This brings us to our final section, looking at initial teacher education.

Initial teacher education (ITE)

The routes into initial teacher education had remained fairly static until the late 1980s, when articled and licensed-teacher pilot schemes were launched by the Government in an effort to increase the available pool of teachers, in some shortage subjects. The scheme, which consists of largely school-based training also acted as a pilot for such school-based methods of teacher education as the Government is currently proposing. The training lasts for two years, but has been on a small scale (447 entrants in 1991/92). Apart from this route, and part-time BEd courses students have two main routes into the teaching profession:

1. Post-graduate Certificate of Education (PGCE) courses which last for one year.
2. Undergraduate courses (BEd or BA/BSc) which provide qualified teacher status as part of the Bachelor's degree programme – a four-year course.

Undergraduate courses have always been the main route for primary teachers, although it seems that the PGCE route into primary education is increasing. As far as those graduates who undertake a Postgraduate Certificate course are concerned, they may or may not have qualifications in science or technology. However, for those who do not, the opportunity to provide some subject knowledge in these areas is severely limited, due to the laid-down criteria for accreditation of ITE courses in primary education. These criteria ensure that subject knowledge is a part of the training, but only in the subject of graduation and only in an applied sense, as far as education is concerned. That is, students with a BSc would be taught not science but science education, so that they could see how their subject knowledge could be applied in a school setting. The criteria were of course prepared before the 1988 Education Reform Act and as such bear little relevance to the needs of teachers facing the National Curriculum in primary schools.

ITE is undergoing revision in England and Wales at present. The critics of teacher education wish, on the whole to dispense with theory and shift training entirely to the schools so that in effect, all teachers will need to qualify is the relevant practical experience. This major emphasis on greater involvement with schools, means more time being spent in schools by students than ever before and contains an assumption that *only* by teaching children can teachers become good teachers. Inevitably, this leaves even less time for the essential subject knowledge to be learnt and understood. In terms of science this is particularly important. Science is a core subject. Headteachers have a right to expect that newly qualified professionals come with the capability to teach the core subjects to the necessary levels in the National Curriculum. Recent pronouncements (Blatch, 1993) at the North of England Education Conference suggest however, that moves may be afoot to alter the need for all teachers to teach science. If the restructuring is to take place as described, the teachers at Key Stage 1 (5–7) would need no degree, and the curriculum in these areas would be much reduced compared to its present structure, to allow more time for reading, spelling, writing and arithmetic. This would remove much of the need for teachers to have specialist knowledge. In Key Stage 2, teaching of subjects would take place predominantly by specialist teachers, rather like the secondary model, so again the danger that teachers may not have the subject knowledge would be removed. This is a rather interesting solution to the problem of teacher knowledge and leaves hanging in the air the place of the core subjects. Either science is a core subject or it is not. If it is, it must continue to be taught at Key Stage 1, and the debate about teacher subject knowledge is firmly back on the agenda.

What is the difficulty about teacher knowledge, particularly of science in Key Stages 1 and 2? In Key Stage 1, for example, the National Curriculum requires that teachers understand that:

> 'size and direction of the resultant force on an object affects its movement, for instance by knowing how forces act on a free fall parachutist at different stages in his descent. (AT3, Level 5.)'

Since a small minority of children score at Level 4 in science SATs at Key Stage 1, all teachers teaching at Key Stage 1 must understand up to at least Level 5. Similarly, this is the case for Key Stage 2, although at the time of writing there was no information about the levels of pupil achievement at the end of Key Stage 2. However, the same argument must follow. Teachers need to understand for themselves science at Level 6 or beyond. This requires for example that teachers understand:

> 'the relationship between an applied force, the area over which it acts and the resulting pressure, in for instance being able to work out the pressure in pascals of objects on a flat surface, or using the concept of pressure to explain how a car braking system works. (AT4, Level 6.)'

Both these examples pose an immediate problem. Research shows that many science graduates are unable to differentiate accurately between force and pressure. For example, understanding that pressure is a scaler quantity while force is a vector. So even if graduate scientists are employed at Key Stage 2 to teach science as a specialist subject, there is no guarantee that they will necessarily understand science needed for Level 6. The current arrangements in PGCE courses allow no time or structure in which teachers' *subject* knowledge in science can be enhanced. Would the supervised practical experience model of more time in schools work better then? Given the state of the art of science subject knowledge amongst the qualified teachers working in schools, it seems unlikely that these teachers will themselves have the level of understanding necessary. A case of the lame leading the blind up a cul-de-sac.

What of undergraduate entrants then? Certainly time is less of a constraint here and teaching of subjects takes place within their degree programme. Which subjects though? Most subject studies demand that students have an A-level in the subject before commencing the work. If one were to teach only science to those students arriving with A-level, then not all teachers would be able to teach science. It should be possible however, to design a course in which students had to take a compulsory second subject such as science. Certainly this is possible. The criteria for teacher education were set by the Council for the Accreditation of Teacher Education (CATE) which accredited courses. One of the criteria was that any subjects taught within such courses had to have content which was at degree level. What it is difficult to do, is to take students with a range of backgrounds in science – many of whom have not studied science for A-level, and teach them, upon their arrival on an undergraduate course at degree level immediately. They need access materials and time to gain confidence and understanding in the concepts, which for many, put them off at GCSE. Courses which offer such arrangements do exist. One such course, in our own institution, the BA with Qualified Teacher Status (QTS) offered students a main subject, with the time for the second subjects split equally between two compulsory subjects – maths and science. In their first year, they were taught at a foundation level, (pre-degree) to provide the basis for further conceptual development. In their second year, students could elect to do either science or maths, or both at degree level. In fact, over 75 per cent of students chose to do both subjects. This sounds like a success story. It has all the elements of what the National Curriculum needs in terms of teachers' own subject knowledge in science. But there is a sting in the tail. The course was refused accreditation by CATE because the foundation science was not at degree level. A Catch 22 situation! The teachers need to enhance their own understandings of science. In keeping with our own, and recognized theories of learning, our Institute began where the learner was – not at degree level in science, in order to enhance subject knowledge. But this was not of sufficient status to be included in a degree course.

The students themselves would disagree with the Government's stance. In an evaluation of the course (Pippola, 1992) when asked if the course had met their personal needs in science, 73 per cent of students felt that they had gained from the course in terms of broadening their scientific knowledge and this had increased their interest and understanding of science. They felt that 'topics that previously baffled me had been thoroughly explained in a non-threatening way'. Those with an already existing A-level scientific background felt that it had been built upon and extended. So the students appreciate the needs they have and felt the arrangements went some way to meeting them. Only the Government's advisers were in doubt about the level of the work.

Is mentoring the answer?

Given that the amount of time in schools is to increase for those in teacher education, can the problem of teacher subject knowledge be solved? There may be some lessons to be learnt from the concept of mentor teaching as it is used in the articled teacher scheme. One such scheme, between the West Sussex Institute of Higher Education, King Alfred College, Winchester, and the Hampshire, West Sussex and Isle of Wight LEAs has been reported by Hill *et al.* (1992). In their concept of mentoring, the mentor takes prominence for the development of the articled teacher and the college and school-based work is jointly planned by college tutor and mentor from the school. Mentors are responsible for supporting the articled teacher in the classroom and the college tutor for assisting the articled teacher to become a competent and reflective practitioner by the end of the training period of two years.

So what is being taught? Hill *et al.* quote Wharfe (1991) in terms of developing competencies of the new teacher:

[competence] involves not just the acquisition of basic . . . classroom management skills, it also requires progressive thinking about the teaching and learning processes, about relationships about theory and practice and about the need to acquire self-appraisal skills the goal of which is continual professional enhancement.

We would not disagree with any of the above – except that in our terms it does not go far enough. Thinking progressively about teaching and learning processes implies that there is an understanding of how to develop these. In the absence of subject knowledge in which the teacher is secure and feels confident, the thinking is unlikely to be progressive.

So what is expected of mentors by the consortium?

Hill *et al.* (1992) have a list of competencies which they have developed in conjunction with their mentors. The general areas include:

- establishing a supportive supervisory relationship with the articled teacher;
- applying counselling skills necessary to become an effective helper;
- maintaining an assessment profile with the new teacher;
- inform colleagues in school about the programme;
- support the development of effective classroom practice;
- identify curriculum specialisms.

It is in the last two of the list (our ordering) that there are some areas that may be helpful. Hill *et al.* define mentor competencies in terms of *classroom practice* to include developing a sound knowledge of the curriculum (pedagogy) and monitoring and assessing children's progress (assessment). *Curriculum specialisms* include planning and supporting specialist contributions to assist in the provision of a broad school experience (content). The latter statement could mean ensuring that new teachers understand areas of the curriculum other than their own. Certainly there is nothing clear and sharp in terms of ensuring that mentors have a responsibility for teaching the mentee content knowledge. This may be well and good if the new teacher has a specialist degree. But our concern is with content knowledge for those who do not. Can the mentor system really support them if the amount of time in schools is to increase dramatically?

Our argument would be no. We can pose models for it to happen. For example, a college tutor could teach in the school for two days a week, releasing the class teacher to teach in the college. After the children had left, the new teachers in the school could then be taught the content knowledge by the college tutor, *in situ*, based around the teaching that the students had undertaken with children. This is possible, but not cost effective, if it means that only three or four students will attend for any one college tutor. Similarly, it means that all students will have to be in the school on the same day, which is not an arrangement which takes place at present.

The future

So what of the future for science and technology in the primary school? As our earlier chapters indicate, there are huge amounts of good practice already. Children do learn and teachers do have conceptual understanding. But with changes in the system can this be sustained? We would argue that it is time to reconstruct. Science and technology education have made great strides in the last five years in primary schools and teachers' content knowledge and pedagogy has increased. But partnership is still needed. A partnership that places true worth on the place of theories such as constructivism and uses it to increase teacher and pupil expertise.

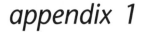

appendix 1

Science policy statement for Spinfield County Combined School

Reasons for the policy

This policy outlines the school rationale for primary science taking into account the demands of the National Curriculum, leading to a shared understanding of what good primary science practice means. It sets out to ensure that every child has the opportunity to engage in scientific activities and thinking, how this will be achieved, and the variety of ways in which this can be best implemented, given the range of abilities and ages of the children.

- It clarifies the way in which we are to deliver our science curriculum.
- It sets out the ways in which a balanced programme of science can be achieved over the course of a child's school life, giving the main aims and objectives.
- It indicates ways in which progress and continuity can be ensured and at the same time meets the requirements of the National Curriculum.
- It provides a mechanism for effective evaluation, recording and review.

How the policy was developed

The school science policy was developed by whole staff discussion, classroom observation, advice and support from the Buckinghamshire Science Advisory Service, consultation between the Headteacher and science co-ordinator and reference to a variety of documents.

What is meant by science in the primary school?

Science means exploiting, discovering and investigating the world around them to help them make sense of it. It should seek to develop the process of scientific thinking and the use of a variety of scientific methods.

(a) Beginning in infant classes, children should grow accustomed to the scientific processes of observing, measuring, describing, investigating, predicting, experimenting and explaining. They should use their science in solving technological problems.

(b) At the same time, children's understanding of some of the central concepts of science should progressively deepen. Teachers need to be clear about which concepts are to be used or developed in particular pieces of work, and to plan their work accordingly.

(c) Primary science should include study of living things and their interactions with their environment; of materials and their characteristics; of energy and materials; of forces and their effects.

(d) Wherever possible the content should be related to the experience of the children. Much of the work should arise from their spontaneous interests and curiosity.

The golden rule

'Why?' said the Dodo. 'The best way to explain it is to do it.'

Lewis Carroll

The one absolute characteristic of good science is that it involves children doing things themselves. This is not to say that there is no place for the demonstration by the teacher, for children consulting books, or even for the occasional straightforward imparting of knowledge by the teacher.

Quote from National Curriculum *Non-statutory Guidance for Science*

Good science education can be recognized when children are involved in:

• practical investigations which capitalize on their own interests, and from which they derive valid and interesting conclusions;
• gaining scientific knowledge;
• cooperating with the teacher and other children in planning, decision-making, investigating and communicating results;
• developing the skills of observing, classifying, recording, making and testing hypotheses, designing experiments and drawing from evidence;
• reflecting on outcomes and the strategies which have led to them, leading to prediction and further planning;
• taking responsibility for an investigation when the outcome is not obvious;
• responding to stimulus provided by the teacher, in ways which show imaginative thinking and that the intellectual demand and pace of work is appropriate for them;
• relating their work to everyday experience;
• enjoying themselves and showing curiosity, perseverance, self-discipline and ingenuity.

We see the role of the teacher as one of structuring and planning a balanced programme of scientific activity; encouraging, guiding and facilitating the scientific process. The teacher's primary function is not one of giving answers but of enabling children to find out for themselves.

The role of the child is that of the primary agent in the learning process. The emphasis is that of developing independent learners.

Aims

1. To equip children for life in a society which will become increasingly dominated by science.
2. To enable children to have the ability to acquire appropriate scientific knowledge, skills and attitudes.

3. To help children to develop a questioning approach that will stimulate curiosity about the natural and man-made world and necessitate investigation in order to formulate generalizations or conclusions.
4. To develop in children an understanding of and an ability to use the scientific process.
5. To enable children to hypothesize about their investigations and to develop the concept of a fair test.
6. To help children to interpret findings critically and communicate them to others.
7. To encourage children to derive enjoyment and satisfaction from scientific activities and thereby develop a positive attitude towards this area of the curriculum.

Our school approach for the teaching of science

We have developed a broad-based and balanced set of topics, each having cross-curricular links, which lend themselves to the teaching of science in a thematic way, making the scientific experiences as relevant as possible and making provision for the varying ability range.

Any scientific processes and skills not accommodated by the topic approach will be taught separately.

Teachers should be aware that they need to provide a positive image of science to both girls and boys. Enough time should be devoted to science-based activities so that children have the opportunity to acquire a thorough understanding of the programme of study. This will be built into each teacher's own timetable.

Attitudes

The attitudes which science should foster in children:

- *Curiosity*
  Showing an interest in new or unusual things; noticing detail; using questions to find out about causes and relationships.
- *Respect for evidence*
  Being prepared to accept evidence even when it conflicts with own predictions.
- *Willingness to tolerate uncertainty*
  Understanding that we do not always know the answers; nor can we always find certain solutions.
- *Critical reflection*
  Being prepared to evaluate one's work or ideas in order to improve them.
- *Perseverance*
  Not giving up when the goal is difficult or the effort required is considerable.
- *Creativity and inventiveness*
  Producing ideas which are from oneself; thinking out own solutions and responding to challenges oneself.
- *Open-mindedness*
  Being prepared to listen to other points of view and accepting new ideas which are convincing.
- *Sensitivity to the living and non-living environment*
  Developing a sense of wonder and respect for living things, and a sense of responsibility towards the whole environment.
- *Cooperation with others*
  Being aware of the needs of others and being prepared to fit in with, or negotiate differences through discussion.

appendix 2

An introduction to National Curriculum technology, Paper I

'Technology' comprises five areas organised into two groups:

Design and technology capability:
1. Home economics
2. Craft/design technology
3. Art and design
Information technology capability:
4. Business and economic awareness
5. Information technology

This paper will deal only with the design and technology capability. Paper II deals with the information technology capability.

There are four Attainment Targets for technology:

AT1 Identifying needs and opportunity
AT2 Generating a design proposal
AT3 Planning and making
AT4 Evaluating what has been done

During each Key Stage each child should design and make:

• artefact (objects made by people)
• system (set of objects or activities which together perform a task)
• environment (surroundings made or developed by people)

Pupils should sometimes work individually, sometimes in groups. At each Key Stage pupils should be given opportunities to work with a range of materials including textiles, graphic media (such as paint, paper, photographs), construction materials (such as clay, wood, plastic, metal and food).

Pupils' work may develop in the order:

identify needs – design – plan and make – evaluate

For example, if you were working on the topic 'Food', you might be thinking about what a child eats at school, how the food arrives, i.e. lunch box food.

To fulfil the technology part of the National Curriculum in this topic and produce an artefact you could:

1. Identify need: We need lunch at school to keep us healthy and fit for lessons. We need to bring it safely from home.
2. Design: We need a container to carry our food. We need to work out what types of food we will eat and what sort of container it will be best to carry them in.
3. Plan and make: A lunch box and finger food – real or imitation.
4. Evaluate: Did the box protect the food adequately? Did it keep it hot/cold? Did the food taste good? Was it nutritious? Did it travel well? Was it fiddly to eat? Was it too expensive? Was it attractive?

In the above example, each of the five areas of technology could have been addressed, i.e.

1. *Home economics*: Work on balanced meals, making attractive presentation, preparing food.
2. *Design and technology*: Making the box, possibly from a variety of materials with different internal sections.
3. *Art and design technology*: Decorating the outside of the box, making models of the food for permanent display.
4. *Business and economic awareness*: Costing the food, running a survey to see how much is usually spent on the contents of a lunch box, balancing budgets, selling recipe booklet.
5. *Information technology*: Word-processing and designing a recipe booklet on *Finger Food* for sale to pupils.

It often helps when planning the technology aspect of your curriculum to use a 'technology web' like the one below.

Note: During their work on one project, pupils may visit several levels of the Attainment Targets, some more than once as technology is not such a hierarchical subject as, say, mathematics.

For more information on how to approach a topic with technology in mind, staff are recommended to look at the Programmes of Study for Key Stage 2 (Levels 2–5) and Programmes of Study for Key Stage 3 (Levels 3–7) in the National Curriculum technology folder.

Foxes Piece Middle School

The National Curriculum states that:

Pupils should be able to use Information Technology to:

- communicate and handle information;
- design, develop, explore and evaluate models of real or imaginary situations;
- measure and control physical variables and movement.

They should be able to make informed judgements about the application and importance of IT and its effect on the quality of life.

The study of information technology (IT) should take place as a cross-curricular activity, as it naturally develops from needs in many curriculum areas, e.g. English and science.

IT should not be solely the province of one specialist in the school, although one member of staff should be available to give advice on hardware and software problems. All staff should have 'hands on' experience of their programs before using them with their pupils. Emphasis needs to be placed on the choosing of suitable software and hardware for the task in hand and staff's familiarity with it.

In order to comply with National Curriculum requirements, software covering the following five areas will be necessary:

1. *Communicating*: The passage of ideas, thoughts and messages.
   Software: Word-processors, e.g. CAXTON, PENDOWN.
   Graphics packages: For example PAINT SPA/PICTURE CRAFT.
2. *Data handling*: Collecting data, interrogating, adding to and creating a database.
   Software: OURFACTS, GRASS, DATASHOW.
3. *Simulations and modelling*
   The use of computers to investigate 'real life' events.
   Software: DRAGONWORLD, SLICK, GRASSHOPPER, DATASUIT.
4. *Measurement and control*
   Demonstrating how computers can control peripheral equipment, e.g. buggies, robots and sensors.
   Software: CARGO, LOGO.
5. *Applications*
   To show how computers are involved in our everyday lives.
   Software: BARCLAYS SCHOOL BANK.

Attention should be given to classroom organization necessary to ensure that all pupils gain equal access to the computer(s) and are gainfully occupied when not at the keyboard.

Note: More time should be allowed for completing activities when the pupils are unfamiliar with a computer keyboard than when they have had more experience.

Records should be kept of individual pupils' progress through each Attainment Target level on the appropriate record sheet. It may also be helpful to keep print-outs and examples of written work, e.g. from newspapers or adventure game projects. In some cases, it may be more useful to take photographs, e.g. when working with a turtle or buggy.

Health and safety

Staff should be aware that those suffering from epilepsy may be at risk when close to a working monitor. Such people should either sit as far back as possible from the screen or delegate a friend to do the 'hands on' part of an IT task. All IT equipment should be maintained so as to ensure pupil and staff safety.

The study of IT is not necessarily a linear experience and as such it may be seen as inappropriate to assign to a particular year one particular IT skill or capability. Rather, staff should endeavour to ensure that pupils address the areas outlined in the attached Programmes of Study, during their normal lessons as and when appropriate. For example:

1. If children are working on collecting information to make graphs in maths lessons – such data could be put on a computerized database and graphs provided by the computer.
2. If there is a school outing being planned, children could use a word-processor to plan and print related correspondence, then save the letters for use in future years.

INSET courses might initially be seen as helpful to staff in the familiarization with hardware and software together with internally run 'twilight' courses after school.

appendix 3

Information technology policy statement at Rokesly Infants School

Nursery

The teacher should develop the pupils' awareness of everyday products – their control and function and where their energy comes from, etc. For example,

A light switch
Control: An on/off switch or dimmer switch
Function: To change the lighting in a room
Energy: Electricity

It is very important, from this early age, to stress the importance of *safety* as often as possible, when talking about electricity. For example, *never* put your fingers in a plug socket. Only use electrical appliances when an adult is present.

Reception

Pupils should:

- talk about and watch how various appliances are used, e.g. tape recorders, TV/video, cooker, vehicles, telephones, kettles;
- learn how to use the tape recorder on/off, volume and play/stop controls and the controls of other simple everyday items;
- use the typewriter to familiarize themselves with the layout and basic functions (e.g. space bar and return key) on a QWERTY keyboard;
- know that information can be held in a variety of forms, e.g. words, numbers, pictures, sounds;
- become familiar with the different parts of a computer and what their different functions are;
- work on the computer.

Year 1 pupils

Pupils should:

- be re-familiarized with the computer;
- know that information can be stored, modified and retrieved in a variety of ways:
  - words on a tape recorder/sound track/computer
  - pictures on film (still and moving)/computer
  - sounds on a tape recorder
  - numbers on calculators/computers
- organize and present ideas using information technology, e.g. create a piece of work on the computer using symbols, words or pictures, so that it can be retrieved later;
- progressively learn to use the BBC Fairy Tales programme:
  - for descriptive writing about the pictures they choose
  - to write a story, then illustrate it
  - to border their own work
  - to begin to plan their own work before they put it on the computer, e.g. where the writing/pictures/borders, etc. will go;
- learn to print their own work on the computer;
- be introduced to the FOLIO program;
- begin to draft and amend their work with teacher support, using the FOLIO program;
- learn to use the mouse on the Apple Macintosh computer. (There are various programs that will help a child learn mouse control, e.g. ALBERT'S HOUSE, MACPAINT, SUPERPAINT and MOUSE PRACTICE.)

Year 2 pupils

Pupils should:

- be re-familiarized with the mouse;
- be introduced to the Macwrite programme;
- become more independent in their use of the computer by learning to:
  - store and retrieve their work
  - draft and amend their work on the computer
  - print their work themselves;
- use the computers for factual documentation;
- describe their use of information technology and compare it with other methods, e.g. explain the differences in procedure between using a programmable toy and giving verbal instructions to another pupil;
- have some experience of using simple databases.

Computers at Rokesly Infants School

At present there are seven computers at Rokesly – three Apple Macintosh computers with printers and four BBC computers with printers.

We also have a Roamer Turtle which can be independently programmed or used in conjunction with the BBC. The Roamer Turtle is used in Year 2 classrooms.

Distribution of computers in school

During the majority of the year, the Apple Macintosh Computers are based in Year 2 classrooms and the BBC Computers are used in Year 1 and Reception classrooms. However, during the year, there are some changes to the distributions of computers in school.

The Roamer Turtle can be used in conjunction with a BBC computer in Year 2 classes. It is up to the individual teachers to organize an exchange of a Year 1 BBC computer with a Year 2 Apple Macintosh computer. The exchange is for the maximum duration of half a term. This not only enables the Year 2 classes to use the Roamer Turtle in conjunction with the BBC, but also gives the Year 1 pupils an opportunity to learn to use the mouse on the Apple Macintosh computer.

Computers in the classroom

There are various issues that arise from having computers in the classroom:

1. *How to introduce the computer or any new program or system on the computer*
   When there is only one adult working in the classroom, the best method to do this is the 'cascade' method. The teacher will show the new program etc. to a few groups of two children. These children will then show the next children, and so on. This method maximizes the use of teacher time and allows the children to consolidate what they have learned and to communicate this information to others in the classroom.
2. *Groups working on the computer*
   Children should work either individually or with a partner on the computer. Groups larger than this cannot effectively involve all the children in the work under progress.

   Pairs working on the computer may be of mixed or similar ability levels. However, when mixed-ability pairs are working on the computer, the groups need to be supervised more to make sure that the more able child does not dominate the situation. Similarly, with mixed-gender groups it is important to ensure that both children have equal opportunity to work on the computer. Therefore, there should be agreed classroom rules for working in pairs on the computer to ensure that both individuals have equal access. When the work is finished both children should receive a copy of their work.
3. *Records*
   It is important for the teacher to keep a record of which children have used the computer even if the children record for themselves who has worked on the computer.
4. *Children's guide*
   To help the children when they are working on the computer, the children could build up a children's guide, e.g. little posters to help them remember the various functions of different keys could be displayed in the class computer area or made into a computer users' manual for children.

Programs available on the BBC computer

FOLIO: a word-processing program
FAIRY TALES: has a picture bank to create your own illustrations and can also add text

Programs available on the Apple Macintosh computer

MACWRITE: a word-processing program
MACPAINT: a graphics program
SUPERPAINT: more complicated graphics
ALBERT'S HOUSE: games around a house, mouse control and use of prepositions

BANNERMANIA: to create very large banners

KIDPIX: a very good graphics program for children

KIDS MATHS FOLDER: maths games such as counting, +, −, ordinal numbers, more/less, capacity games, etc.

MOUSE PRACTICE: mouse practice

NUMBER MAZE: complete the maze using +/−, multiplication and division problems at different levels that can be set

READING MAZE: complete the maze using progressively harder reading skills

THE PRINT SHOP: graphics program for letterheads, signs, greetings cards and banners

XPLORATORIUM: this folder contains a lot of different programs, mainly

MY DATA – a simple database

MACDOODLE – graphics

BROKEN CALCULATOR – work out problems with numbers missing

BROKEN TEXT – work out the text from word shape and guessing groups of letters

appendix 4

Science equipment

Much of this should be available in each classroom. Only those marked with*
will be needed infrequently. Again, this is a baseline list.

For measurement

Thermometers

Scales

Weights – hanging and placing

Force meters

Stop watch

Trundle wheel

Metre and half-metre rules

For observing

Bioviewers or microscope

Magnifying lenses

Concave, convex and plane mirrors*

Prism*

Candles and nightlights for heating

Sand trays for placing nightlights in

Petri dishes

Plastic beakers

Plastic funnels

Pond net*

Syringes

For magnetic and electrical work

Bulb holders*

Bulbs*

Batteries*

Battery holders*

Crocodile clips and leads*

Magnets*

Compass*

Iron filings*

Theme plan, Olney Middle School

Title: —————————
Date: ————————— Duration: —————————
Age Group: ——————— Key Stage: —————
Teachers: ——————— Classes: —————————

National Curriculum Attainment Targets Accessed

English
1. Speaking/Listening
2. Reading
3. Writing
4. Spelling
5. Handwriting

Science
1. Scientific Investigation
2. Life and Living Processes
3. Materials and Properties
4. Physical Processes

Maths
1. Using and Applying Maths
2. Number
3. Algebra
4. Shape and Space
5. Handling Data

Technology
1. Identifying a Need
2. Generating a Design
3. Planning and Making
4. Evaluating
5. I.T.

History
1. Knowledge/Understanding
2. Interpretations
3. Historical Sources
   Core Study Unit

Geography
1. Geographical Skills
2. Knowledge of Places
3. Physical
4. Human
5. Environmental
   Locality/Region/Country

Music

P.E.

Art

Modern Language

KEY SKILLS REFERENCE

1. Following Instructions
2. Planning and Organizing
3. Investigating
4. Problem Solving
5. Using Trial and Improvement
6. Modelling
7. Questioning
8. Hypothesizing
9. Predicting
10. Developing Fair Tests
11. Controlling Variables
12. Quantifying Variables
13. Observing
14. Measuring
15. Classifying
16. Recording

17. Note Taking
18. Considering Safety
19. Interpreting Data
20. Analysing
21. Making Artefacts etc.
22. Interacting
23. Collaborating
24. Decision Making
25. Communicating Findings
26. Summarizing
27. Empathizing
28. Detecting Bias
29. Sequencing
30. Working Independently
31. Expressing a Viewpoint
32. Evaluating

ORGANIZATION/DELIVERY

A. Whole Class Activity
B. Individual Work

C. Group Collaboration

CROSS-CURRICULAR DIMENSIONS

Citizenship

Health Education

Environmental Education

Multicultural Education

Equal Opportunities

Personal and Social Education

ENGLISH

Tasks	A.T.	Key Skills	Organization

Differentiated Activities	Special Needs Provision

Assessment Opportunities	Evidence Kept

Ousedale Liaison Group Assessment Sheet

AT	1				2						3						4					5					6				
	A	B	C	D	A	B	C	D	E	F	A	B	C	D	E	F	A	B	C	D	E	A	B	C	D	E	A	B	C	D	E
1 Speaking and listening			▓					▓						▓																▓
2 Reading																				▓										
3 Writing		▓	▓	▓				▓						▓																
4 Spelling		▓	▓	▓				▓					▓	▓			▓	▓												
Presentation																								▓	▓					
5 Handwriting		▓	▓			▓	▓	▓				▓	▓	▓			▓	▓												

SCIENCE

Tasks   A.T.   Key Skills   Organization

Differentiated Activities   Special Needs Provision

Assessment Opportunities   Evidence Kept

Ousedale Liaison Group Assessment Sheet

MATHEMATICS

Tasks	A.T.	Key Skills	Organization

Differentiated Activities	Special Needs Provision

Assessment Opportunities	Evidence Kept

Ousedale Liaison Group Assessment Sheet

TECHNOLOGY

Tasks	A.T.	Key Skills	Organization

Differentiated Activities	Special Needs Provision

Assessment Opportunities	Evidence Kept

Ousedale Liaison Group Assessment Sheet

AT	1		2			3					4						5					6					
	A	B	A	B	C	A	B	C	D	E	A	B	C	D	E	F	A	B	C	D	E	A	B	C	D	E	F
1 Identifying needs and opportunities																											
2 Generating a design																											
3 Planning and making																											
4 Evaluating																											
5 Information technology																											

HISTORY

Tasks   A.T.   Key Skills   Organization

Differentiated Activities   Special Needs Provision

Assessment Opportunities   Evidence Kept

Ousedale Liaison Group Assessment Sheet

GEOGRAPHY

Tasks	A.T.	Key Skills	Organization

Differentiated Activities	Special Needs Provision

Assessment Opportunities	Evidence Kept

Ousedale Liaison Group Assessment Sheet

MUSIC

Tasks	A.T.	Key Skills	Organization

Differentiated Activities	Special Needs Provision

Assessment Opportunities	Evidence Kept

Ousedale Liaison Group Assessment Sheet

PHYSICAL EDUCATION

Tasks	A.T.	Key Skills	Organization

Differentiated Activities	Special Needs Provision

Assessment Opportunities	Evidence Kept

Ousedale Liaison Group Assessment Sheet

ART

Tasks	A.T.	Key Skills	Organization

Differentiated Activities	Special Needs Provision

Assessment Opportunities	Evidence Kept

Ousedale Liaison Group Assessment Sheet

MODERN LANGUAGE

Tasks	A.T.	Key Skills	Organization

Differentiated Activities	Special Needs Provision

Assessment Opportunities	Evidence Kept

Ousedale Liaison Group Assessment Sheet

RESOURCES

TEACHERS' REFERENCES

MATERIALS

VISITS

SPEAKERS

CLASSROOM SUPPORT

TOPIC COLLECTIONS

MUSEUM COLLECTIONS

OTHER RESOURCES

EVALUATION

(work completed from theme plan highlighted on planning pages)

References

Adey, P., Bliss, J., Head, J. and Shayer, M. (eds) (1989) *Adolescent Development and School Science*. London: Falmer Press.

Alexander, R. (1991) *Primary Education in Leeds*. Mimeograph, University of Leeds.

Alexander, R., Rose, J. and Woodhead, C. (1992) *Curriculum Organisation and Classroom Practice in Primary Schools*. London: Department of Education and Science.

Asoko, H., Leach, J. and Scott, P. (1993) Learning science. In Hull, R. (ed.) *ASE Secondary Science Teachers' Handbook*. Hemel Hempstead: Simon and Schuster.

Barber, B. and Michell, M. (1986) *Better Science: Building Primary–Secondary Links*. London and Hatfield: Heinemann/Association for Science Education.

Barnes, D. (1976) *From Communication to Curriculum*. London: Penguin Books.

Beat, K. (1991) Design it, build it, use it: girls and construction kits. In Browne, N. (ed.) *Science and Technology in the Early Years*. Milton Keynes: Open University Press.

Bell, B. (1992) *Questions and Responses. A Teacher's Pack*. Wellington, New Zealand: Department of Education.

Bell, D. (1992) *Coordinating Science in the Primary School: A Role Model*. EriE Special Issue on Primary Science.

Bell, D. (1993) The role of the Science Coordinator. In Sherington, R. (ed.) *Science Teacher's Handbook*. Hemel Hempstead: Simon and Schuster Education with Association for Science Education.

Bentley, D. and Watts, D.M. (1989) *Learning and Teaching in School Science: Practical Alternatives*. Milton Keynes: Open University Press.

Bentley, D. and Watts, D.M. (1992) *Communicating in School Science: Groups, Tasks and Problem Solving 5–16*. London: Falmer Press.

Biggs, J.C. and Collis, K.F. (1982) *Evaluating the Quality of Learning. The SOLO Taxonomy*. London: Academic Press.

Blatch, B. (1993) Address to the *North of England Education Conference*. Blackpool, January.

Bloom, B.S. (ed.) (1956) *Taxonomy of Educational Objectives*. London: Longman.

Bonnet, M. (1988) *Topic and Thematic Work in the Primary and Middle Years*. In Connor, C. (ed.) Cambridge: Cambridge Institute of Education.

Brandes, D. and Ginnis, P. (1986) *A Guide to Student-centred Learning*. Oxford: Basil Blackwell.

Brighton Women and Science Group (1980) *Alice Through the Microscope.* London: Virago Press.

Browne, N. (1991) *Science and Technology in the Early Years.* Milton Keynes: Open University Press.

Bruner, J. (1966a) *Language and Learning.* London: Pelican.

Bruner, J. (1966b) *Studies in Cognitive Growth.* New York: Wiley.

Budgett-Meakin, C. (1992) *Make the Future Work. Appropriate Technology: A Teacher's Guide.* London: Longman.

Chomsky, N. (1985) In Wells, G. and Nicholls, J. (eds) *Language and Learning – An Interactional Perspective.* London: Falmer Press.

Copeland, I.C. (1992) Patterns of girls' and boys' attainment in the first SATs. *Education Today*, 42(4), 38–42.

Cosgrove, M. and Schaverien, L. (1992) The child as technologist. Paper presented to the *Annual Conference of the Australasian Science Education Research Association, University of Waikato, New Zealand, July 1992.*

Cosgrove, M., Osborne, R. and Carr, M. (1985) Using practical and technological problems to promote conceptual change. In Duit, R. (ed.) *Aspects of Understanding Electricity, Proceedings of an International Workshop, Kiel, Institut für die Pädagogik der Naturwissenschaften.*

Croner's Manual for Heads of Science (1993) London: Croner.

Crossman, M. (1987) Teachers' interactions with boys and girls in science lessons. In Kelly, A. (ed.) *Science for Girls?* Milton Keynes: Open University Press.

Cummins, P. (1984) In *Language and Education*, (1989) 3(2), 109–30.

Davies, J. and Brember, I. (1991) The effects of gender and attendance period on children's adjustment to nursery classes. *British Education Research Journal*, 17(1), 73–82.

Department of Education and Science (1967) *Children and their Primary Schools* (The Plowden Report). London: HMSO, Central Advisory Council for Education (England).

DES (1977) *Education in Schools: A Consultative Document.* London: HMSO.

Department of Education and Science (1989) *Discipline in Schools* (The Elton Report). London: HMSO.

Department of Education and Science (1991) *Statutory Orders for the Teaching of Science.* HMSO: London.

Donaldson, M. (1978) *Children's Minds.* London: Fontana.

Driver, R. (1981) *Children's Ideas in Science.* Open University Press: Milton Keynes.

Driver, R. (1984) A review of research into children's thinking and learning in science. In Bell, B., Watts, D.M. and Ellington, K. (eds) *Learning and Doing in School Scene: The Proceedings of a Conference.* London: Secondary Science Curriculum Review.

Driver, R. (1985) *Pupils as Scientist?* Milton Keynes: Open University Press.

Driver, R. (1989) Changing conceptions. In Adey, P., Bliss, J., Head, J. and Shayer, M. (eds) *Adolescent Development and School Science.* London: Falmer Press.

Elstgeest, J. (1985) The right question at the right time. In Harlem, W. (ed.) *Taking the Plunge.* London: Heinemann.

Fisher, R. (1987) *Problem Solving in Primary Schools.* Oxford: Basil Blackwell.

Floyd, A. (1976) *Cognitive Styles.* Open University Course Unit: *Personality and Learning.* Milton Keynes: Open University Educational Enterprises.

Floyd, W.D. (1966) *The Language of the Classroom.* Columbia University, NY: Teachers' College Press.

French, J. and French, P. (1984) Gender imbalance in primary classrooms. *Educational Research*, 26(2), 127–36.

Galton, M., Simon, B. and Croll, P. (1980) *Inside the Primary Classroom*. London: Routledge, Kegan and Paul.

Gilbert, J.K. and Watts, D.M. (1983) Concepts, misconceptions and alternative conceptions: changing perspectives in science education. *Studies in Science Education*, 10, 61–98.

Goddard Spear, M. (1989) Differences between the written work of boys and girls. *British Journal of Educational Research*, 15(3), 223–41.

Gollitt, V. (1993) Energy at Kingswood House School. In Edwards, P., Watts, D.M. and West, A. *Making the Difference: Environmental Problem Solving in School Science and Technology*. Godalming: World Wide Fund for Nature UK.

Hammersley, M. (1990) An evaluation of two studies of gender imbalance in primary classrooms. *British Journal of Educational Research*, 16(2), 125–43.

Harlen, W. (1993) Children's learning in science. In Sherrington, R. (ed.) *ASE Primary Science Teachers' Handbook*. Hemel Hempstead: Simon and Schuster.

Hill, A., Jennings, M. and Madgewick, B. (1992) Initiating a mentorship training programme. In Wilkin, M. (ed.) *Mentoring in Schools*. London: Kogan Page.

Hirst, P.H. (1974) *Knowledge and the Curriculum*. London: Routledge and Kegan Paul.

HMI (1991) *Education Observed. The Implementation of the Curriculum Requirements of ERA*. London: HMI.

Howe, C. (1990) Grouping children for effective learning in science. *Primary Science Review*, 13. Hatfield: Association for Science Education.

Hunn, K. (1993) Providing resources for primary science. In Sherrington, R. (ed.) *ASE Primary Science Teachers' Handbook*. Hemel Hempstead: Simon and Schuster.

Johnson-Laird, P.N. (1983) *Mental Models*. Cambridge: Cambridge University Press.

Jones, A.T., Simon, S.A., Black, P.J., Fairbrother, R.W. and Watson, J.R. (1992) Open work in science. Hatfield and London: Association for Science Education and King's College.

Juniper, D.F. (1989) *Successful Problem Solving*. Slough: W. Foulsham.

Keil, F.C. (1989) *Concepts, Kinds and Cognitive Development*. London: MIT Press.

Kelly, G. (1955) *The Psychology of Personal Constructs*, Vols 1 and 2. New York: Norton.

Kempa, R.F. and Aminah, A. (1991) Learning interactions in group work in science. *International Journal of Science Education*, 13(3), 341–54.

Keogh, B. and Naylor, S. (1993) Progression and continuity in science. In Sherrington R. (ed.) *ASE Primary Science Teachers' Handbook*. Hemel Hempstead: Simon and Schuster.

Kerry, P. and Eggleston, J. (1988) *Topic Work in the Primary School*. London: Routledge and Kegan Paul.

Kyriacou, C. (1989) *Essential Teaching Skills*. Oxford: Blackwell.

Langer, J. (1969) *Theories of Development*. New York: Holt, Rinehart & Winston.

Layton, D. (1988) Revaluing the T in STS. *International Journal of Science Education*, 10(4), 367–378.

Layton, D. (1991) Science education and praxis: the relationship of school science to practical action. *Studies in Science Education*, 19, 43–79.

Layton, D. (1992) Values in design and technology. In Budgett-Meakin, C. (ed.) *Make the Future Work. Appropriate Technology: A Teachers' Guide*. London: Longman.

Leibschner, J. (1992) A child's work. Freedom and guidance. In *Froebel's Educational Theory and Practice*. Cambridge: The Lutterworth Press.

Licht, B.G. and Dweck, C.S. (1983) Sex differences in achievement orientations: consequences for academic choices and attainments. In Marland M. (ed.) *Sex Differentiation and Schooling*. London: Heinemann.

Makiya, H. and Rogers, M. (1992) *Design and Technology in the Primary School. Case Studies for Teachers*. London: Routledge.

Morgan, V. (1989) Primary science – gender differences in pupils' responses. *Education 3–13*, 17(1), 33–7.

Moyer, J.R. (1966) An Exploratory Study of Questioning in the Instructional Processes in Selected Elementary Schools. PhD Dissertation, Columbia University, NY.

Murphy, P. (1991) Gender and assessment. In Woolnough, B. *Practical Science*. Milton Keynes: Open University Press.

National Curriculum Council (1989a) *Curriculum Guidance 1: A Framework for the Primary Curriculum*. York: NCC.

National Curriculum Council (1989b) *Cross-Curricular Themes*. York: NCC.

National Curriculum Council (1989c) *Non-statutory Guidance for Science*. York: NCC.

National Curriculum Council (1991) *Science for Ages 5–16*. London: HMSO.

National Curriculum Council (1993) *The National Curriculum at Key Stages 1 and 2: Advice for the Secretary of State for Education*. York: NCC.

National Primary Centre (1990) *Topic Work 3–13*. Oxford: National Primary Centre.

National Primary Centre (1992) *Primary Schools in Action: 'I Don't Care What We Call "It" As Long As We Do It'*. Oxford: National Primary Centre.

National Union of Teachers (1983) *TVEI: Extension of the Pilot Scheme*. Circular 392/ 83.

Newman, D., Griffin, P. and Cole, M. (1989) *The Construction Zone: Working for Cognitive Change in School*. Cambridge: Cambridge University Press.

Nott, M., Watts, D.M. and Oakes, M. (1992) Ideal INSET. A report of a survey of science teachers. *Education in Science*, 150 (November), 16–17.

Osborne, R. and Tasker, R. (1985) *Science Teaching and Science Learning*. London: Unwin.

Papert, S. (1980) *Mindstorms: Children, Computers and Powerful Ideas*. Sussex: Harvester Press.

Peacock, A. (1991) *Multi-cultural Science in the Primary School*. Basingstoke: Macmillan.

Perkins, D.N. (1986). *Knowledge As Design*. London: Lawrence Earlbaum Associates.

Peters, R.S. (1967) *The Concept of Education*. London: Routledge and Kegan Paul.

Perrott, E. (1982) *Effective Teaching. A Practical Guide to Improving Your Teaching*. Harlow: Longman.

Piaget, J. (1932a) In *Experience and the Growth of Understanding* (1978). London: Hamlyn, D.W. International Library of the Philosophy of Education.

Piaget, J. (1932b) In *Paradigms Lost* (1989), Casti, J. (ed.) London: Cardinal.

Pippola, P. (1992) *BAQTS Foundation Maths and Science: A Preliminary Evaluation*. Mimeograph. London: Roehampton Institute.

Pope, M. and Keen, T. (1981) *Personal Construct Psychology and Education*. London: Academic Press.

Pope, M. and Watts, D.M. (1988) Constructivist goggles: implications for process in teaching and learning physics. *European Journal of Physics*, 9, 101–109.

Rennie, L.J. and Parker, L.H. (1987) Detecting and accounting for gender differences in mixed-sex and single-sex groupings in science lessons. *Educational Review*, 39(1), 65–73.

Roberts, M.R. (1989) *Serendipity. Accidental Discoveries in Science*. Chichester: John Wiley.

Rogers, C.R. (1969) *Freedom to Learn*. Ohio: Charles E. Merrill.

Russell, T. *et al.* (1988) *Science at Age 11: A Review of APU Survey Findings*. London: Assessment of Performance Unit.

Safe, B. (1990) *Some Aspects of Safety is Science and Technology in Primary Schools*, 2nd edn. Hatfield: ASE.

Schools Examinations and Assessment Council (1989) *A Guide to Teacher Assessment, Pack B. Teacher Assessment in the School*. London: SEAC.

Scott, P. and Asoko, H. (1990) A study of students' understanding of sound 5–16 as an example of action research. Paper presented to the *BERA Conference, September, Roehampton Institute, London*.

Sherrington, R. (1993) Science and language. In Sherrington, R. (ed.) *ASE Primary Science Teachers' Handbook*. Hemel Hempstead: Simon and Schuster.

Simon, S.A. and Jones, A.T. (1992) *Open Work in Science: A Review of Existing Practice*. London: Centre for Educational Studies, King's College, University of London.

Smail, B. (1993) Gender issues. In Sherrington, R. (ed.) *ASE Primary Science Teachers' Handbook*. Hemel Hempstead: Simon and Schuster.

Smail, B. and Kelly, A. (1984) Sex differences is science and technology among 11-year old children, ii: affective. *Research in Science and Technology Education*, 2(2), 87–106.

Smillie, I. (1991) *Mastering the Machine*. London: IT Publications.

Smith, D. (1992) The incidence and nature of cross-sex bullying amongst pupils of junior school age. *Education Today*, 42(2), 31–36.

Smithers, A. and Zientek, P. (1991) *Gender, Primary Schools and the National Curriculum*. Manchester and London: University of Manchester, NAS/UWT and Engineering Council.

Solomon, J. (1981) *Getting to Know About Energy*. London: Falmer Press.

Spear, M. (1987) Teachers' views about the importance of science for girls and boys. In Kelly, A. (ed.) *Science for Girls*. Milton Keynes: Open University Press.

Sutton, C. (1992) *Words, Science and Learning*. Milton Keynes: Open University Press.

Tough, J. (1977) *The Development of Meaning*. London: Unwin.

Turvey, C. (1973) *Sydney Microskills – Series 1*. Sydney: University of Sydney.

Vygotsky, L. (1978) *Mind and Society*. Harvard, MA: Harvard University Press.

Vygotsky, L. (1986) *Thought and Language*. Harvard, MA: MIT Press.

Watts, D.M. (1991) *The Science of Problem Solving*. London: Cassell.

Watts, D.M. and Bentley, D. (1991) Constructivism in the curriculum. Can we close the gap between the strong theoretical version and the weak version of theory-in-practice? *The Curriculum Journal*, 2(2), 171–182.

Watts, D.M. and Bentley, D. (1993) Humanising and feminising school science: reviving anthropomorphic and animistic thinking in constructivist education. *International Journal of Science Education*, in press.

Webster, K. (1992) Appropriate technology? Appropriate economics. In Budgett-Meakin, C. (ed.) *Make the Future Work. Appropriate Technology: A Teachers' Guide*. London: Longman.

Wharfe, L. (1991) A new approach to teacher training. *Higher Education News*, No. 13, Spring.

Whitby, V. (1991) A Study of Effective Questioning in Science. MA Thesis, Roehampton Institute, London.

White, R.T. (1988) *Learning in Science*. Oxford: Blackwell.

Whyte, J. (1983) Non-sexist teachers evaluating what teachers can do to help girls opt in to science and technology. *Second GASAT Conference, Gran, Norway*.

Whyte, J. (1988) *The Language of Science*. Hatfield: Association of Science Education.

Zylbersztajn, A. (1983) A Conceptual Framework for Science Education. Investigating Curriculum Materials and Classroom Interactions in Secondary School Physics. PhD Thesis, University of Surrey.

Index

SPECIAL EDUCATIONAL NEEDS IN THE PRIMARY SCHOOL
A PRACTICAL GUIDE

Jean Gross

Local management of schools and cutbacks in central support services mean that the responsibility for meeting special educational needs is resting ever more squarely on the shoulders of ordinary classroom teachers. Yet few feel wholly confident in their ability to adapt work within the National Curriculum to meet the whole range of needs, or coordinate successful action plans for children who – for whatever reason – are not learning as well as they might.

This book will increase that confidence. Aimed at busy class teachers, special needs coordinators, heads and teachers in training, it shows how the teacher can build differentiation into planning lessons and schemes of work. It describes workable strategies for managing the most common behaviour difficulties and meeting special needs in language and mathematics.

At a whole school level, it offers practical guidance on developing special needs policies, assessment, record keeping, and the management of time, roles and resources. The focus is on the ways in which schools can do a good job in meeting special needs themselves, within everyday constraints of time, money and energy, and in doing so hold back the tide of increasing marginalization of vulnerable children within the education system.

Contents

Current perspectives on special educational needs – Developing a whole school policy – Special needs and the National Curriculum – Assessment and special educational needs – Action planning and record keeping – Managing time – Managing roles and resources – Managing behaviour – Communication and classroom relationships – Special needs in speaking and listening – Special needs in reading – Special needs in writing – Special needs in maths – Beyond the school – References – Index.

240pp   0 335 19035 9 (Paperback)

READING THE CHANGES
Eleanor Anderson

In the context of changing perspectives on and experience of language, learning and schooling, Eleanor Anderson suggests a new model of the reading process and how it may be applied to classroom practice. She provides an overview of research and development in the field of language and literacy over the past forty years, a new framework for the reading process, and practical suggestions for use by teachers. She discusses, for instance, strategies for reading whole texts and complete texts, reading 'real books', reading and information handling, reading across the curriculum, and reading within national curricula. She also tackles how to develop a school reading policy, how to communicate such a policy within the community and to other professionals, and the challenge of reading for teacher education. She constructs a theoretically sound model which teachers may adapt to their own needs in trying to make sense of the myriad changes with which they are being asked to cope, and in the daily decision making in which they are involved.

Contents
Changing views of children's language and learning – Reading in this changing context – Applying a new model to classroom practice – Teaching and developing reading in this changing context – Teaching reading within national curricula – The challenge for teacher education – Communicating with colleagues, community, parents and other professionals – Epilogue – Appendices – References – Index.

128pp   0 335 15642 8 (Paperback)   0 355 15643 6 (Hardback)

ORGANIZING FOR LEARNING IN THE PRIMARY CLASSROOM
A BALANCED APPROACH TO CLASSROOM MANAGEMENT

Janet R. Moyles

The primary classroom is the context in which a wide range of teaching and learning experiences occur – and not just for the children! What is it that underlies classroom organization, routines, rules, structures and daily occurrences? What are the prime objectives and what influences the decisions of teachers and children? What is it useful for teachers to consider when contemplating the issues of classroom management and organization? What do different practices have to offer?

Organizing for Learning in the Primary Classroom explores the whole range of influences and values which underpin *why* teachers do *what* they do in the classroom context and what these mean to children and others. Janet Moyles draws on several different research findings to examine the evidence in relation to the underlying issues of teachers' beliefs and values. She examines teaching and learning styles, children's independence and autonomy, coping with children's differences, the physical classroom context and resources, time management and ways of involving others in the day-to-day organization. Practical suggestions are given for considering both the functional and aesthetic aspects of the classroom context. Opportunities are provided for teachers to reflect on their own organization and also consider innovative and flexible ways forward to deal with new and ever increasing demands on their time and sanity!

Contents
Introduction: Polarizations and balance – Teachers and teaching: beliefs and values – The learning environment: organizing the classroom context – The children and their learning needs: balancing individual and whole class approaches – Grouping children for teaching and learning: providing equal opportunities and promoting appropriate behaviour – Time for teaching and learning – Deploying adult help effectively in the classroom: delegation and responsibility – Evaluating classroom organization and management – Conclusion: the primary classroom, a place and a time – References – Index.

208pp   0 335 15659 2 (Paperback)   0 335 15660 6 (Hardback)